iron eye's family:

THE CHILDREN OF JOSEPH LA FLESCHE

by norma kidd green

sponsored by
the nebraska state historical society

johnsen publishing company • lincoln, nebraska

TO

Marguerite La Flesche Farley Conn
who first told me of the family letters and in
whose memory the letters were placed in the
Nebraska State Historical Society by her sons
Dr. Fletcher F. Conn and C. William Conn.

FOREWORD

The story of the Omaha Tribe and their long and colorful history is poorly known despite their exposure to European culture prior to 1800. Certainly they were residents of the area that is now Nebraska in the eighteenth century and controlled much of Eastern Nebraska during the exploration period.

Relations with these American explorers and settlers date from the Lewis and Clark Expedition of 1804. A few Spanish explorers knew them even earlier. They provided land and assistance to the military personnel at Cantonment Mission in 1819 and at Fr. Atkinson. They befriended the Mormons in the 1840's and with territorial settlement in 1854 they peacefully withdrew to a reservation.

Stories are told of the infamous Chief Blackbird but the achievements of the distinguished La Flesche are less well known. The La Flesche papers include many intimate letters of the family in the first generation venturing beyond the tribal life pattern. They are, therefore, in that rare group of Indian papers where Indians talk to Indians without the self-consciousness of impressing white people or the awkward and disturbing presence of an interpreter.

Norma Kidd Green has performed an outstanding service to Nebraska history by the extensive compilation she has made from the detailed study of this outstanding family.

We are pleased to have been of service in this achievement.

Marvin F. Kivett, Director
Nebraska State Historical Society

v

PREFACE

In 1960 I wrote short biographical sketches on Susette La Flesche Tibbles (1854-1903) and Susan La Flesche Picotte (1865-1915), members of the Omaha Indian Tribe, daughters of Chief Iron Eye, Joseph La Flesche. These were for the biographical encyclopedia, *Notable American Women, 1607-1950,* which Radcliffe College planned to publish in 1970. It was remarkable that two American Indian women from the same family met the achievement standards of this editorial board.

Two grandnephews of these women allowed me to study the family papers saved by their grandmother, Rosalie La Flesche Farley and their mother Marguerite Farley Conn. These letters, diaries and account books led me to the newspapers of the period, to government records and to other collections of letters.

Joseph La Flesche, often called by the direct English translation of his Indian name, "Iron Eye," was the last man to obtain Chiefship of the Omaha under the age-old rites and rituals. His participation in these rites followed his own adoption as a son by the old Chief Big Elk. The story of this remarkable family is one part of the history of white men's settlement of the Great Plains.

While still a territory Nebraska had a Historical Society and made an effort to collect books and pamphlets and various papers. For a few years there were two societies producing more confusion than order. The need to preserve State papers was debated in 1878 but no publications are dated earlier than 1885. Ex-Governor Furnas was President of the Society and was active in establishing a more smoothly working organization.

The La Flesche name is conspicuous by its absence in this first publication. It is strange since other writing shows Joseph La Flesche was a leader and had one of the largest farming operations. Could it be because Furnas had been the Agent for the Omaha fifteen years earlier and had had disagreements with the leader La Flesche?

Now, nearly one hundred years later several new sources have been found and a more rounded picture may be gained of certain events. They are about minor events but until now only one interpretation has gotten into tradition and into print.

This book is built upon three groups of unpublished letters. The first group is made up of the La Flesche family papers. The letters between brothers and sisters are supplemented by letters from their friend, Alice C. Fletcher. Most of her letters are in the Bureau of American Ethnology in the Smithsonian Institution. Still others are in the Peabody Museum at Harvard and at the Women's Archives at Radcliffe College.

A second group was saved by the Presbyterian Church in their great collection "American Indian Correspondence." The State Historical Society of Nebraska has several microfilm rolls of letters from or about the early Mission to the Omaha. I have read most of these in Lincoln, using those from 1846 to 1895. For brevity I refer to them as "Missionary Letters." I wish to thank the Presbyterian Historical Society for permission to quote from them.

The third group comes from the Office of Indian Affairs, papers now deposited in the National Archives. They are the "Letters Received" in Washington from the Council Bluffs Sub-Agency (1836-1857), from the Omaha Agency (1856-1876) and a few later ones from the combined Winnebago and Omaha Agency.

Besides correspondence I have consulted Annuity Rolls, Census and Allotment Rolls and Court Records of the County Courts of Burt and Dakota counties in Nebraska, of the Supreme Court of Nebraska and several files of the United States District Court, District of Nebraska. The last were retrieved from storage through the kindness of Judge Robert Van Pelt of the United States District Court, District of Nebraska.

I have made use of the famous 27th Report of the Bureau of American Ethnology, *The Omaha Tribe* by Alice C. Fletcher and Francis La Flesche to gain understanding of the Omaha tribal life, of names, customs and ceremonies. A few stories are taken from Fannie Reed Giffen's *Oo-ma-ha Ta-wa-tha* since they agreed with government records and personal letters. Added to these sources I have studied a few New England newspapers and magazines no longer published.

Personal interviews contributed a great deal and when no source is cited for intimate family incidents, the material has come from such interviews. Each interview has been checked with documents, news reports, other personal memories whenever it was possible. My greatest debt is to Winnie Wood Farley, Mrs. Edward Farley who came into the family after Rosalie's death and cared for Ed Farley and his family. She preserved the papers which she found Rosalie had kept together and passed them on to Rosalie's daughter Marguerite. "Grandma Winnie" talked intimately with me several times and I was fortunate to have known her. I wish I might have worked more rapidly that she might have read the whole story.

I wish to acknowledge the help I have received from the present generations of the La Flesche family—Joseph's grandaughters, his great-grandchildren, and from the spouses of the Farley family. Thanks are also due to many residents and former residents of Pender, Walthill, Bancroft and Macy, Nebraska.

I am indebted to Dr. Donald Danker, formerly Historian for the Nebraska State Historical Society and Dr. John Champe, former head of the Department of Anthropology at the University of Nebraska for reading part of the manuscript. I extend thanks to Dr. James C. Olson, Chancellor of the University of Missouri at Kansas City for his suggestion that I edit these papers. I owe much to the early encouragement of the late Mari Sandoz, who constantly said, "The quiet stories are hard to dig out."

I wish to thank the helpful staffs of the many libraries where I have worked, the college libraries, the historical group libraries, the public and the private ones. The interest and patience of these people have added to the whole pleasure. My gratitude goes to Virginia Opocensky for assistance in research and gratitude to her daughter, Claudia for typing. This last item includes Wynn Miller, Eunice Stout, Ramona Lang and Elizabeth Thiel who typed portions of the manuscript in its several forms.

Of utmost importance has been the continued interest and support of my husband, Roy M. Green and other members of our family.

Lincoln, Nebraska　　　　　　　　　　　　　　NORMA KIDD GREEN
October 1, 1969

NOTE ON THE LA FLESCHE FAMILY

Joseph La Flesche was half French and half Indian and lived with the Omaha, the Otoe, the Ponca and the Pawnee tribes during the most of his boyhood. As a man he cast his lot with the Omaha and was called E-sta-mah-za (sometimes written as Inshtamaza), "Iron Eye" but was generally known by his father's name, Joseph La Flesche. I have used "Iron Eye" for the chapters on the Tribe where the Indian name is most fitting. Omahas of the mid-twentieth century who knew him or his children spoke of "Joe La Flesche." His principal wife, in those days of multiple wives was Mary Gale, Hinnuagsnun, The One Woman, a title of great honor. She, too, was half white and half Indian; her father was Dr. John Gale of the United States Army and her mother Ni-co-mi, an Indian woman highly respected on the frontier. They had four daughters who grew to womanhood. The eldest was Susette, or Yosette whose Indian name was In-shta-the-umba, Bright Eyes. The first two syllables were like the first of her father's name meaning "eye" and the rest meant "bright." The other girls were Rosalie, Marguerite and Susan.

The only other wife to leave children was an Omaha woman, Ta-in-ne who became known as Elizabeth Esau or as Lizzie La Flesche. Her children by Joseph were Francis, named for his father's brother; a daughter, Lucy; and another son Carey, the youngest. Lucy married Noah Leaming who took the name of La Flesche since his family was of lower position than Lucy's.* Carey married La-ta-da-we, later called Phoebe Cline. Susette, Lucy and Frank had no children so the descendants are from Rosalie (Farley), Marguerite (Diddock), Susan (Picotte) and Carey La Flesche.

Evidently Rosalie attended no school but the Presbyterian Mission School on the Reservation. The Mission School provided Frank's only formal education until, during the years he worked in the Indian Bureau and the Smithsonian Institution in Washington, he studied law. Rosalie and Frank, however, became truly educated persons. Susette, Marguerite and Susan all attended an excellent

---

*Some accounts say Noah's name was Stabler. Many incidents suggest that he was closely related to the Stabler Family.

school for girls in Elizabeth, New Jersey. Marguerite and Susan with Lucy Noah and Carey went to the Hampton Industrial and Agricultural Institute at Hampton, Virginia. Susan later graduated from the Woman's Medical College of Pennsylvania in Philadelphia.

None of the seven children ever severed their ties to the Tribe, although they moved very much among white people. Susette, Rosalie, Marguerite, Susan and Francis—to a lesser degree—Lucy with her husband Noah always worked for the development of the Indians and for their adjustment to the white man's world. Carey was a participant in tribal life for nearly fifty years. Francis, connected with the Bureau of American Ethnology, was widely recognized for preserving the ceremonials and the ancient songs of the Plains Indians.

Susette's and Rosalie's marriages to white men were only thirteen months apart and their deaths occurred within three years. Therefore, I have discussed them in the chapters which cover approximately the 1880's and the 1890's, giving less space to the others. Marguerite and Susan both worked under the Indian Bureau at the Omaha Agency, both married and had children and were pioneer residents of Walthill, Nebraska when that town was formed in 1906. They worked together in many civic projects at the same time giving attention to and lending assistance to those on the Reservation; always being a family with Rosalie's children, with Lucy and Noah and with Carey and his family. Susan died in 1915 and Marguerite added Susan's two boys to her own family of two girls and two boys. The chapter about them roughly ends with 1917 when Susan's boys went into service in World War I.

Before 1930, the Picotte and Diddock children, progeny of Susan and Marguerite had scattered, most of them were married as were their Farley cousins, and Marguerite went to live with a daughter, another Marguerite. She, one of the older ones, lived almost as long as the youngest, Carey. The chapter on "Ta-in-ne's Children" covers as far as possible the less documented lives of Lucy and Carey on the Reservation and the distinguished career of Francis (called Frank by the family) in the field of ethnology.

On the whole they were short lived; Susette, Rosalie and Susan died before they were fifty, Lucy lived a little more than a decade longer, and Frank, Carey and Marguerite reached more than their three score years and ten. It was hard to be born into one life and move into another. While they were no longer subjected to the hazards of the hunt and a semi-nomadic life or faced a fluctuating food supply, they did not live as long as preceding generations. Short lives which cast long shadows. I hope I have depicted them as individuals worthy of remembrance.

LA FLESCHE FAMILY LINES

Since the following family lines cover many decades and two or three cultural systems, the sign "====" indicates a marital union. It is impossible, and unnecessary, to determine the exact customs and rites in each case.

Joseph La Flesche, Jr. had other wives, one was either a Pawnee or an Otoe; several children died; only those mentioned below reached maturity.

A. **Line of Mary Gale La Flesche**

NADAWIN (Omaha)====HAVING MANY HORSES (Otoe Chief)
　　Child: One daughter Kazawin (Omaha-Otoe)

　　　1. KAZAWIN====VILLAGE MAKER I (son Chief Blackbird, Omaha)
　　　　　Children: Son Village Maker II
　　　　　　　　　　Daughter Memetage (Madeline Wolfe)

　　　2. KAZAWIN====WACHIN-WASCHA (Iowa Head Chief)
　　　　　Children: Son Nicohi (killed by Sioux)
　　　　　　　　　　Daughter Nicomi (Omaha-Otoe-Iowa)
　　　　　1. NICOMI====DR. JOHN GALE (U.S. Army)
　　　　　　　Child: Daughter Mary (Omaha-Otoe-Iowa-Caucasian)

　　　　　2. NICOMI====PETER SARPY (trader at Bellevue)

B. **Line of Joseph La Flesche, Iron Eye**

JOSEPH LA FLESCHE, SR. (French trader====WA-TUN-NA (Ponca or Omaha)
　　Child: Joseph La Flesche, Jr. (French-Indian) 1822-1889

　　　1. JOSEPH LA FLESCHE, JR. 1822-1889====MARY GALE (Omaha-Otoe-
　　　　　　　　　　　　　　　　　　　　　　　　　Iowa-Caucasian) 1826-1907
　　　　　Children: Louis 1848-1860
　　　　　　　　　　Susette 1854-1903====T. H. TIBBLES
　　　　　　　　　　Rosalie 1861-1900====EDWARD FARLEY (3 girls 7 boys)
　　　　　　　　　　Marguerite 1862-1945====CHARLES PICOTTE
　　　　　　　　　　　　　　　　　　　　====WALTER T. DIDDOCK (2 girls
　　　　　　　　　　　　　　　　　　　　　　　　　　　　　　　　　3 boys)
　　　　　　　　　　Susan 1865-1915====HENRY PICOTTE (2 boys)

　　　2. JOSEPH LA FLESCHE, JR.====TA-IN-NE (Elizabeth Esau) Died 1883
　　　　　Children: Francis 1857-1932====Alice Mitchell (Divorced)
　　　　　　　　　　　　　　　　　　====Rosa Bourassa (Separated)
　　　　　　　　　　Lucy 1865-1923====Noah (Leaming) La Flesche
　　　　　　　　　　Carey 1872-1952====Le-Da-We (Phoebe Cline (4 girls
　　　　　　　　　　　　　　　　　　　　　　　　　　　　　　　2 boys)

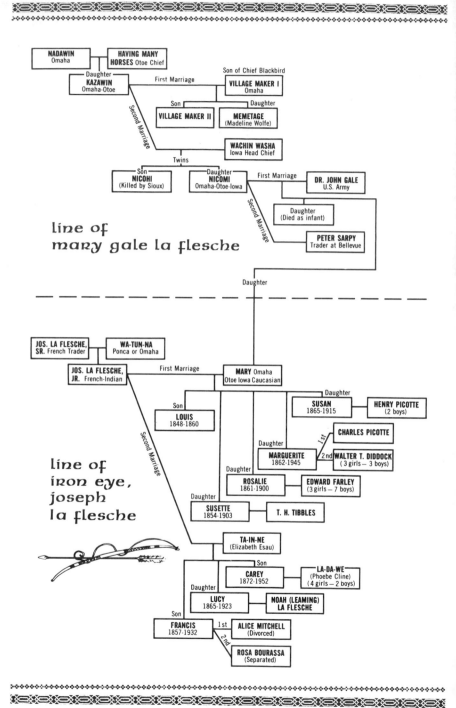

line of mary gale la flesche

line of iron eye, joseph la flesche

CONTENTS

CHAPTER I

INDISTINCT BEGINNINGS

The parentage and childhood of Iron Eye, Joseph La Flesche, are as difficult to date exactly as are the early movements of the Omaha tribe. The Omaha are certainly the "Maha" of the early records. This name is used in the Lewis and Clark *Journal* of 1804 and in the treaties of 1815 and 1825. In the tribal language the name Oo-ma-ha was spoken with the first syllable sounded like oo and the accent on the second syllable, "u-ma'-ha." The white men, with ears untuned to the soft Omaha speech, failed to catch the first syllable and understood the word as "Maha." By 1830, however, the United States Government was calling the tribe Omaha.

For over one hundred years before Jefferson sent Lewis and Clark up the Missouri, European explorers and hunters spoke of the Maha located near the Missouri, or at the mouth of the Big Sioux. At one time they were observed trading as far north as Lake Winnepeg. Tribal traditions even indicate an early home in the Ohio Valley and a much later move west and north, probably up the Des Moines River and across to the Missouri.

The name Omaha means "against the current," "above the stream" or "upstream." In 1514 De Soto met a tribe whose name meant "down stream," the Quapaw. The stories vary but it is assumed that at some time related tribes had separated, or one tribe had divided, with one group going up a stream and the other moving down in the stream of the current. This parting may have been fairly recent, as history measures time, for the Omaha and Quapaw, together with the Ponca, Osage and Kansa make up one small group within the large division of the Siouan language family.

At the time Americans on the eastern seaboard were turning envious eyes toward the Indian hunting grounds, trade and warfare between the tribes had increased as the use of horses had spread from one tribe to another. Formal visits and, at times, extended sojourns with other tribes were a large part of Indian life. Among cognate groups, at least, there was intermarriage. At times with realistic acceptance of fate, prisoners who saw no means of returning to their own band simply became part of the conquering tribe. Adoption was frequent, moved by affection or necessity and even extended to members of other tribes and races. All of this led to a series of interlocking relationships making it difficult to designate the exact tribal origin of certain words and customs, and even of exact blood lines.

No one questions but that the father of Iron Eye was Joseph La Flesche, Sr. (in earlier records written, "La Fleshe") a French fur-trader. Like others of his countrymen from many walks of life, he came along the Missouri River, by the hunting grounds of the Omaha and on to the mountains. The French evidently accepted Indian ways more easily than the English and Americans and were called "white natives" by the Indians to distinguish them from other white men. Like most traders who stayed any length of time in the Indian country, La Flesche made an alliance with an Indian woman.

Printed statements are divided in claiming that this woman was an Omaha or that she was a Ponca. Whatever may be the case, certainly Iron Eye's son, Francis, considered his father's mother was an Omaha. Francis La Flesche, the son of Joseph, Jr., was the only person close to his father, Iron Eye, who had actual living experiences in tribal life, yet spoke fluent English and was well enough educated to write about his people in the terms used by the whites. For nearly forty years he studied the Plains Indians. He lived among educated people and moved in scholarly circles of Washington and other eastern cities.

Years after the death of both Joseph, Jr. and his son, Francis, a memorandum on Joseph's mother was found among the private papers of Alice C. Fletcher, the anthropologist with whom Francis had been closely associated. They were co-authors of the most authoritative detailed study of his people, *The Omaha Tribe*.[1] The memorandum appears to be in Alice Fletcher's handwriting. It relates a conversation held in her apartment in 1906 with Wa-ja-pa, an Omaha Indian.[2] Wa-ja-pa's name and picture are given in *The Omaha Tribe*. He is listed as one of the Omaha "soldiers and braves" in Indian Bureau records. Throughout his life, he was close to Joseph and to the next two generations of the family.

In this conversation Wa-ja-pa related the events of Joseph's boyhood and said that he, himself, had known Joseph, Sr. He definitely stated that Joseph's mother was an Omaha and related to his (Wa-ja-pa's) mother. He named the gens (the tribal division) to which his own father belonged and that of which Joseph's mother was a member. He explained that when Joseph, known as Iron Eye, was adopted by the Omaha chief, Big Elk, he entered the gens of Big Elk which was contrary to custom, for since his father was a white man he would have belonged to his mother's gens.[3] This, of course, was in keeping with the custom of adoption. The account of Iron Eye given in *The Omaha Tribe* is plainly based on this memorandum.

The lifetime relationship between Wa-ja-pa and the La Flesche family would indicate that he was as close a source of information on Iron Eye's origin as could be obtained. Numerous records attest to Wa-ja-pa's respectable position in the tribe and newspapers mention several trips to Washington. The La Flesche family and other members of the tribe spoke of Wa-ja-pa's children as "some sort of cousins" of Iron Eye's even as late as 1926.[4]

Still later another account of Joseph's parentage was discovered among a daughter's papers. Although this, too, came from within the family it states that his mother was a Ponca, by the name of Wa-tun-na. The information for this paper must have come from Joseph's wife, Mary, or from her mother, Ni-co-mi. It would be impossible to tell whether their ideas should carry greater weight than the statement of Wa-ja-pa who grew up with Joseph and must have been either a first or second cousin according to white English-American kinship terms.

One of the earliest ethnologists to study the Omaha gave his story of Joseph's background. Rev. J. Owen Dorsey mastered the Siouan dialect spoken by the Omaha tribe and thus drew closer to many individuals than did most white men. He said Joseph had been born a Ponca but grew up among the Omaha, Otoe and Pawnee; he had long been considered an Omaha, having held the highest position in their system of government. His half-brother Frank, known as White Swan, became a chief among the Poncas and some sources state definitely that Frank was born of a different mother.

In 1962 the Office of Indian Affairs made a special study of the blood lines of all on the Omaha Roll before an indemnity was to be paid and the Roll officially closed. This study declared that Joseph was a Ponca and the names of several descendents were removed from the Omaha Roll. Even a superficial effort to trace any family line of the Omaha tribe, before and during the 1820's shows a constant intermingling and intermarriage between the Yankton, Omaha, Ponca, Otoe and Iowa tribes. It would be impossible to determine the exact tribal membership, or blood strains of the forebearers of Joseph's mother. One Omaha in 1880 spoke of the Ponca tribe as "our relatives—we lived together as one family." A few years later the Government restored the names of these grandchildren to the Tribal Roll.

But aside from conflicting statements and possibilities, the fact remains that a half-French, half-Indian boy was born in what is now northeastern Nebraska sometime in the early 1820's. At his death his family gave the birth date as 1822. Later his son gave the date as 1818. The latter date would coincide with the one indicated in the allotment roll of 1871.

Four or five years either way could make little difference. The child came into a tribal world at one of its difficult periods. After 1790 or 1800 the Indians were pressed into constant westward movement. The Plains tribes were buffeted by eastern, formerly Woodland, tribes moving to the West, driven by the land hunger and military power of white men.

The small boy's mother did not like her French husband's long absences on trading expeditions and when the child was about five years old she married a man of the Omaha tribe. Little Joseph was cared for by two aunts, whose brother had been captured by the Sioux long before. This Omaha had grown up with the Sioux and became a man of considerable influence in the tribe. After Joseph's mother was married to the Omaha, the aunts took him to visit this brother. They stayed for several years and Joseph learned the Dakota tongue. They returned to the Omaha at some unverifiable date (probably in the early 1830's), and Joseph La Flesche, Sr. came again trading among the Omaha. He was allowed to take his son with him when he left and apparently they were together from the lad's early teens until he was a young man.

Young Joseph shared his father's life of hunting and trading with many different tribes and probably spent some time in St. Louis. He did learn to speak French and the languages of still other Indian tribes besides the Omaha and Dakota with which he was familiar. This knowledge was extremely important later and allowed him to interpret by putting the words of a white man speaking one Indian tongue into another native dialect.

Joseph had not been born or was quite small when the United States planned a series of forts along the upper Missouri, striking deep into hostile Indian country. The first establishment to materialize was Fort Atkinson, built in 1820 at the site of the present-day town of Ft. Calhoun, some ten miles north of Omaha. With the troops that came to the fort was a highly respected and attractive Army doctor, John Gale. Besides wrestling with difficult health problems at this advanced post, Dr. Gale looked about at the Indian women. He was married to a pretty Omaha-Oto-Iowa girl called Ni-co-mi, going through the proper Indian procedure of approaching her nearest male relatives and giving and receiving presents. Dr. Gale and Ni-co-mi had two little girls; the younger one died as a baby. The older, Mary, was still quite small when Ft. Atkinson was abandoned and the garrison was ordered on boat to return to St. Louis.

Dr. Gale thought he had persuaded Ni-co-mi to let him take Mary with him and had even plotted to detain the child on the boat until it had left the wharf, but the interpreter warned Ni-co-mi and she ran away and hid the child. Then Gale appealed to Joshua Pilcher and John Cabanne of the American Fur Company to keep an eye on the child and to see that she received an education.[5] Dr. Gale, himself, died not long after returning to St. Louis. After four years Peter Sarpy, the local trader for the Fur Company, asked permission of Ni-co-mi's family that he might marry her. Dr. Gale, Sarpy said, had saved his life and he wished to care for Ni-co-mi and Mary.

So it came about that Sarpy took care of John Gale's daughter by marrying her mother, who, in turn, frequently took care of him. Ni-co-mi was a vigorous and determined woman, a well-known figure along the frontier for several decades. Sarpy was always thoughtful of Ni-co-mi and Mary, and saw to it that Mary was sent to St. Louis to school where she learned to speak French and may have learned some English. However, as an old woman, she would never attempt to use English before English-speaking people.

Sarpy had a trading post on each side of the Missouri. St. Mary, for the white trade, was on the eastern side, a bit south of the present Council Bluffs, Iowa. Bellevue, for the Indians, was on the western side at the old American Fur Company post, south of Omaha, Nebraska. By 1836, the government had set up an agency at Bellevue to care for the Omaha, Otoe and Missouri tribes. Sarpy dealt with the fur-traders, the French, the Indians, the English and the Americans; with the would-be white settlers, the soldiers, the travelers and the missionaries; and became a pivotal figure in many matters, large and small. Mary spent much of her girlhood with her mother in Sarpy's rather pretentious house—pretentious for the time and place. Joseph La Flesche became an employee, possibly a partner in some of Sarpy's several ventures. Thus Sarpy was the means, intentional or not, of bringing together these two young people, each half-white and half-Indian.

As an old woman, Mary told her married daughters a story of

the two Joseph's their father and their grandfather, assisting the
Indian Agent in a difficult task. The two La Flesche men, the son
probably not quite twenty, had returned from a long hunt to the
Omaha village near the present day Homer, Nebraska.

Almost immediately the Omaha chief, Big Elk, sent word to
Joseph, Sr. that an Omaha Indian and his brother had killed a
crippled French hunter, Beauchamp.[6] Although he was holding the
brothers under guard, Big Elk, always desiring peace, feared the
whites might become angry at the whole tribe and that in retaliation
the Omaha might commit acts of violence. He wanted the help of the
Frenchman, La Flesche, in taking word to the authorities. He knew
that the Agent stationed at Bellevue would take the prisoners to St.
Louis and he wished them to get on the way as quickly as possible.

Mary related how she had stood on the balcony of their two-
storied house in Bellevue and had seen the Indian captives led to the
boat landing. The murderer had stopped, looked up at the sky and
had sung a tragic, haunting song.

> Where can I go
> That I might live forever?
>
> The old fathers have gone to the spirited land
> Where can I go
> That we might live together?[7]

A raft was built upon two great log boats with provisions for
the long journey down stream. Besides the prisoners, the party was
made up of the Agent, Joseph Hamilton; his guide, a half-breed Joe
Robideau; Village Maker and Big Elk; and several Mexican youths
recently taken from the Pawnee who had captured them. Hamilton,
in his report, also includes "Joseph La Flesche, the interpreter" and
"two witnesses from the Omaha tribe." The "Joseph" was obviously
Joseph, Sr. since his name is signed as interpreter to documents near
this date. The Agent did not name Joseph, Jr., Wa-nun-sun-da, or
Village Maker, whom Mary mentioned. Probably the last two were
the "witnesses" and Joseph, Jr. so young that he was not distinguished from the young "Spainards."

Near the mouth of the Nodaway River the boat capsized in a
storm; Big Elk, the Agent and others swam to shore. The Indian
considered the most guilty made a mighty effort and broke his hand-
cuffs, then lifting his heavy chain he jumped into the water. Young

Joseph tried to save him, even grasping the man's long hair, but the weight of the chain was too great and the man was carried to the bottom. The other prisoner, Wa-o-ga and the La Flesches clung to the boat and were carried to the shore.

Orders were given to put Wa-o-ga under guard and to give him only bread and water. Joseph, Jr., showing the pity and compassion which marked much of his life, would cut open a loaf of bread, hollow out a part of it and insert a piece of meat to take to the prisoner. Wa-o-ga was set free by the authorities and with the two Josephs walked back to Bellevue, passing no dwellings save a few log houses at St. Joseph. Months later Hamilton presented a bill to the Indian Office for the expenses of this trip which included cash paid to Robideau for the use of horses and the purchase of one for Big Elk, the chief.[8] No mention is made of the rest of the party. Probably it was thought that trappers and Indians were accustomed to walking and could walk; but the chief who should be paid for his help in enforcing the law was given a horse, and, of course, he might prove to be useful in the future. Mary remembered after many years to tell her daughters that their father and grandfather had carried with them many useful things for the household at Bellevue.

It may have been after this that Joseph, Jr. traveled less and less with his father hunting and trading, but spent more time with the Omaha who were constantly harassed by raiding parties of the Sioux who were being attacked by tribes east of them. The Omaha moved from the location near Homer to the south near the mouth of the Platte to be farther away from the Sioux country and closer to the government agency. The father suspected his son was courting the Omaha girls but actually the younger man was winning the confidence of the Omaha chiefs.

Through his experiences with many tribes and his observation of the increasing power of the white men, Joseph had come to believe that the white men would increase in numbers and that their manner of living would prove stronger than that of the Indians. He felt the future meant only sorrow for the red men unless they learned the new ways and worked with the white men rather than against them. He felt every person must change and that the Indian leaders must be convinced of the necessity. Therefore, he deliberately spent time with the older men, listening to tribal traditions and learning about the rites and ceremonies so that he might understand how changes must be made.

He decided to live as an Omaha and win a place of influence

that he might assist in this change. The chieftainship was partially hereditary but it was possible for a man to attain the position through a series of certain ceremonies and the presentation of proper gifts or by adoption which also included ceremonies and gifts.

It is impossible to say whether his belief that the Indian must learn the white man's ways attracted the attention of Big Elk, or whether Joseph's own conviction led him to seek the favor of Big Elk. Big Elk had often told his people that the approach of the white man was like a flood which would grow greater and greater and might completely overwhelm them. The incident of the prisoner taken to St. Louis shows that Big Elk had confidence in the older La Flesche and he began to show confidence in the son.

Big Elk had a son of his own who was expected to succeed him; but the boy was never strong. While his son was still a minor, Big Elk adopted Joseph and indicated that if his own son did not survive him, Joseph was to be his successor. At one time, when a hunt was being planned, Big Elk invited Joseph to join the council and seated the young man by his side. This was a definite mark of favor and since the other chiefs made no objections, they tacitly accepted Joseph as one of them.[10]

Probably by 1845 or 1846, Mary, daughter of Dr. John Gale and step-daughter of Peter Sarpy, married Joseph La Flesche, Jr., son of the Frenchman. Two years later Big Elk formally "pipe danced" Mary. This ceremony included the presentation of gifts and brought honor to the person for whom it was "danced." Then by public crier, Big Elk declared that Joseph was his "oldest" son and that he was to inherit the chieftainship. Then he caused Joseph to give the four ceremonial feasts required by this announcement.[11]

At this time, or possibly earlier, Joseph, called Iron Eye, was assigned to or in some way placed in the Wezhin-chte gens, that of Big Elk, and (according to Wa-ja-pa) not to the gens to which his mother had belonged.[12] This gave added acknowledgement of Iron Eye's position in the tribe. He is listed as Esta-ma-za, Iron Eye, in the Omaha tribal census of 1848.

These steps toward chieftainship must have come between 1840 and 1848, but dates remain indefinite. This is not surprising, since from the time when he accompanied his father to St. Louis until the appearance of his name in the Omaha Census, the years when he was twenty (more or less) to nearly thirty, were times of great confusion for the Omaha tribe.

The semi-annual hunts which brought food, clothing, and

shelter became more and more difficult. Fur bearing animals whose pelts were traded for ammunition and supplies became more and more scarce. The poor hunt of 1844 left both the Otoe and Omaha "in a state of destitution." During these years the Omaha moved several times and then moved again as other tribes claimed their village sites.

From 1840, year by year, the agents asked that something be done. The Omaha "have no resting place"; they "are a poor dispirited people" almost starving and beset by diseases and enemies. The Superintendent of Indian Affairs at St. Louis wrote about "the butchery of the Omaha."13

The Mormons, themselves surrounded by hostility, were forced out of Illinois and settled west of the Missouri on Indian land. They were given permission to stay until the spring of 1847; many remained through a second winter and presented a problem to the Omaha.

Brigham Young, the Morman leader, offered to raise food for the Indians to keep them from helping themselves to Mormon supplies. As early as 1845, John Miller, the Omaha Agent, replied that this would be useless since the ground to be used was claimed by both the Omaha and the Otoe. Moreover, it would not remove the Indian's greatest complaint, the loss to them of game and timber. Miller advised the Mormons to leave the Indian country as quickly as possible.14

For years the Agents pleaded for a detachment of soldiers to afford some protection against the Sioux, and Big Elk visited tribe after tribe trying to make peace. The government duly recorded that his efforts had been properly rewarded by presents of a gun with powder and balls.15 But while giving gifts on one hand, the white people appropriated land with the other and continued to develop villages and establish farms on what had long been the Omaha hunting grounds.

As early as 1842 the Omaha leaders talked of selling some of their land and of being granted a definite place of their own. The Agents repeatedly sent this request to Washington, but other matters claimed first attention. The government maintained the policy that the Indians were separate nations and made treaties with tribe after tribe, much as European countries had long signed treaties with each other. Negotiation between independent nations, however, assumes that in each nation there are definite persons who can exercise authority and speak for the whole group. Also, such negotiation is

possible only when two parties understand each other through a
common language or through some person who can take the ideas
expressed in their one language and give the same meaning in the
other language.

Agreement\with Indian tribes rested on the translation of extremely different languages. Everything depended on the interpreter
who was often a half-breed, able to carry on daily affairs but who
understood spoken English much better than he did written English.
In a large proportion of cases he was unfamiliar with the white man's
legal terms and phraseology. There was seldom any way to be assured
that the Indian "nation" actually understood what the strange
scratches on paper meant, or that the persons signing by mark really
knew what they were signing. Too often it developed that they had
thought they signed something quite different from the actual written
statements. A frequent source of error was the fact that the Omaha
dialect had no word which could be used as "territory." They did
not understand the distinctions the white men made between "states"
and "territories" and "public domain" and if they had understood,
they had no words to express the ideas. In discussions about removal
to the Indian Territory nothing could be said but "the Indian
country," a term which meant almost the whole country to the
Indians. Tribes signed treaties agreeing to future residence in the
"Territory" only to discover that they were placed far away from the
spot they had had in mind.

Moreover, since their earliest contacts with the Plains Indians,
the whites had followed a practice which under-cut tribal authority.
In an effort to create friendly relations, white men had "made"
chiefs by presenting medals or elaborate and (to the Indians) unintel-
ligible papers. Through the days of the all-powerful Agents, chiefs
were "made" and "unmade" almost at the Agents' whim. These were
called "paper chiefs" by the Indians. At first it was rather amusing
for they knew how a man became a chief and they also knew the
character and abilities of the individual "paper chiefs" better than the
white men did. The ethnologist Dorsey said that in 1843 there were
sixty subordinate chiefs, many of whom were government appointments. As a rule, however, the Agent considered them as distinct
from the regular chiefs.

In January of 1844, Daniel Miller, Agent at the Council Bluffs
Sub-agency (at Bellevue) was visited by "the Elk and others of the
first men of the Omaha." They made formal complaint that the
traders were presenting medals to some of the young braves and

utterly destroying the authority of the chief. Big Elk said that he felt like "an old scabby buffalo—separated from his own band on the prairie." He said that when the "Great Father" (the President) had given him a medal he had been told to be good to both the white and the red people and to set a good example for his tribe, and he had remembered this. But now these rash young men, who had never gone through any process of discipline or of ceremony leading to chieftainship, claimed they had equal rank with him.[16]

Miller realized the dangers and on investigation found that a pewter medal, costing fifty cents in St. Louis might have as great an influence as the gift of a fine horse. Therefore, he urged the government to place greater restrictions on the traders. He added that in his opinion this medal vending was next to the liquor traffic in producing dissensions and difficulties.

While the practice had been started by the government, its representatives were late in seeing that it swept away the basis of authority; probably no one saw that it also destroyed the true meaning of the word "chief." The word continued to be used and is still used, but without the original tribal significance.[17]

Vague wording in the treaties also became a source of misunderstanding. Many treaties reflected an ignorance of the terrain and of native custom on the part of the white writers. Western and northern boundaries were frequently poorly defined, showing that the area was not known. But it would seem that after fifty years experience with the wayward Missouri, the treaty-makers would not have chosen "the center of the main channel" as a "permanent reference point."[18] One hundred and twenty-five years later the Omaha tribe laid claim to land that had been west of this point as it was in 1854, although the wandering Missouri had long before placed the point far on the eastern side of the river in the state of Iowa.

This, however, was a minor defect among several in the Omaha treaty. The location of the reservation had not been thoroughly explored. The tribe had repeatedly expressed a dislike of going too far north—too near to the Sioux. The location chosen did not please them, although provision was made that if it were not suitable another place could be selected.

A major point of confusion lies not in the treaty itself but the uncertainty over the actual leadership of the tribe when the treaty was made. If the facts of Joseph La Flesche's origin and childhood are undated and indefinite, his exact position in the tribe early in 1854 is equally uncertain. His son, with the ethnologist Alice

Fletcher, said, ". . .he became one of the two Ni-kagahi u-zhu chiefs,"[19] but no exact date was given.

A year earlier Big Elk had discussed the possible terms of a treaty and the sale of the Omaha hunting grounds. Sometime during 1853 he became ill and died. It is said that he called for Joseph, gave him his "papers from Washington" and said "you will occupy my place" and also, speaking of his own son, "when your brother is older you must do for him what is best."[20] But in some way, Joseph's immediate recognition did not follow, at least not among the white men and probably not within the tribe.

Another half-French, half-Indian was an accepted member of the tribe and had yielded considerable influence for years with the whites. Logan Fontenelle was the son of Lucien Fontenelle who came from a distinguished French family. Lucien Fontenelle was a prominent figure during the height of the fur trade and saw that his children were well educated; therefore, Logan Fontenelle handled English with greater facility than most of the interpreters. He carried himself as a man of the world and was a natural spokesman. He had been particularly vocal in protest over the site considered for the new Reservation.

Government records show four lists of the recognized chiefs of the Omaha during the year of 1854 when the treaty was signed in Washington, and no two lists are alike. A study of the treaty delegation by Melvin Gilmore, a highly respected ethnologist, adds still another name.

Late in 1853, Major James M. Gatewood had been appointed Agent to the tribes at and near Bellevue. He was specifically instructed to meet with the Omaha in Council and arrive at a general understanding on the terms which might be incorporated in a treaty and to have the tribe appoint a delegation with full power to act "as if the whole nation were present." Details were spelled out, but the delegation was to be able to "ratify, confirm, to slightly modify, alter or amend any of the stipulations."[21] The Indians were apparently reluctant to give such liberty of action. Gatewood, at least, insisted that he could not get them to sign such a statement. He, therefore, reported to the Commissioner of Indian Affairs that he had "made a treaty with the tribe."

Now treaties were made in Washington and by the Commissioner himself acting for the Secretary of the Interior and the President, not by newly appointed agents. It may be that the distinction between making a treaty and the granting of authority to a delegation was not grasped by the Indians. They were accustomed to important action being taken only by the Chief Councilors, Headmen, Braves and Warriors assembled together. Moreover, since newspapers in St. Joseph talked of Gatewood making a treaty before the gentlemen had landed at Bellevue, it might appear he had had such an idea in the first place.

George Manypenny, Commissioner of Indian Affairs, reported to Robert McClelland, the Secretary of the Interior, that Gatewood had disobeyed orders and the "so-called treaties" should be disregarded. He, himself, felt that if the matter had been properly handled, the Indians would have signed the papers sent to Gatewood.[22]

Records of the Indian Bureau give a full account of the council, with the names of the designated delegates and the signators of the "treaty." The names of the delegation were: Logan Fontenelle, Joseph La Flesche, Village Maker, Standing Hawk, Little Chief and Yellow Smoke, six in all. But the group of tribal leaders had always numbered seven. The signatures to the unauthorized "treaty" were: Logan Fontenelle, Joseph La Flesche, Village Maker, Standing Hawk, Little Chief, Yellow Smoke and the Cross Elk (Opan-wai-pegi), numbering the traditional seven. After these first seven signatures there is a long list of nearly fifty names apparently of Braves and Warriors, but four are set off by themselves and might be interpreted as belonging with the first seven names. These four are Peg-ga-ha, Wa-a-hi (Big Eyes), Te-san (White Cow) and Man-tu-ni.

The signatures to the actual treaty signed in Washington on March 16, 1854 are: Son-ga-ska or Logan Fontenelle, E-sta-mah-za or Joseph La Flesche, Gra-tah-nah-je or Standing Hawk, Gah-he-ga-gin-gah or Little Chief, Tah-wah-gah-ha or Village Maker, Wah-no-ke-ga or Noise and So-da-mah-ze or Yellow Smoke. It is to be noticed that here again the number is seven and that the name of Noise takes the place of Cross Elk as signed to the "Gatewood Treaty." It might seem that Logan Fontenelle was included in the delegation, but the Indians clung to the ancient rule of hereditary chieftainship by including Cross Elk, the son of Big Elk.

The fourth list of men in authority in the Omaha tribe came from Gatewood's successor, Major George Hepner. The Commissioner asked him to make a thorough investigation into the organization of the Omaha. Accordingly Hepner called a large council and asked the tribe to tell him which ones among them he should recognize as chiefs. He wrote down the names given to him, read them back to the whole group and no objections were raised. This list has eight names: Standing Hawk, Mixed Fire, Little Chief, Village Maker, Ernois*, Big Eye, Joseph La Flesche and Logan Fontenelle. He further explained that all the chiefs who had gone to Washington were of equal status and that at the time they had no principal chief, since the hereditary chief, Cross Elk, was a boy about eight years of age, "under care and protection of Joseph La Flesche."[23]

It might be noted that Big Eye in this list given by the tribe was one of the four names after the seven signed to the "Gatewood Treaty." The question remains as to the identity of "Ernois" or "Arnoise"—can this be a white man's interpretation of the Indian's "Noise"? Noise was a signator at Washington but in other documents is spoken of as Wah-no-ke-ga. Were Fontenelle and La Flesche mentioned last because they were half-breeds?

Hepner's letter described several ways in which one might become a chief, besides heredity, such as rites and gifts and "acts of charity." He said:

> Logan Fontenelle was no doubt recognized as chief from the fact of his liberality and in making feasts for the headmen and braves together with some other influence which the department will understand—he will be discharged at the end of this quarter as interpreter.

The relative position of these men has puzzled careful students of the Omaha for many years. When Fannie Reed Griffin, in 1898, edited her little booklet called *Oo-Mah-Tha Ta-Wa-Tha* (Omaha City), she worked in close collaboration with Joseph's eldest daughter Susette (Bright Eyes) and Susette's husband, the journalist, Thomas H. Tibbles. Mrs. Griffin lists the signatures of the treaty in the order given in official records and presents a short sketch of each one. She mentions Fontenelle's facility in English and the qualities which made him at greater ease among whites. She indicates that he made the most notable speeches to the President, but since Louis Saunsoci was the official interpreter, Fontenelle spoke in Omaha and Saunsoci translated. She also says that Fontenelle was "elected chief for the express purpose of helping the Indians to make the treaty."

In 1919, Melvin Gilmore, disturbed by the erroneous ideas presented when a memorial tablet had been placed in the Fontenelle Hotel in Omaha, fully discussed before the Nebraska Historical

*Note: This might be "Arnois," the script is difficult to read. In Early Baptismal records the name Hannois appears.

Society some earlier studies that he had made among the Omahas. Gilmore was a painstaking researcher accustomed to meticulously recording his findings. He recognized Fontenelle as an important historical figure; but felt the honors bestowed in the twentieth century were inaccurate, praising things he had not been and neglecting the work for which he deserved to be remembered.

Gilmore had worked among the Omaha when many of the tribe who had known the treaty delegation were still living. He was aware that a contribution to *North American Ethnology*[24] contained a narrative by an Omaha, Two Crows, in which the departure of the chiefs for Washington was discussed. Two Crows, had said, "Louis Sunssoci (sic) and Logan Fontenelle went along as interpreters."

The same volume contains a story by Big Elk, the nephew of the Chief Big Elk, who in describing the death of Fontenelle said, "They killed the white man, the interpreter." Gilmore mentions that full bloods frequently referred to half-breeds as "white" and as has been said, the Frenchmen were often called "white natives." Gilmore's point was, however, that Fontenelle had always been associated with his father from the Indians's point of view and had never been made a chief by the accepted rites.

Gilmore talked to all the contemporaries of the delegation that he could find and asked them to name the chiefs who went to Washington. They always gave the same names: Two Grizzly Bears, Joseph La Flesche, Standing Hawk, Little Chief, Village Maker, Noise and Yellow Smoke. The name of Two Grizzly Bears is not on the treaty, yet long before a plaque to Fontenelle as a chief was placed in the city of Omaha and long before Gilmore asked his questions, Two Crows had named Two Grizzly Bears as one of the group who went to Washington.

Gilmore goes on to say that when the Indians arrived in Washington, Logan Fontenelle was unaccounted for and Commissioner Manypenny asked why he was there. Two Grizzly Bears said, "to interpret for me." Gilmore believed that in this way, Fontenelle's name was first on the treaty instead of Two Grizzly Bears', whom the Indians always named as the first of the delegation.

Yet in spite of this, we notice that Two Grizzly Bears' name is not included in the Gatewood lists. Whatever may be the weight of evidence in these lists, there can be no question about the great disturbance throughout the tribe over the ceding of land and where leadership should lie after the death of Big Elk. Eight years earlier the Indians in council had said to the Presbyterian missionaries that they hesitated to speak in the absence of "Big Elk with whom we always advise."[25] "The Elk" of some generation had signed papers with the United States Government since 1815. It is often difficult to distinguish which "Big Elk" is meant, since dates for succession to the chieftainship do not exist or are extremely vague.

When Hepner in December 1854 tried to find which Omahas were the ruling authorities he found evidence of these earlier disturbances. He believed that in the council which he called, the difficulty was brought into the open and in some way must have been resolved. Regrettably the heated exchanges were in Omaha and Hepner had felt it best not to press for a detailed interpretation.

> This question of chiefship is a delicate one and when it was mentioned old White Cow took the floor; his first expression was "now you shall hear it," you could hear a buzz around the room. All hands seemed to be somewhat electrified, but in the end it all passed harmoniously.

White Cow was one of the four names added on the Gatewood list. Elsewhere he is spoken of as elderly and highly respected, although he seems not to have been of high rank.

Then follows Hepner's discussion of Fontenelle and the implication that he used "some other influence that the department will understand," and concludes with, "Joseph La Flesche spoke in Council and seemed to be pleased with the result."

Did White Cow bring out matters which had only been whispered about? What was this "influence" wielded by Fontenelle? Was Two Grizzly Bears present? Did Iron Eye make peace, assert authority or was he given some definite recognition? What led Hepner to feel that Iron Eye was "pleased with the result"?

CHAPTER II

THE EARLY RESERVATION:
IRON EYE AS A TRIBAL LEADER

Surveys of early Nebraska history and accounts of the Plains Indians usually relate that early in 1854 the Omaha tribe ceded to the United States their hunting grounds north of the Platte and west of the Missouri. In exchange they received some 300,000 acres of land bordering on the Missouri about seventy miles north of the present day city of Omaha.

It sounds very simple and easy. The average reader may visualize the tipis taken down, the travois packed and the tribe in picturesque parade moving off to the north to settle happily in their new home. But it was far from simple and the move was not made quickly or easily. The Omaha had not wanted to go so far to the north; they felt they were being turned over to their enemies, the Sioux.

The treaty had said that the tribe, in consideration of the new reserve, would release all claim for money granted under former treaties, but that they were entitled to one unpaid balance of $25,000. The delegation had understood that this over-due annuity would be paid when the treaty was signed, but the chiefs were told it would come "later" and be given in commodities—food, clothing and implements. They had had such payments before when the supplies consisted of clothing they did not want and of food, if it arrived unspoiled, too often not to their taste.

The Indians were rebellious and resentful in their disillusionment and refused to go past St. Louis on the return journey until money was paid. Plainly the actual words and their implications had not been clearly and exactly explained. Alfred Cumming, the Superintendent at St. Louis, said, "...the Agent professed to know nothing." They were, however, persuaded to proceed to the village west of Bellevue.

By this time the corn should have been planted and the treaty was still on the President's desk awaiting his attention. Moreover, if they might still consider an alternate choice for the reserve,[1] exploration must be made and the corn would have to be planted at Bellevue. Because of the uncertainty, many did not plant. The promised goods in lieu of a cash annuity did not come, and in hunger and disappointment the Omaha too often helped themselves to the stock and supplies of the settlers.

The settlers were quick to file claims for damages and demand payment, but at the same time rejoiced over the Indians' land becoming "public lands." The few eagerly read newspapers of the frontier triumphantly announced that "all land above the Nemaha was open to settlement"[2] and that the area where white men could make new homes "was nearly equal to all six of the New England states."[3]

In November, Major Hepner and several of the chiefs went to explore along the "Aoway" (Iowa) river seeking possible locations for a village. They decided it was poor country, but at last chose a spot near the Missouri between the two Blackbird Creeks which afforded a slight protection.

The *Nebraska Palladium,* the first newspaper in the Nebraska Territory, proudly published by Bellevue citizens, reported on November 18 that the Indians would move next spring and that at the time, they were away on the fall hunt. The hunt was most successful and on their return they found abundant crops—and the belated goods from the government. Now there was no need for them and there was no possible way to store them.

The *Palladium* further proclaimed as a sign of progress that the sale of public land that year would amount to almost six million acres. And still the Omaha were not supplied with their permanent home, or with the mill and the blacksmith shop and the armed protection which had been promised.

Negotiations for the treaty were a year past when Hepner reported to his superiors that white men were objecting and exerting pressure because they did not like the Blackbird Hills site. He, himself, had thought the "choice was to be made by the Indians" who still asked that further exploration be made. But the government made no decision and sent no definite orders. In February 1855, the Omaha again requested a cash annuity payment and a sympathetic editor impatiently asked "how does the government know best" what the Omaha require? He answered his own question with an emphatic statement that "the government cannot tell what kind of food or clothing the Indians need."[4]

In April and again in May the tribe asked for the cash annuity insisting they would stay where they were until the money was assured. Two weeks later the word came that the Blackbird Hills site was approved and that the annuity would be paid on the new reservation. They were eager to move in spite of the fact that some had planted corn for the second year in their old fields.

By the 11th of June, Hepner wrote with satisfaction, "they are placed at Blackbird Hills." He had experienced difficulty getting them past Ft. Calhoun where Ft. Atkinson had stood thirty years before. One band, or a faction, had announced they would stay there and that the money should be paid on the spot. A few even began to select areas for their individual fields. Hepner said, "Logan, La Flesche, Saunsocee and a few others were with me with the money; the opposition was too strong and they finally struck for the Hills."

The payment was made on May 31 in a place near the river and a little south of Blackbird Hills. "It amounted to $20,000 and some hundreds." Before the payment a group of white traders from the east side of the river created a disturbance by insisting that they be paid for horses allegedly stolen by the Omaha. When no money was given them, they did all they could to frighten the Indians with threats of sending the Sioux to kill them off.

This was the end of May and on July 5, 1855, the Omaha left for the summer hunt. A week or ten days later, Logan Fontenelle became separated from a small party, was set upon, killed and scalped. The tribe fled southward in terror. The thing they had dreaded had happened and they refused to return. They had been at their new home less than six weeks and the treaty had been signed, amended, ratified and enacted into law for a full year.

By November, they were told that they might stay "near the mouth of the Horn"[5] (the Elkhorn) for the winter. Henry and Tecumseh Fontenelle, brothers of Logan, together with Lewis (sic) Saunsocee and James Cleghorn petitioned for their shares of the Half-Breed Reservation between the Nemahas. They may have contemplated leaving the tribe and its uncertainties, but on October 1, Henry was appointed interpreter for the Omaha and remained with them.[6]

George Hepner, the Agent, mentioned the generally broken morale to Alfred Cumming, the Superintendent at St. Louis, and his fear that the Sioux might drive the Omaha off the plains during the fall hunt. He said, "...800 raised no corn; 130 odd acres of crops were abandoned for the summer hunt." It is not clear, at this date, where these crops were, near Bellevue or north at Blackbird Hills. If the former, the tribe had been ordered and urged to leave them and go to the new reservation. If they had planted to that extent on the new location, fear of their enemies and not the hunt caused them to abandon the fields. The age old habit had been to plant the corn and then leave for the hunt, harvesting green corn on the return. But the official report gives no indication of any other reason but the hunt for the lack of a harvest.

Alfred Cumming, as Superintendent, in the usual sequence, reported this to George Manypenny, the Commissioner of Indian Affairs, who duly informed Robert McClelland, the Secretary of the Interior, specifically stating that the "country above the Aoway is not satisfactory to the Omaha." Nevertheless, the balance of the report is full of plans for the next spring (1856) at the location; land would be broken, a saw mill would be erected, a school would be opened.

The school would be in the hands of the Presbyterian Board of Foreign Missions and the church moved more quickly to make plans and start construction than did the government. The Presbyterians had been operating a Mission and school at Bellevue for nearly ten years. Now that school was to be reestablished farther south for the Otoe and Missouri, and a new Mission and school would be opened for the Omaha on the new reserve, wherever that might be.

Walter Lowrie, secretary of the Board and Rev. William Hamilton, the missionary in charge at Bellevue, had made an extended trip into the new area during the tribe's short stay there in 1855. They visited the proposed village site, observed "breaking" being done in the rich bottom land for a common farm, and held a council with twenty-nine chiefs and head men. The missionaries wanted the Indians' opinion on the location for the school. But the Indians, convinced that they were unprotected, feared the Sioux would harm their children and would not answer.

The tribe returned to the Reserve in May of 1856 but Hamilton "passed them on the way up." They stopped him and wanted to know where the school would be, but he replied that they should first study several possible sites. Hamilton waited for Joseph to join him and for several days they rode over the hills, along the streams, discussing advantages and disadvantages of each location. These men talked easily together in the dialect of the Iowa, for Hamilton had served the Iowa before crossing the river. There were few other instances at that time when a white man and an Indian, without the presence of a third party, could talk directly and with as great understanding as could this chief and this missionary.[7]

Iron Eye wanted the school to be fifteen or eighteen miles away from the village making it harder for the children to run away.

But, at last, Hamilton selected a spot not far above Blackbird Hills on a high wooded bluff overlooking the river. A good spring nearby was an advantage as was the plentiful supply of wood and the possibility of access to the river and shipping.

Wasting no time Hamilton planted a garden; then camped that night with the tribe. Iron Eye consulted with the others and the next morning assured Hamilton that with one exception, the chiefs approved. The exception had been a report that a friend of Louis Saunsoci wanted that place for a farm. But the man had not been present and the others were eager for Hamilton to go ahead. He started for Bellevue with his head full of plans—the problems of building material, sources of supply, the need for a sawmill, for carpenters, for a field and fencing, for a farmer and teachers, the task of furnishing and heating a large building and feeding the staff it would house.

Major Vanderslice, who was to relocate the Indian tribes along the Missouri, sent word that it was his prerogative to select the site for the Mission and that Hamilton should meet him and they would settle the matter. But the Major did not keep his appointment. Hamilton went back to the Reserve trying to find the officer, who was always reporting as having been "somewhere" in the neighborhood or just recently left. Rumor said Vanderslice had selected the same spot for the Agency, but he never confronted Hamilton face to face with such a statement—and immediately left the country.

Feeling that the Indians were the ones concerned and assured of their desires, Hamilton was again on the scene in June with wagons and teams and six laborers. Once more he consulted the chiefs, telling them that the place was wanted for the Agency. The Indians had always thought the Agent would live with the Missionary, but accepted the fact that this was not to be and told Hamilton to go on with his plans. They wanted him there and expected no payment from him.

Rumors, some far fetched and some easily credited, built up over this move of the Government. Hamilton brought his years of experience serving Indians and dealing with government to bear on these rumors and wrote to his superiors in New York. One of his informants had been in a position to catch the under surface machinery of the Bureau's planning and Hamilton was concerned. He was told that Vanderslice was opposed to La Flesche as chief saying he was fanatical. But Hamilton's interpretation was that those dealing with the Omaha knew they could not use La Flesche, "the only strictly honest and intelligent chief" for ulterior purposes. He was convinced that white men intended to disregard the treaty, place the Omaha with other tribes and gain land for themselves. No doubt, some members of the tribe resented the prestige given Iron Eye by Big Elk and made dire predictions as to Iron Eye's fate if he were acknowledged as chief. Hamilton felt the white men intended to use this resentment to satisfy their own cupidity and indicated that Joseph had been pushed aside at the time of the treaty. He reported in September that "La Flesche has never been . . reinstated." However, a petition for the mill promised two years earlier was made in June and Joseph's name was the first on the list although no designation of principal chief was made. Iron Eye was officially known by the Indian name; however, the one used on government records is always Joseph La Flesche.

Credence is given Hamilton's suspicions by Superintendent Cumming's official recommendation that the Ponca tribe be located on the reserve with the Omaha,[8] thus avoiding the creation of still another reservation. Cumming also asked instructions for action because the Rev. Hamilton of the Presbyterian Mission was occupying the site selected for the Agency Building, and although he had been notified of the government's wishes, he was "going on to improve it."

In fact, the walls of the Mission were rising steadily when at last a new Agent, not provided with a building or a dwelling, was appointed in July after the tribe had left for the annual summer hunt. Again no annuity had been paid in the spring when the move had been made north and winter supplies were running low. Through Hamilton, we know that there had been real suffering, some going without food for several days. Iron Eye came to the rescue by using his savings from his trading business to buy meat. He was resented by many of the tribe and was unrecognized by the Government; he still maintained leadership by advising many individuals. His sense of duty led to personal sacrifice; for, besides buying a beef for the tribe, he, himself, seldom ate, so that there might be more for others. The only report reaching Washington was in the fall in the Commissioner's annual report.

> The Omaha. . .have ample supplies for the coming winter. . .had a successful hunt. . .have buffalo and deer meat; 800 buffalo robes and plenty of deer and other skins.[9]

The practice of making annual reports in the autumn after the summer and fall hunts, and after the vegetables and melons were stored always put a brighter light on the Indians' condition than if they had been made in the meager season of a long-delayed spring.

Late in the fall of 1856, Hamilton made a last trip north. He spent several weeks at the Mission, working, directing and planning. There were early storms and he was forced to leave, knowing the building could not be roofed; the upper floor and part of the lower one would be exposed to the weather. He had purchased a sawmill, operated by oxen, since the Government still had not supplied one. It would be ready by spring and would speed the work of finishing the building, of making large pieces of furniture and erecting outbuildings.

One man remained on the site all winter, working in the covered rooms, fashioning school desks, tables and chairs. The mill was in operation by March. Then in April the Agent wrote that he would consult on a location for the Mission. Influential white men made fun of the Mission and extended their scorn to Iron Eye, its most devoted supporter. Many of the Omaha were completely bewildered, thinking in agreement with the last person to whom they had talked. Joseph was constantly explaining and counseling, trying to show how the school would help them and their children; saying, over and over, that they must learn to farm and help their children live in a new world; reminding them that Big Elk had said the flood of white men would overwhelm them.

Hamilton saw matters from the point of view of the Indians and did not feel that the chiefs should be appointed by the government. But as pressure grew greater, he saw that the employees of the government frequently worked only for themselves, not for the Indians or the Indian Office. He began to feel that recognition from Washington gave added prestige and authority. He felt it should be granted to Iron Eye, for without it his plans to lead the people might fail. This recognition was given Iron Eye a few months later.

The fifteen years before coming to the Reservation had been hard on the Omaha, pushed about by encroaching white men and their old enemy, the Sioux. All continuity was gone from the tribal system. At the same time, they were faced with both a complete change in the pattern of living and the new, powerful temptation offered them by the white men. Like all other American Indians, the Omaha had had no knowledge of alcoholic drinks before the advent of the white men. Alcohol, however, became the essential in the traders' stock; no rules or regulations could control its sale on the sparsely settled frontier. Agents spoke of the Indians having "a drunken frolick," which was usually accompanied by shooting and knifing, as drinking became a common practice.

Iron Eye consulted with the wiser, more thoughtful men of the tribe and took a bold step. With the consent of the council he took about $1,000 from tribal funds to equip and pay a police force. Thirty men were organized and uniformed and pledged to keep order. They were to whip severely any drunken Omaha whether he came on the Reservation after drinking or if it be proven he had been drunk while away. This penalty was inflicted without regard to rank or personal favor. Iron Eye allowed it to be administered to a close friend. The Omaha became a sober people, widely recognized as such by the government workers.

This was the first native police force on the plains and it was later copied by Agents until it became part of the usual organization of a Reservation. The uniforms of this first police unit were of green broadcloth trimmed with red facings. Typically, the material was furnished at Iron Eye's personal expense and the suits were made by Mary. She still had the patterns she had used, when fifty years later, she told the ethnologist, Melvin Gilmore, about them and gave him the names of the police force.[10]

The year of 1857 was a memorable one for the Mission and for Iron Eye. The building was almost complete and the Missionary and his family arrived in May. A head teacher and several assistants came a few weeks later. The Missionary was the Reverend Charles Sturgis, a devoted laborer, sincerely dedicated to the advancement of the Indians. A modest person, he never felt equal to the task and suffered acutely over his ignorance of the language. From the first, he asked that a younger man might be found who could master this strange tongue, for at his age of fifty it was impossible and the pressing matter of "religious conversations" was baffling with an interpreter.

He struggled on, visiting the lodges and asking for another horse to facilitate these visits. He invited chiefs to the Mission, and tried to explain the Truth that he so sincerely believed, to these leaders who met him with dignity, tolerance and often with admiration. He rejoiced in taking Iron Eye as a private pupil in English, for the man "was anxious to learn. . .and such a man, if educated would be a great benefit to the Mission and a great influence among the people."

The school made progress under J. D. Rolph who passed on the roll of the school which has been preserved. There were twenty-five boys and four girls. The girls were all from Henry Fontenelle's settlement near Decatur. The Mission wanted more girls but the chiefs said they were needed at home. This roll gives the name of Louis La Flesche, age nine years. Letters of a near date speak of "Joseph La Flesche" being in school. The name may have been Louis Joseph or the writer was accustomed to writing "Joseph" with "La Flesche," for Joseph (Iron Eye) was a private pupil and would not have had time to have been in the school.

The Missionaries, of course, were largely responsible for the English names given to the school children which were passed on to their children and their families. To be sure, as in the case of the La Flesche, Fontenelle, Pilcher, Cabney and Barada families and others, the non-Indian name came from a white progenitor, but at times, full bloods were given names or took names of white men whom they knew or admired. Later a distinction was often made between the Indian name and the "citizen name." Rolph reported in October 1857:

> Silas Wood, Edison Rockwell, James Buchanan and Thomas McCauley commenced in June. . .in their a, b, c, d's. . .and are now reading and spelling in Webster. . .Francis Brush came in July, aged four and reads in words of three or four letters.[11]

When the tribe was settled on the Reserve, Joseph built an earth lodge, forty feet in diameter, about one mile south of the Mission. He had drawn about him a group known as "the young men's party." He planned a whole village of frame houses in order to show how the white men lived. During the summer of 1857, he started his own frame house, using his own oxen to operate the Mission saw mill and paying a "service charge" in cash. The two story house (family home and stopping place for travelers) was completed and occupied by November. This was the first time a Plains Indian had built his own frame house.[12] In 1861, there were nineteen inhabited houses in the village, eight having been built that year—seven more than were in the predominantly white settlement of Decatur. In 1869, after the "young men's party" had lost influence, the government men still spoke of the place as "Joe's village," and one man described it as "not unlike (villages) seen through Virginia during the late war."[13]

Iron Eye continued to be a trader as he and Logan Fontenelle had been with Peter Sarpy. On the new Reserve, Logan's brother Henry and Iron Eye were associated, serving as traders for the tribe— a lucrative and often coveted position. The tribe liked having them there, and as long as possible, resisted the post being put in the hands of white men.

One Agent, in describing the payment of an annuity, said there had been no trouble except that Joseph and Henry had stood by the official paying table to collect amounts due them. The collection of debts at the time of payment became standard practice, for the merchant or banker could not be sure of getting the amount due him unless he had the first chance at the money. The tribe always wanted payment in money rather than goods and it was reasonable in many ways. However, many Indians had no concept of money values and their share disappeared quickly with little to show that they had briefly handled the cash. Ignorance of values and this collection at the payment made the uneducated Indians easy prey for the unscrupulous white men. White men would list an Indian's debt at an increased figure, and at times, they entered the side door of the Agency in order to be in the first place as each member of the tribe came for his portion of the payment. In years to come, Iron Eye's daughters would take the accounts of certain merchants and the record of debts incurred by Indians. They would then see that the money was honestly collected and paid out properly to both red men and white men.

Iron Eye had worked for cash payment in more ways and for a longer time than others, and he had been liberal with his savings when the tribe had been in want. He often had funds beyond his own immediate needs and loaned money to others at the high interest rates of the frontier. He had learned these things about the white man's money economy, but he had not understood that a man was not personally involved when he acted for an organization. He had loaned $1,800 to Rev. Hamilton and then became impatient when the loan was not promptly paid. He could not understand why Hamilton did not have the means at hand to meet the debt. Hamilton was constantly spending money around the Mission, at times rather large sums and the Indian could not see that at times Hamilton acted for the Mission and at other times for himself.

He was encouraged in his confusion and his impatience by certain of his own white employees who hoped to weaken the connection between the Mission and this influential chief. Iron Eye's impatience became deep resentment. It was sometime before Sturgis discovered the underlying reason and was able to bring about some approach to reconciliation. But the whole episode tended to instill a suspicion of white men and an overcaution which increased year by year in his dealing with them.

While Iron Eye and the Mission had been making progress and building, the government had still reached no decision on the location of the Agency. It is difficult to know whether this was a red-tape entanglement or deliberate stalling, with the hope that the Mission would give up. Two succeeding Agents built their own houses in Decatur and requested an Agency building on the Reserve.

The tribe continued to ask for the sawmill and the gristmill promised long before. At last in February 1858, the government announced that the Agent was supplied with funds for a grist-sawmill, to be placed near the land. It was understood that an engineer had been appointed. Before it was erected, however, a new Agent was appointed; he thought the mill would be working "at the original site" by the middle of August. Then one Sunday in July, just as Rev. Sturgis started the church service, the mill was unloaded within thirty yards of the Mission. The Missionary did not abandon his service to supervise, but offered to have it moved the next day. This was to no avail—the mill remained.

Several times Iron Eye stayed home from the hunts, trying to show the people that they must learn new ways to make their living for they could no longer rely on hunting. Game was scarce. The white man's concentration on killing the buffalo had almost exterminated that source of food and clothing. There were repeated attacks on hunting parties by other tribes. In 1864, responsible white men from the Mission and from Bellevue went out to the Platte to rescue the Omaha hunting party from the enraged settlers who were frantic over the Sioux depredations and the frequent intertribal battles.

Iron Eye led in making temporary alliances with friendly tribes so that they might protect each other. One year, a detachment of soldiers was sent with the hunting party, and the commanding officers throughout a large territory were sent word that the Omaha tribe was allowed to hunt over a certain area and along a certain route. The problem of restraining the young braves who welcomed the hunt as the opportunity to prove themselves and their prowess, complicated managing the hunt. But in spite of these discouragements, the Omaha continued to go on the hunt until strictly and finally forbidden in 1876, more than twenty years after reaching the Reservation.

Iron Eye led his people in seeking new knowledge of all kinds. He believed the Missionaries were good people who truly wished to help the Indians, and urged his people to listen to what these men said and to give careful thought to the things in "God's book." When

Sturgis visited the villages, he found the largest gathering at Joseph's and felt that both Joseph and his wife Mary were striving to understand.

Then in the fall of 1859, Joseph (as Dr. Sturgis came to call him) met with an accident which brought a permanent disability. This increased his deeply thoughtful and philosophical turn of mind. It was an accident of the new world—the new way of life—not a matter of a tomahawk blow or an arrow shot from ambush as the romantic writers might supply. He stepped on a nail and neglected the wound! The tools of the white man were at hand, but his medicine could not cure the leg. Within a few weeks it was amputated below the knee.

Sturgis spent a great deal of time with Joseph conversing as best he could.[14] One day Joseph asked Sturgis to pray for him. When the minister asked what he wished him to pray, Joseph said to pray that if he was to die that God would be his friend and that if he was to get well that God would help him to "live in the good road." Even though he thought God had afflicted him for some reason, he still believed that "God was good." From that time on, Joseph asked to have the religion of the Book explained to him. It was a long, hard road to travel for a deeply sincere man when so many of the precepts were contrary to those under which he had been trained.

The amputation had been done awkwardly, and Joseph continued to suffer. Several requests for a trip to Washington or New York were ignored, and the staff at the Mission feared that the further spread of infection might cost Joseph his life. All he wished to live for, he told the Missionary, was to see his people on the road to improvement, their money matters made straight and the Mission in full favor. At last, in 1861, permission was granted and Iron Eye led a delegation to Washington to discuss the complete fulfillment of the 1854 treaty.

He went on to New York, and under the guidance of Walter Lowrie of the church board, he had proper surgical care and was fitted with a cork leg. He brought home with him a small electric device and a magneto with handles attached, thinking he had found a way to impress his people with the need for education. He gave a feast for the chiefs and the headmen telling them that he would show them something of the white man's great power which surpassed anything done by their medicine men. He had several chiefs hold hands and one at each end grasp the handles of the apparatus. He turned on the current and quietly watched their contortions; then he turned it off and without being seen, put on his leg and walked among them. He sat down, moved his foot; got up and walked again. Their amazement was mounting to fear when he quieted them. He showed them his wooden leg, and explained it and the electrical device. He assured them that this was not magic, but the result of white men working and sending their children to school.[15]

He never ceased to emphasize the school, sending his own children and doing everything he could to encourage others. He brought other children to school, and often came to visit and watch them all. He had the tribal police find the runaways and bring them back. He persisted until the Agent arranged for two of the older boys to spend half a day in school and half a day working with the blacksmith. Here was an opportunity, close at hand, for them to learn one of the white man's skills.

The Omaha tribe was known as an industrious tribe and was the most temperate and peaceable on the fronteir. In 1861, the Commissioner of Indian Affairs reported to the Secretary of the Interior, ". . .much of the progress of the Omaha is due to Chief La Flesche and the excellent school in their midst."

The leaders at the Mission spoke with high praise of Joseph's intelligence, his sense of responsibility and his leadership, but they must have felt that his actual union with the church was long delayed. It was a matter of many years before he became a church member. William Hamilton was back again at Blackbird Hills and in charge of the Mission, and Joseph had suffered sorrows and humiliation. The first Sunday after Joseph joined the church, Father Hamilton was amazed to have the room suddenly too small to hold all the Indians present. This continued for several weeks and at last Hamilton asked Joseph why so many had suddenly decided to come to church. He replied that it was good for them to go to church and he had ordered them to go. The minister tried to explain that this was not the way the work of the church was extended. Joseph insisted that the words they had formerly heard were not good words but when Hamilton explained "God's Book" to them it taught them to "walk in the right way."

The discussion went on for some days, for Joseph always probed deeply into a new idea until he could find its full meaning and discover which ideas he could make a part of his life. One day Hamilton read to him, "My kingdom is not of this world." Joseph said that was enough but he must think that over. Days later he

returned and said he saw that the Book told two things. It taught
how to do things in order that men could live on the earth, that was
for the body, but that it also taught things for the heart. He realized
that he could tell a man to build a house and to live there instead of
in a tent, but he could not tell that man to have a good heart and
the man's heart would be good. He thought only God could do
that.16

One of Iron Eye's great moments of outward recognition as
chief, at least of which any record was left, was in June 1861 when
Orasmus H. Irish replaced Dr. George B. Graff as Agent. The Civil
War was in progress and the government was uneasy over the attitude
which might be taken by the Indians in the territories outside the
States. A great ceremony was made of the raising of the flag—the
Union flag.

Rev. R. J. Burtt of the Mission reported the event:

> The whole tribe was in their best attire, the soldiers in uniform with
> their muskets. The Chiefs were decorated with their medals and many
> pretty things. In procession they marched, preceded by La Flesche
> as principal chief on horseback with Henry Fontenelle as marshall.
> Many whites assembled from thirty miles around—such another sight
> was never seen. Several addresses were made and the Union Flag
> hoisted. Among the speakers, La Flesche gave us quite a treat, regular
> American or Union speech to the Chiefs, soldiers and braves.
>
> "My white and red friends. Today our fathers (the Agents)
> call us together. . .and have hoisted this flag over us. The flag
> signifies freedom and equal rights. When we were at Washington at
> our Great Father's we saw this flag floating in the breeze. . .Our
> Great Father gave us this on our departure. . .Before he gave us
> this flag. . .we were not a people. Since then we think we are a
> people. . .(with) this flag he gave us strength. . .as long as this flag
> waves over us so long, I think we will be a people."

Burtt felt certain that white men stirred up ill feeling over Iron
Eye and obviously many within the tribe disliked his influence. Too
often Iron Eye and the Mission were thought of as one. Predatory
would-be settlers sought underhanded ways by which they might
attain their desires, but they knew Joseph and the Mission were
against them. The rumbles continued and dissensions increased. The
Indians were well aware of conflicts related to the Civil War, and
knew that they were closely watched to prevent any added trouble.
Nearly one hundred of their young men were serving in the Union
Army. It was through political turns rising out of the War that
tension on the Reservation came to a climax.

In September 1863, the Second Nebraska Cavalry Regiment was mustered out of service and the Colonel, Robert W. Furnas, was without any business connection. (Furnas later became an important figure in Nebraska history and served ably as governor from 1873 to 1875.) Before entering the Army he had edited *The Nebraska Advertiser* at Brownville and had actively supported Samuel G. Daily for the territorial representative to Congress. About the same time, Irish was moved to the position of Superintendent of Indian Affairs with headquarters in Salt Lake City and it was possible for Daily to pay his political debt by securing the Agency for Furnas.[17]

Furnas was a vigorous man, accustomed to action and recently accustomed to command. He entered his new position, apparently feeling he was the highest authority and able to command obedience from all. He was faced with an emergency immediately. Several hundred Winnebagos sought refuge with the Omaha tribe. For over a year the Winnebago tribe had been expressing its dissatisfaction over the reservation given them on Crow Creek in Dakota Territory. They were hard pressed by the Sioux, almost constantly on the move and frequently quite destitute. One citizen wrote to the Indian office that they were "scattered along the Missouri River from Ft. Randall to the Omaha Agency", that they must be collected, fed and controlled.

The Winnebago asked that a small group might stay with the Omaha for a time. Furnas moved to hasten Omaha consideration of this request. It was granted, and a large field was set aside for the visitors to cultivate. Under Iron Eye's direction they were given a set of laws by which they were to live. These especially prohibited dancing and gambling and the use of "spiritous liquors."

Instead of a group numbering less than two hundred Winnebagos, however, they kept coming by the canoe load—always more and more until there were over seven hundred, and then early in September almost the whole Ponca tribe arrived with no provisions except a little buffalo meat. The Omaha had no meat, for the early hunt had been a failure and they were glad to exchange corn for meat. Neither tribe, however, had enough to last more than a few weeks. Although the Ponca left before winter, for almost two months, Furnas had over 3000 Indians from three different tribes on his hands. Emergency rations from the government were obtained and the Omaha tribe and Joseph shared all they could.[18]

With characteristic vigor, Furnas moved towards plans of longer range and in accord with the government plan to settle each tribe in a definite place. In spite of the War, white settlement was advancing

and approaching the limits of the more easily cultivated land. Locations for more reservations were becoming scarce. Furnas, as a few
before him, saw the solution in placing this discontented, unsettled
tribe with the Omaha. In less than a year after he assumed his duties,
he started to Washington with a delegation authorized by the chiefs
and headmen to sell part of their reservation to the United States for
the use of the Winnebago. Rumor said it would include the Ponca
and they would be under one Agent, Robert Furnas.

Many of the Omaha disliked the idea. Their treaty had said
their reservation would be surveyed and they would be given individual farms; but nothing had been done. Moreover, they would have
preferred to have their relatives the Ponca rather than the Winnebago.
Joseph, as the leader, was greatly opposed to any lessening of the
reservation.

The treaty was signed on March 18, 1865, but was not ratified
and enacted into law for nearly a year later. By then the Nebraska
Territorial Legislature, in its lower house, had passed an act to force
the removal of all Indians from the State. Furnas, Joseph and Rev.
Burtt of the Mission worked together to secure a large petition that
the survey be made for the Omaha tribe as assurance that they would
not be moved.

In the meantime, Furnas had turned his attention to the
Mission school although strictly speaking he had no authority over
the school. The government contracted directly with the Presbyterian
Board of Missions and the Mission had worked to the limit of its
contract ands facilities.[19] Furnas said they did not reach enough
children; there must be more schools and provision must be made to
include the Winnebago children. Furnas had made appropriate and
generous gifts to the church and the school, but Burtt began to
doubt any real interest, although he agreed with Furnas that some
kind of extended service was needed.

The threat of removal, the knowledge that part of their Reservation was gone, resentment over Furnas' arbitrary authority and his
requirement of military passes restricing their movements were added
to groundless gossip about Joseph and about Rev. Burtt and to dis-
sention in the Mission family until all produced a turmoil building up
to an explosive climax. Both Rev. Burtt and Joseph were removed
from their positions in the spring of 1866.

Too little material exists after one hundred years to even
venture reasons for Burtt's sudden dismissal although one letter indicated that Furnas was involved. In February, Burtt had written

about his affection for the children, the welcome he received from the adults, his own growing use of the language and the increasing number of church and prayer meetings held in the villages. Then in April he wrote, "God give me grace to bear this trial. No one knows its severity." But putting aside his own humiliation and sorrow he adds, "Joseph La Flesche has been deposed and removed from the Reserve. . .pretended friends are enemies."[20]

Later he wrote, "There must be some specific charge against me. May I ask what it is?" and again, ". . .had a conversation with Col. Furnas and have denied every charge. . .because I am innocent. . .he has gone so far as to admit that they were made upon rumor."[21]

Two months earlier Furnas and Jospeh had worked together to present a petition for allotment and under Furnas' direction, Joseph as principal chief had signed the paper. By July, Burtt was in New Jersey at his old home and there is no record of Joseph's whereabouts.

One letter[22] from Furnas to Dr. Lowrie of the Church Board throws some light on the matter and yet from another angle only makes it more confusing. This is in the Historical Records of the Presbyterian Church and has not before been considered with Furnas' work as agent, since it is not among his papers in the Nebraska Historical Society. It is a curious document when read in the light of the many other comments on Joseph from agents, military men, traders and missionaries over a period of thirty years. It alone sounds a derogatory note and nearly every statement in it can be contradicted by another source. Joseph was "accidentally" chief; he continued to bribe others for his own ends; "he is shrewd, cunning and ambitious," . . . no friend of the school, he has arrayed himself against every effort of mine to elevate the tribe."

The key to understanding may lie in the words "every effort of mine." It may be that Joseph had asserted his own convictions against the plans of the recent army officer. Several times the phrase "was never subordinate to the Agent" was used. Furnas insisted he had not ordered Joseph to leave. Joseph had taken his children out of the school, had packed up and left with his whole household. He might return whenever he wished but he must "conduct himself properly and be subordinate to the Agent."

Furnas showed he was not well versed in Indian background by using the wrong terms for certain tribal customs and speaking of "Little Elk" when he evidently meant Big Elk. He said Ma-ha-min-ga had followed Joseph and forced him to surrender the tribal "archives." Ma-ha-min-ga (No Knife) was captain of the police, who lived in the "make-believe-white-man's-village" in a frame house. He had been a member, with Joseph, of the last delegation to go to Washington. He was of the Elk gens and took Joseph's place as chief until that confused position was abolished in 1880.

Furnas started his letter by claiming that his present position was not of his own choosing. He took it because he might be able to do some good. He may not have started out to be an Indian Agent, but he could not disclaim the fact he had sought a federal appointment in return for favors he had shown Daily. Two other items might cast light on this letter aside from Furnas' complete reliance on interpreters.

When he had accepted Daily's offer of the agency, he had been told he might appoint a trader, although this was a "delicate matter."[23] La Flesche and Fontenelle had remained as traders under increasing difficulty in raising the needed capital to make cash payments and meet the freight bills. Irish, the Agent, had asked if the government might advance the money to them, since he felt that at the time it was best to leave the trading in the hands of tribal members, athough he thought an outsider might be in a better financial position.

At about the same time (May 1863) Burtt, speaking for Joseph, asked if Lowrie would loan the money for the freight. Burtt added, "I give no promise. . .but Joseph is honorable and meets his payments promptly." In February of 1866, Burtt sent money from Joseph to Lowrie, remarking it was the "last payment."

The whole situation made it feasible to appoint an outsider as trader and the "delicate matter" consisted in the plan to find one for the lowest possible pay so that more profits might be divided between Furnas, Daily, the Territorial Representative to Congress and William Dole, the Commissioner of Indian Affairs.

Such arrangements were common at the time and even when the agents were not directly concerned with reservation business they frequently used the Agency as a step for personal advancement. The greatest impact on the local situation was that it deprived Fontenelle and La Flesche of their means of livelihood, the business which they had conducted for nearly six years. They continued to sell for a time which only made them less popular with the new business firm, who were all in authority over the tribe. A year after Furnas arrived, Burtt wrote to Lowrie that Joseph was no longer in the merchantile business and must meet his obligation through the management of his beef cattle and horses of which he had many.

It may be at this time that La Flesche and Henry Fontenelle drew away from each other. Joseph had been a friend of Henry's older brother Logan, an outstanding leader, and on removal to the Reserve had become a partner of Henry's. From this time on, however, they apparently turned in different directions and at last came into bitter disagreement and competition. Henry, because he had a facility with English, became the unofficial spokesman for his people even after he was no longer the official interpreter. In this way he attracted the continuing attention of the white men. All this contributed to the fact that the name Fontenelle is well noted in the area today—streets, parks and a hotel are named "Fontenelle," while nothing is named "La Flesche."

The second item which might have bearing on Furnas' vehement letter about Joseph grew out of the treaty ceding part of the Reservation for use by the Winnebago. On September 28, 1866, Furnas wrote to E. B. Taylor, the Superintendent of Indian Affairs stationed at Omaha, saying, ". . .in regard to the $2,500 provided in the treaty for La Flesche," the tribe feels since he "abdicated his position" no money should be paid. But no such stipulation appears in the treaty. Any agreement of this sort must have been by verbal agreement or a private memorandum which is not part of the record. Joseph had objected to giving up the land and feared clashes with the Winnebago. Incapacitated physically, he had been forced to give up his business as trader and Furnas had profited by the change.

Late in 1866, after the treaty was the law, Furnas reluctantly conceded that this payment could not be avoided although, he added, La Felsche had left his position in the tribe. He did not mention that the agreement to pay Joseph was made at least thirteen months before Joseph had left. The Indian Bureau records contain a letter from George M. Doane of Omaha trying to collect this money for Joseph. He said that Furnas promised the amount of $2,500 to Joseph if he would cease his opposition to vacating the land for the other tribe:

> La Flesche, supporting this promise to be authoritative, as it was made by the Agent in Washington while he was in constant communication with the Commissioner and others in authority, . . .ceased his opposition. . .had La Flesche continued his opposition to the Treaty it would never have been concluded for his influence with the tribe was. . .potent. His opposition being based upon pecuniary considerations alone it was entirely proper that he should yield his opposition. . .(for a like consideration).

Did these matters lie behind Furnas' willingness to listen to rumors or did he yield to irritation because of what one contemporary called his tendency to be "wedded to his own theory"? Did Joseph sink into confusion over the incomprehensible ways of white men with money? No complete answer can be given. While history tells *what* has happened, many times it is silent on *why* it happened.

Whatever the reasons, whatever the faults, here and there, the name of Joseph La Flesche ceased to appear on official Omaha documents. He returned to his village sometime later and his leadership continued as it had existed before formal recognition of his chieftainship—through advice, through example and eventually through his children. He turned more and more to the teaching of the missionaries and became one of the strong members of the little Presbyterian church at the Agency. He was a long time reaching this point for he always thought over ideas and problems for a long time before he analyzed them and could express his conviction.

This habit indicates that Joseph was philosophically an Omaha whether or not he was one by blood. The Omaha had always placed a high value on serious thinking, and believed that careful study could bring about reasonable conclusion. Their Sacred Legend which related their origin and development is explicit in its statement that whatever forward movement they made, whatever arrangement that worked for betterment came from thought. Repeatedly the Legend said, "And the people thought."[24]

Ten years after Joseph ceased to be chief, the Ponca tribe, closely related to the Omaha, was bereft of their old home and faced with forced removal. At the same time many of the Omaha and other tribes thought the Omaha were moving entirely too fast in the white man's ways. The Otoes sent a delegation to talk with them and to give support to those who wanted to retain old ways and customs.

This, of course, had been largely in Joseph's thinking for many years and now he formed a statement of his ideas on the Indians' future action. Later he had someone, probably his oldest daughter, send these ideas to his brother, White Swan, who was a chief with the Poncas.

He said:

There are some good things by which we live.
First—The God above made this world and gave it to us to live in.
Second—The white men have been sent to teach us how to live.
Third—God has made the earth to yield the fruit to us.
Fourth—God has given us hands with which we can work.

Look back on the lives of your fathers and grandfathers; then look at yourselves, and see how far you have gone ahead, and seeing this, do not stop and turn back to them, but go forward. Look ahead and you will see nothing but the white man. The future is full of the white man, and we shall be as nothing before them.

Do not think that if anyone cheats you or does you wrong, that you will do the same to him. Look out for yourselves. Take care of yourselves. [25]

These were the precepts, the basic philosophy on which he lived and in which he trained his children.

CHAPTER III

JOSEPH AS A FAMILY MAN

Children were the most precious possession of an Omaha Indian family. Every stage of their development was marked by ceremonies of poetic beauty and deep significance. Each child was carefully disciplined and trained to take his or her place in the family and in the tribe. The fables which each child learned emphasized the qualities of truth and dependability. Only a well trained and disciplined child could contribute to the future of the tribe for children would shape the future.

The pleas accompanying one petition for land allotments expressed this feeling of the children's importance. One leader after another asked for allotments for the sake of the children, knowing their own generation would not benefit. "I may never know the good but my children will know." Another said if the titles were not secure, ". . .our children will suffer even a greater wrong than would befall us. . .do not let our children be sufferers because of the inaction of those who do not seem to care for the future."[1]

In their system of education girls were trained by their mothers and grandmothers and boys by their fathers, uncles and grandfathers. They were fitted for a system that rested on both hunting and agriculture, depending entirely on handcrafts, all within the tribal organization. By the middle of the 1860's it was clear that this way of life was disappearing rapidly. The roles of men and women were often reversed as certain duties were rendered obsolete. Why train a boy to hunt and wage war when there was little game to hunt and war had become the business of the United States Government? Why teach a girl to dress skins and fashion garments of leather and fur when these materials were no longer available? And how could men till the soil when it had always been the duty of the women? How should children be trained under such circumstances?

As a young man Joseph had realized that the Indians must learn to speak English, to dress as white men, to live in houses and in settled villages, but he had not foreseen how rapidly the more fundamental structure of their life would change. He said he had often gone for a year or two without seeing a white man and then suddenly they came in vast numbers, ". . .just as the blackbirds do, and spread over the country. Some settled down, others scattered on the land. . .We Indians see you and want to take our steps your way but it seems as though the Government pushes us back."[2]

We do not know how far Joseph had developed his ideas when he first found a wife and had children as we cannot be entirely sure how many wives he had. Multiple marriages were more common among the leaders of the Omaha than through the whole tribe. The maintenance of status and influence came largely through making gifts and giving feasts. This entailed a great deal of labor by the women of the household and plural marriages provided the necessary hands to serve the required feasts, to care for the animal pelts and to fashion and decorate the garments and equipment which would become gifts. The system also cared for the widows and the women who were left fatherless.

Wa-ja-pa told Alice Fletcher and Francis La Flesche in 1906 that Joseph had been married to an Otoe woman and that she and a child had both died when the baby was born. When the family enters the period of more complete records, these records show that Joseph was married to Mary, the daughter of Ni-co-mi and Dr. Gale. Another wife, Ta-in-ne, an Omaha, later known as Elizabeth Esau, bore him three children. A third wife is listed in the records, but not named. Of the last, nothing seems known except that later one of the missionaries said she was "giddy."[3]

Apparently Joseph had taken a new wife early in 1862 and had been caught up in a wave of scandal and gossip which swept through the tribe, the mission family and the group at the Agency. It largely concerned Rev. R. J. Burtt and became so damaging to his reputation and influence that Walter Lowrie of the Mission Board in New York asked Father Hamilton to come from Bellevue to find out the truth and make an effort to correct matters.

Part of the gossip centered on Burtt supposedly carrying on an improper affair with an unmarried woman teacher at the Mission. It became embroidered with the additional touch that Joseph had said on taking a fourth wife, "If the missionary can do so—so can I." In August Hamilton wrote that there were no real grounds for the tales. He felt it might all be traced to a former Agent, who desired to get rid of the Mission, with other additions being made by a teacher or by one or two disgruntled Indians. He did know that the Agent, O. H. Irish, had felt that Burtt could have prevented Joseph from taking the fourth wife, but Burtt felt nothing could be gained by going against an emotional and deep-seated custom. He knew that when another wife had died, Joseph had promised her father at the grave that he would marry her sister.[4]

This was according to an established rule of the tribal structure; when a wife died the husband could marry any of her sisters, aunts or nieces. It was not mandatory but it was considered a laudable act to thus preserve family ties. Was this wife who died the Otoe of whom Wa-ja-pa spoke and the fourth wife her sister of the historical record? Or was the Otoe woman still another wife unknown to history?

Evidently Joseph's and Mary's first child was Louis born in 1848. The baptismal book used by both Father De Smet and Father Hoechen, Jesuit priests who served the area in the before-treaty days, is preserved at St. Marys College in St. Marys, Kansas. It has the notation that Louis La Flesche was baptised by Father Hoechen on December 27, 1850—"Father, Joseph La Flesche; Mother, Omaha; Sponsor, Burgiere." Louis died when he was a child attending the Mission school. Joseph and Mary were away on a visit to the Pawnee. His sister Susette wrote about this long afterward, saying that the parents had been met a day's journey from home by a runner bearing the sad news. Her mother told her that her father lay all that night with the child's body in his arms. This must have been within a year or eighteen months after Joseph's leg was amputated, for one of the Mission workers had written to Louis about the accident late in 1859. Joseph visited the Pawnee tribe several times from 1860 to 1862, for twice the missionary mentioned such visits and the tribes combined their strength for the summer hunts in 1861 and 1862.

Accompanying this story, which she tells in Fannie Reed Giffin's *Oo-ma-ha Ta-wa-tha,* is a charming sketch of a chubby cheeked little boy, which, she said, had been made by a traveling artist. Mary and her small son had been at the landing in Bellevue as a boat was preparing to leave. A passenger hastily made the drawing and handed it to Mary as he went on board. Could this have been the Swiss artist, Rudolph Frederich Kurz, who in search of picturesque native life, spent the winter of 1851-1852 at Ft. Berthold? Kurz was at Bellevue in 1851 and his journal mentions Joseph as an employee of Sarpy. Then on his return the next year he had dinner with "his friends Joseph and Mary La Flesche."[5] The picture might well be that of a child two and one half to three years, as Louis would have been if we accept the date on the Mission school roll, which gives him as nine years old in 1857.

Susette felt her mother would be glad to have these things published so that Louis would always be remembered. The Mission roll, the baptismal record, a letter, the picture and Susette's story bear witness. It might be added that twenty years later, Louis' sister Rosalie named a son Louis and one hundred years later another Louis La Flesche, a great-grandson of Joseph's made visits to the old reservation in Nebraska. The original sketch of Louis is with the La Flesche papers in the Nebraska Historical Society.

In 1866 when Joseph lost the chieftainship, he was responsible for a large family. Mary had four daughters, Susette born in 1854, Rosalie in 1861, Marguerite in 1863 and Susan in 1865. Ta-in-ne, who was much younger than Mary, had two children, a son Francis born in 1857 and a daughter Lucy born in 1862.[6] A letter from the Agent to the Indian Bureau in 1860 calls attention to the fact that two of Joseph's children "Harriet and Francis, ages six and five"[7] were omitted from the list for allotments in the Half-Breed Tract. Later a letter from the Mission says, "Joseph buried another child today; he says, she is with God." Was this child Harriet, or a newborn, unnamed baby? Harriet is mentioned in no other place but her birth year would be the same as Susette's. Could it be that the name was "Harriet Susette?" It is not surprising to find a daughter by this name, for "Harriet" was Ni-co-mi's English name. Some seven years later Ta-in-ne had another son, Carey.

These all made up one family; each encompassing all the others in their love, each child sharing in the care and attention given by the adults. Joseph told Rev. Burtt that each one was as dear to him as Burtt's family was to him; he could not bring himself to send any of them away. He knew he must care for them all. The family ties held them close in their growing up, the older sister Susette, the first to step into the outside world; then the brother Frank who must play the part of two sons, since Louis had died; then four little girls within four years; and at last the little brother, Carey. There seemed to be little distinction between the children of the two mothers until they were grown and each took a slightly different path in the white man's world.

They all knew love but they also knew discipline. Omaha children were taught to respect older people, address them courteously and never pass in front of a person seated in the tent unless permission was granted. They must never stare at visitors or strangers and must always say "thank you" when a gift was given to them. When several children were together with a group of adults, as was usually the case, they were to play quietly and speak in low tones. When he was a small boy inclined to mischief, Frank said his father would take him aside at times and talk seriously with him. If it were a more serious infringement of the rules, he would tie the lad to a chair and tell him to sit absolutely still or he would strike him.

Susette remembered that once when all the tribe was on the hunt another child had given her a small bird. She held it and played with it and tried to feed it. Joseph called her to him and told her to bring the bird. He took it in his hand and stroked it gently saying:

> Daughter I will tell you what you might do with this bird. Take it carefully in your hand, out yonder where there are no tents, where the high grass is, put it softly on the ground and say as you put it down: "God, I give you back your little bird. Have pity on your bird."
> I said, "Does it belong to God?" He said, "Yes, and he will be pleased if you do not hurt it, but give it back to him to take care of."[8]

In these ways Joseph tried to train his children while Mary taught the girls the housewifely tasks. Mary must have acquired many housekeeping ways of the white world, probably in the indefinite time she may have been in St. Louis; or possibly from the white neighbors when she and Ni-co-mi were with Sarpy in Bellevue. It was said later that the most progressive Indian families would send their daughters to her to be taught. When the children were grown and far away they still looked to Joseph and Mary for guidance. They would write to Rosalie who remained near by and have her ask Father and Mother to give advice on some problem.

Joseph had hoped to help the tribe change to new ways but now he had no authority. He had assumed that since all white men were Christians they all acted upon the teaching of the Book, that Hamilton, Sturgis and Burtt explained to him. Now he found that all white men did not study the lessons of the Book and at times those who did would talk in one way and act in another. How could he help his children in such an unpredictable world?

He apparently came to the conclusion that they must learn all they could from the white people.[9] He became confident, in spite of disappointments, that on the whole the Indians would learn good things, for he believed that God had sent the white men to teach them. In the first place they must study English, to read and write it. He consistently supported the school. At one time he brought five new recruits including one of his own daughters. It was probably Rosalie who would have been just under five years of age. She wanted very much to go to school and insisted she was "Ta-pa-ka's girl." Burtt explained she could not say "Ta-puth-ka," which apparently meant "teacher." This sounds like the way Rosalie might have started her education, immensely eager to learn—always wanting to learn more.

When support was withdrawn from the Mission and the school closed in 1869, Joseph insisted that Frank read the Bible to him and make translations from it, so that the boy would not forget the English he had learned. By the time he was twenty, Frank was one of the best interpreters. Joseph knew Susette should have more help or better teachers, as she had gone as far as the overworked teachers at the Mission could take her. She helped Rev. Burtt with translations he was making, but there were no other resources through which her eager mind might explore.

These questions for the children's future were in Joseph's mind as he developed his own analysis of man's place in the world, the relation of the races to each other and faced his personal difficulties—the loss of Louis, a severe illness suffered by Frank, his own injury, money matters that confused and annoyed him and then the loss of the chieftainship.

At the same time together with many others, he was touched by a wave of religious feeling which stirred the tribe during the winter of 1866. Since he was a young man, Joseph had observed the missionaries and had listened to them. For many years religious meetings were held in his earth lodge and then in the frame house. In 1860 Joseph had told Dr. Sturgis that he often prayed but it lacked something; he felt that God was probably angry with him. Mary had felt she belonged with the Christians for some time. Then there was a time when Burtt had larger and larger meetings in the villages and more individuals came to discuss religious matters. Although Burtt's use of the language had improved, he felt he could not fully communicate with these people who asked about a great life and sought to understand a whole new philosophy. He thought of studying French so he could talk to Mary and Joseph; but this concerned many more. So he sent for Father Hamilton, knowing he would speak in Iowa to Joseph and Joseph could carry the message directly to the understanding of the people.

They held what sounds like an old-fashioned revival meeting, but Hamilton spoke of the "week of prayer." There were nightly meetings of sixty to eighty people in the villages or at the Mission, where the school children also attended. During the day Hamilton

went into the lodges and houses to talk to individuals and often
Joseph had meetings with the men and Mary with the women. More
and more Indians asked that prayers be made for them and many
added their own prayers to those of the ministers.

The missionaries were amazed at the deep feeling shown,
although at times they were met with reserve on the subject of the
white man's "Good Book." Village Maker, in true Omaha fashion,
said his band would think about it. Fire Chief's band also wished to
think and to wait; they did not want to say they would do a thing
and then fail. They understood that a few from La Flesche's village
offered prayers and then hunted rabbits on Sunday.

One night Hamilton was impressed and excited when he asked
if any of them would speak and Joseph rose. Facing the people he
preached a short sermon on the text that Hamilton had used, expressing his own thoughts from his own approach to the subject. This
was during the days of Frank's illness and the uncertainty over the
signing of the Winnebago treaty.

When Frank was ill, one of his sisters, probably Marguerite who
was three years old, would go to a window near Frank's room, kneel
down and whisper several words in Omaha. She said she was praying
to Ta-put-ka's God to maker her brother well and she believed he
would do so. Burtt could not resist the opportunity to point out to
Joseph that a child-like faith could plunge deeply into the truth.
They talked at some length about Joseph's situation with the three
wives and Joseph admitted he sometimes felt he would be glad if all
but Mary would leave but he could not tell them to go.

Burtt urged friends in the church office to write letters of
encouragement to Joseph who was carrying a heavy load with "many
powerful persons working against him." He felt that at times Joseph
wondered if he should continue his efforts for the tribe. Probably all
these things built up to that time when Joseph "packed his household goods and left." But in some way through all of this, Joseph's
conviction grew that God had given good gifts to men and "hands to
work with" and that white men and red men must go on together.

More than a year elapsed with no mention of Joseph in correspondence from the Mission or the Agency. This might be because
new people were in charge in both places, for the first mention
indicates he had been back for some time. He must have felt that he
could care for the children better by remaining with the tribe. Furnas
had left in December of 1866 and W. P. Callon did not assume the
duties until the following July. The Mission had been without a

minister. S. Orlando Lee who was acting as Superintendent had come as the farmer; then was a teacher, and as Superintendent seemed to enjoy carrying all the duties of the minister which he could without being ordained. After the stir of feeling a few months earlier it was a woeful change to attend his church services. Finally in the summer of 1867, Father Hamilton came back to serve in the place he had done so much to establish. Religious meetings were held again in Joseph's house but they were attended only by his band as others were "hostile to him."

In one of his first long letters to Church headquarters, Hamilton mentioned that Joseph had sent one wife home, "the youngest who had no children."[10] The others, he added, had families and all were kind and affectionate to each other. The first wife (Mary) felt more than ever that she was a Christian and the other (Ta-in-ne) "gives evidence of change."[11]

It might seem that Joseph met his problem a little at a time for the last child, Carey, was born in 1873. The date of Ta-in-ne's separation from the family group remains a mystery. The children of Joseph's children were told that Joseph "provided for her." Years later, after Carey was past forty, Francis made formal claim for an allotment of land for himself, his sister Lucy and his brother Carey as heirs of "Elizabeth La Flesche," their mother. He said she had been given a grant in 1871 within a narrow strip which was later sold for the use of the Winnebagos. Her allotment had been canceled without her knowledge or consent and no new allotment, to which she was entitled, had been made. Howard W. Partch, Superintendent at the Mission from 1880-1883, wrote to John C. Lowrie in April 1883, saying that Lizzie La Flesche had died; that she was Mr. La Flesche's second wife, "Frank's mother." Partch himself had conducted a burial service "as Mr. La Flesche wished." There is nothing to indicate whether they all still lived together but Joseph was still taking care.

The panic created by the Government's pressure for the Winnebago treaty and the State's threat of removal was by no means relived when the Government canceled its contract with the Mission for a school. Government day schools were established, however, and later the Mission school re-opened as a boarding school for girls. A degree of assurance came with the first allotment of lands in severalty in the fall of 1867, although the certificates of title were not delivered for nearly three years during which time there were constant rumors of removal.

The Indians thought these certificates meant security and stability. But in the clash of many conflicting influences—an increase in the tribe, in the number who had some education, the too close association with another tribe, several drastic changes in government policy and the acceleration of white settlement—stability was impossible. Those years from 1869 to 1879 were years of uncertainty and anxiety.

It must have been a difficult time to train a family with five girls and a boy passing through their earlier teens and entering adulthood. Each step had to be tested. Did it move in the tribal pattern or boldly away from it? Susette and Frank certainly experienced the formal and traditional rites which tiny Omaha children had known for generation after generation. In some degree they must have moved in the tribal form until they were approaching twenty, which would have meant the middle of the 1870's. This might have been true of Rosalie but less so of all the younger ones.

Both boys and girls of the Omaha were the center of one beautiful ceremony, "The Turning of the Child." This took place when a child could take steady steps alone and could go in the direction he wished. Until this time a child was held as precious but was considered more in the light of another living organism among the many in the natural world. Now he had become a personality, an individual; quite as white men say "he is on his feet" or "on his own."

As a distinct person he must be given a definite place within the tribe; his baby name was discarded and he received his "ni'kie" name, the one he would be called by in the tribe, and symbolically he was started on his journey of life. The songs spoke of the "four hills of life" and the child was turned to face all the four directions whence came the four winds which could assist him on his way. Carrying a pair of new moccasins, the child entered the ceremonial tent alone; no adults came in except those who performed the ceremonies. The parents and others looked on from a distance, through the open east side of the tent.

The story was told that when Susette started toward the tent and a priest came to meet her, she became frightened and started back toward Mary and Ni-co-mi. Ni-co-mi stepped forward, took the little girl by the hand and led her nearer to the tent before releasing her. Ni-co-mi was accustomed to acting quickly and firmly. (It was said everyone respected her because she could subdue even the fiery Peter Sarpy.) She steadied the little girl on that day and it might seem that she imparted a certain firmness to the child who took important steps that day and years later when she took courageous steps for her people along the white man's road.

Her father made a far-reaching decision when Susette was twelve or thirteen. Under the tribal system it would have developed that Joseph's daughters would have carried the "mark of honor." This consisted of symbolic marks tattooed on the forehead and neck of a young girl. It was granted only to the daughters of men who had many "counts," that is a record of many laudable acts, usually acts of kindness toward the unfortunate or which contributed to the welfare of the tribe.

This should have come to Susette in the late 1860's, just at the time of Joseph's deepest troubles and the need to decide which way the family was to move. Joseph refused the honor and held firmly to his conviction that the Indian way was of the past. He was sure his children would live in a white man's world and he did not wish his daughters to be permanently marked as belonging to a worn-out tradition. How his five daughters must have blessed him in the future as they went East to school, appeared in the white courts of law or addressed the Congressional committees and large public gatherings!

All this was far in the future and the Mission school was almost wrecked by the siege of gossip and the uncertainty after Rev. Burtt left. When it closed, Susette became more restless with too little to do; she knew there were other things to learn and she longed to study them but now all hope was gone. Fortunately there was one teacher who was alert to her need and asked Susette what she would like to have as a Christmas gift. The girl could think of nothing but her longing to get an education.

The teacher had relatives in the East who were connected with an excellent school for girls. The teacher asked if, in any way, they could help the eager, intelligent but baffled young Indian girl. The money was found and plans were made which were but the beginning of plans and gifts opening new doors for the La Flesche family. In 1869 Susette made her first journey away from the Missouri River country and went to Elizabeth, New Jersey to enter the Elizabeth Institute, conducted by the Misses Nettie Reed and Susan Higgins. Later Miss Higgins was married to Rev. Pingry, headmaster of a neighboring school for boys. In many places it has been incorrectly stated that Susette went to "the Pingry School," but the schools never were united; the Institute merged with other schools and the name was lost, but the Pingry School (for boys) was continuing nearly one hundred years later.

The Elizabeth Institute was a good school and its heads were women of character and ability. It was a fortunate introduction into a new social and intellectual world. Susette had excellent training in written English and in literature. She developed a passion for good reading and wrote so well that the last of her essays in the school were printed in a New York City newspaper.

In sharp contrast, her return to the tribe in 1875 was disappointing and frustrating. The Omaha as a group were in a state of apathy and despair. She had nothing to do and almost nothing to read. She had brought back a handful of books from Elizabeth. Two were gifts from the school, probably awards of some sort—*Travels in Arabia* by Bayard' Taylor and *Personal Reminiscences* edited by Henry Stoddard. She read these over and over. Did she find a note of kinship in Taylor's account of a nomadic people who lived in tents, who had adjusted to a harsh environment and who had perfected the process of packing and setting up camp even as had her own people? Did the biographical experiences that Stoddard had collected bring a desire for action on this girl who had glimpsed wider horizons?

She had one other book which meant a great deal to her. Although William Hamilton frequently blundered in dealing with people, he did enter into the experiences of his charges in a remarkably sympathetic fashion. When she had gone to Elizabeth, or shortly after she arrived there, he had given her a book, *Within and Without,* a long dramatic play in verse by George MacDonald. This was what Susette needed, and even more during the first months back on the Reservation—the beauty of words and phrases, inspiring ideas and lofty thoughts that she had begun to find in literature. Of course it is sentimentally stated; it was a sentimental age and writers depended upon sentiment. Susette read the book many times, as shown by its worn binding and its many marked passages today. She memorized some of these lines and they exerted an influence over her life: "Go and do the deed," "Weep and work, for work will lead to song." She wrote five lines in Marguerite's autograph album, ten years later.

> And should the twilight darken into night
> And sorrow grow to anguish, be thou strong.
> Thou art in God, and nothing can go wrong
> Which a fresh life pulse cannot set aright
> That thou dost know the darkness, proves the light!

Susette had had some severe tests of courage in those ten years.

She had found comfort in the last line at times when things seemed dark. She could straighten her shoulders and move to act with the line "be thou strong" and "a fresh life pulse." She knew that their situation between two worlds would bring despair and the need for courage to Marguerite as well.

But she had a sense of humor, too, and appreciated other qualities in this delicate and extremely pretty younger sister for she wrote at one side:

Mag is a sunflower
Mag is a daisy
Mag is the very gal
To set "herself crazy."

The rest of the page is taken up with a fine lined sketch of a leafy branch, with each leaf bearing a letter of her own name: S-U-S-E-T-T-E.

Books could fill only a small bit of time. It was hard to return to household tasks in the combination fashion Mary had made from both white and Indian ways, when she had seen and experienced a different way of living. She could not leave the Reservation without obtaining a pass from the Agent, several miles away. She wanted to teach and had an opportunity to do so in the Indian Territory; she would help others along the white man's road, but she was still held by the old ways. Two Crows, her uncle by adoption who had equal control with her parents, said she could not go.

After a time she found that the Indian Bureau would give preference to Indians if they were properly qualified; after another long wait she was hired to teach on the Omaha Reservation for $20.00 a month. The government was emphasizing day schools in an effort to reach more children and large promises were made for school buildings, but they were slow in materializing. Susette gathered a few children and was allowed the use of a small rough building at the Agency. Because of the need to be near her work, Susette kept house by herself in this building. Not content with just a school, she opened a Sunday School and out of her own small savings bought an organ so she might bring music into both schools.

During the years Susette was at school and beginning to teach, Frank had become more a part of the tribal life, entering into the experiences which had been common to generations of Omaha boys. Certainly he had been the center of the "Turning of the Child" rite and he must even have been sent out to seek his vision. The initial ceremony of a lonely vigil was required of every male; then each

might choose whether or not be continued to live by the rite. Every
Omaha boy knew the opening prayer:

O Great Mysterious Power,
I stand here, humble and needy,
Praying to Thee.12

A youth went out alone to the hills or the open prairie, to fast and
to pray for four days and four nights. Although, as he left, his father
handed him a bow and arrow, it was only an added test of his
endurance for he was not to use it, no matter how hungry he might
become. If he fell in a trance or seemed to see or hear anything
unusual, it appeared to be the answer to his pleas. It was said to be
accompanied by a definite rhythm and the vision and the cadence
were that individual Indian's connection with the vast universe and
were never spoken of to the others.

Later after resting and eating and reporting that he had had a
vision to some trusted older man, he traveled about until he met a
bird or animal or felt again that underlying cadence. If it were an
animal or bird, he killed it and saved a part of it as his particular
symbol. He did not talk about this either, but it might be worn as
part of his costume on the special occasions of ceremonies and feasts.
If his vision had come from a cloud or was a sound, it was represented by symbolic figures on his clothing.

Frank would not have been old enough to undergo this test
until the family had returned to the Reservation after Furnas' regime.
Since it was a matter never discussed in the tribe, he did not talk
about such secret, personal experiences when, as a man, he did all he
could to preserve the Omaha ceremonies and traditions and wrote
about them for white people.13 But among his personal papers and
possessions found after his death, in the Washington, D. C. apartment
where he had lived for some thirty years, there was a long feather
with a strong shaft, probably the tail feather of a hawk. With it was a
strip of red felt with slits in one end so that it could be made to
hold an ornament. Could this have been Frank's personal symbol? It
was saved for more than half a century along with the patent for his
land on the Reservation and all his appointments to government posts
in the Office of Indian Affairs and the Bureau of American
Ethnology.

Under the tribal pattern all the families, all the tribe, went on
the hunts. Frank told Rev. Dorsey that he had gone on the buffalo
hunt three times;14 evidently he meant that he had gone as a

working member with the hunters three times, for several times he spoke of events on the hunt when he must have been quite a small boy. On the first occasion when he was grouped with the men, he was set to work with other boys of his age caring for the pack horses while the hunters surrounded the herd. At probably a later hunt, after the surround had been made and the men were prepared to shoot, Frank suggested that he might join them. But Joseph said, no, it was much too dangerous, for he might be thrown by his horse and gored by a buffalo. Seeing that the boy was much out of sorts, Joseph went with him to a hill and sat with him to watch the hunters. But Frank continued to sulk and would not reply to any of his father's attempts at conversation.

Suddenly, they saw coming directly toward them an enraged bull pursued by a mounted hunter. At times the buffalo would turn and start to charge at the man. Joseph suggested they move on a bit farther, but Frank must have thought this was his opportunity. He roped a large red mare, picked up his father's light gun and rode toward the buffalo. For the moment the savage bull was standing motionless; then the hunter let fly an arrow. But it only penetrated the hide along the back, inflicting a wound of little consequence, except that it excited the buffalo. Frank's horse lunged wildly from side to side and he was thrown. The buffalo dashed toward him, then swerved to one side and went past the startled boy before he could shoot.

After those few moments of action it was humiliating to have to walk back to the circle of tents. The bridled horse arrived before he did and when Frank entered the tipi his mother, trying to cover her own anxiety was roundly scolding his father. Joseph made no reply, but sat laughing at his daring son, probably secretly enjoying Frank's courage and relishing the fact that a lesson had been learned.

"Well," he said, "Did you kill the buffalo bull?" Long afterward Frank related, "I did not speak."

Before the hunts were entirely abandoned, at least once, Frank was the runner. The runner went ahead to locate the buffalo herd before the whole party moved out in hunting order. At fifteen he covered one hundred miles in some eighteen hours on this mission; at seventeen he killed his first buffalo. This was accompanied by a definite ritual and was a recognized step in a boy's growth toward manhood. These events must have taken place between 1872 and 1876 before the Omaha tribe at last recognized that the hunt was impossible and submitted to the government's orders.

Frank's mention of three hunts may be a partial measure of the amount that Joseph's family shared in this event in the days of its decline. Shortly after reaching the Reservation in the late 1850's Joseph had tried to discourage the hunt, thinking the tribe should learn other ways to make a living. But the majority had ignored his advice and only the actual disappearance of the herds and the resulting poverty convinced them the hunt was a thing of the past.

The final acceptance of this fact threw the tribe into despair and confusion. They felt some dreadful and malevolent power was operating against them. The hunt not only meant the year's supply of meat and robes but it was intricately woven into the governmental, religious and ceremonial life of the people. Their most cherished symbol, the Sacred Pole, called the Venerable Man, was necessary to the existence of the tribe, but it could not operate without certain ceremonies which depended on the buffalo. They lost unity and security and all reason for morality when these rites were neglected and suffered a complete loss of standards to measure right and wrong.

Certain men felt the buffalo had disappeared because the hunts had brought small returns and had not had the full support of the tribe. As a result, the proper respect had not been shown to the Venerable Man and disaster had followed. They advanced the idea that they might substitute cattle for buffalo, perform the sacred ceremony and thus enjoy a return of plenty. This would require thirty head of cattle and the chiefs asked the Agent to make a purchase with money due the tribe for certain ceded lands.

This presents a typical case of the white man's misunderstanding of the real inner Indian life and philosophy; for the Agent, obviously not appreciating the religious significance, wrote to the Secretary of the Interior:

> The Omaha have a tradition that when they do not go on the buffalo hunt they should at least once a year take the lives of some cattle and make a feast.15

The cattle were purchased at a cost of nearly one thousand dollars, not just one year, but for three years and still it did not bring back the buffalo. The Sacred Pole stood for years in its Sacred Tent revered as mysteriously powerful but for some reason unable to use that power for the people.

In this way the loss of old customs brought strain and distress; stability and meaning went out of life. The reasons for ceremonials were gone and the articles needed for their celebration could not be found. The ritual was no longer used and the men who knew the ancient forms and the sacred words did not teach them to younger men. Little by little much knowledge of the form was lost and only vague memories of spectacular events remained.

Frank had gone far enough in the tribal ceremonies to have caught their force and beauty. He began to grasp enough of the white man's culture to see that it furnished few counterparts that might be quickly absorbed by his people. He came to believe the old rituals should be preserved and that he might be the person to get the songs and ceremonies from the old men. Then he could put them into English so that the white men might know his people. In a way this seems contrary to his father's insistence that they learn the white man's way, but it actually was a supplement. Joseph said, ". . .let us put aside the old ways and go along the new path." Frank acquiesed in this major thesis but added, ". . .let us save the old as we move toward the new, in order that as we learn white ways the white people may learn about our ways."

The next major event of Frank's life partook of the mixture forced on a generation caught in the rapid shift from one culture to another. On July 20, 1877, he was married to Alice Mitchell, a member of the tribe. It was of the old way, in that he married an Omaha girl; it was of the new way that the ceremony was performed by the Christian minister, Rev. William Hamilton of the Presbyterian Mission. Moreover, it was reported in the white man's newspaper, the euphoniously named *Vindicator* of Decatur, Nebraska. It was said that after the ceremony the "bridegroom's relatives sat to a table prepared by the groom's sisters that would have done credit to any family and they had no help or instruction from any white person in preparing it."

Ten years earlier the distress of the Winnebago and their settlement next to the Omaha had brought various repercussions to the Omaha Tribe and to Joseph's family. The later part of the 1870's brought trouble to the Ponca, a more closely related tribe which distressed the Omaha and deeply involved Joseph's children. Joseph's brother Frank, White Swan, was a chief of the Ponca and with others of the tribe turned to Joseph for assistance. Susette and Frank had become good interpreters and had reached the age where they acted with the adults in the Omaha efforts to help the Ponca.

Between 1877, the year when both Omaha and Ponca became aware of approaching danger, and the year 1883, several separate incidents shaped the lives of the La Flesche family and determined the direction that Susette, Frank, Rosalie, Susan and Marguerite would follow. To a lesser degree the same events brought changes to Lucy and to the small brother Carey, who was seven years old in 1880.

Frank's marriage was of short duration for he and Alice separated within a year. A child was born and Frank angered his wife's father—and the missionary—by taking little notice. He evidently did not consider the child his own, for in 1884, after the white men's courts were established, Frank asked for a divorce. The early records in the old reservation neighborhood are none too exactly filed, but in the folder containing Frank's petition, there is a penciled note that he was granted a divorce on the grounds of infidelity. Alice Mitchell married another man of the tribe soon afterward.

As an interpreter Frank had come to the attention of Senator Samuel J. Kirkwood of Iowa, who later became Secretary of the Interior, the Cabinet member directing the Office of Indian Affairs. Kirkwood remembered this intelligent young Omaha and had him appointed as a copyist in the Indian Office, feeling Frank's knowledge of the Omaha and of Indian ways would be most valuable.

Friends of the Elizabeth Institute made arrangements for two other sisters of Susette to enter the school. There is an indication that it was to have been Rosalie and Marguerite, but for some reason it was Marguerite and the youngest sister Susan. Both Rosalie and Lucy must have had other plans.

In 1877 the Decatur *Vindicator* mentioned that "Mr. Edward Farley is selling organs." Did the organ Susette had for her school pass through his hands? It is certainly possible for there would hardly have been other organ salesmen in sparsely populated northeastern Nebraska in 1877. Moreover, the next generation of Farley's often heard how Ed had sold organs. By the next year, Farley was harvesting grain on a contract basis and hiring Indians as his crew. Although no other contractors hired them, he insisted they were able and reliable workers. He grew to know many of the tribe and worked at the Agency for a time. There were many ways he might have learned to know Joseph's family and the graceful second daughter, Rosalie.

The family was growing up. Soon Frank was in Washington busy in the Indian Office. He continued to work and study there for over forty years. Marguerite and Susan were in New Jersey and more than one young Omaha was casting interested glances toward Lucy. Sometime within these few years she was married to Noah Leaming, who took the name of La Flesche because her family was of higher rank than his.

The education Joseph felt was so important was coming to the children. He never found time from the demands of the tribe and the family to continue long with the study he had started under Dr. Sturgis and was never able to use English with any assurance. He apparently gave up trying and, like many parents caught in a change of cultures, he began to depend upon the children. This lack of English, which he had urged the tribe to learn, probably kept him from his rightful place in history. The account of the plains and the Plains Indians have been written by white men who depended on government records, which were written by other white men. They all depended on the few Indians with whom they could talk; frequently they misunderstood the limited English of the Indian interpreters and often the interpreters deliberately misinformed them. As Joseph became less and less active, his children in many ways became the teachers and the leaders of the tribe.

CHAPTER IV

SUSETTE AND ROSALIE:
THE INDIAN PROBLEM AND THE LAND

Shortly after the Omaha settled on their Reservation, the Ponca, living sixty miles or more to the north and northwest ceded their hunting grounds to the United States. They reserved for their home the land around their old village sites near the Niobrara River. This transaction was reconfirmed by the Government in 1865. But three years later the Government mapped out a large reservation for the Sioux which included the area given to the Ponca. None of the negotiations concerning this new move were known to the Ponca, when in 1877, with no warning and with no explanation, they were told their leaders might go to the Indian Territory to select a location for the resettlement of the tribe. The Ponca chiefs insisted that they thought they were being taken to the Omaha Reservation. To them "Indian Country" meant the Omaha Reservation, the only place near them which they felt belonged to the Indians.

The chiefs who accompanied the government officials to the Arkansas valley were not pleased with what they saw and refused to make a choice. They asked that they might return to their families but permission was denied. Therefore, with only a few dollars and one blanket apiece, the Ponca leaders started to walk the five hundred miles back to northeastern Nebraska. On their arrival at the Niobrara, the Agent sent for the Army and on May 1, 1878, the whole tribe was moved to the Indian Territory by military force.

Joseph's brother, White Swan, had been one of the Poncas who had made the return journey to Nebraska. Joseph had tried to persuade him to stay on the Omaha Reservation when the chiefs had stopped there on their way north. However, White Swan had gone on, only to be faced with this eviction of the whole tribe. He sent word to Joseph that the group would be at the crossing of the Platte near Columbus, Nebraska on a certain day. Joseph and Susette with eight or ten other Omahas rode the seventy-some miles to again meet their relatives. They arrived before the Ponca party, but the soldiers were there, erecting their tents and preparing the camp. This show of military watchfulness disturbed the Omahas and when the bedraggled, weary line of Poncas came in sight they were all in tears. Susette did not sleep that night because one sick old Ponca wept and cried out for the homeland he was leaving. Joseph again tried to persuade his brother to bring his family and come to him—but they went on. The Poncas did not trust the official interpreter and even the Agent was not satisfied for he asked Susette to take the man's place. Fortunately she refused and was later able to serve the cause of the Ponca in a much larger way.

On arrival at the Territory neither rations nor tools were issued for some time. This enforced idleness and hunger added to temperatures of 95 to 100 degrees proved disastrous to the tribe. In less than a year one-third of their number died. This again aroused the Omaha's fear of a similar fate. If this could happen to their relatives, could it happen to them? They took their land patents to attorneys and were told they were worthless.

In the winter of 1878-1879 Chief Standing Bear's son died. The father felt he could not bury the boy so far from the land of his ancestors and, although no permission was granted, he told the Agent he was going and prepared again to return to the Niobrara. About thirty people accompanied him, seven of whom were very ill. Besides the bones of the chief's son they carried those of other family members. Traveling in three covered wagons and with a "treasury" of twenty dollars they started on the long journey north.[1] A few months earlier the Northern Cheyenne had broken away from the Territory and, successfully evading posses of citizens and the United States Army, had fled 1500 miles toward the Yellowstone. Even after this dramatic demonstration of Indian determination the Ponca were not followed. They were too few to cause concern. In ten weeks they reached the Omaha Reservation and begged for a plot of ground and seed that they might grow their own food.

Once more, the Omaha, although still suffering over the tragic close of the hunt, took in suffering wanderers. As the Ponca were about to plant, Army officers arrived and arrested them. After a night of anxiety, the leaders consented to go to Ft. Omaha and talk to General Crook, the commanding officer. They, themselves, led the way, escorted by the military, moving off south toward Ft. Omaha. The leaders were placed in the prison and the others camped near the barracks. This time, action toward the Indians could not be ignored or hidden as was often the case and public sentiment was deeply stirred. A petition asking that the order to return the Ponca to the Territory be rescinded was sent to Carl Schurz, Secretary of the

Interior, signed by five leading clergymen of Omaha. A citizens'
committee was formed, headed by Bishop Clarkson of the Episcopal
Church. Rev. Hamilton wired the Indian Office asking that attention
be given to the Ponca tribe—and received no answer. Rev. J. Owen
Dorsey, a missionary-ethnologist, wrote to the eastern magazine, *The
Council Fire,* which was devoted to the Indian problem. Thomas H.
Tibbles, assistant editor of the *Omaha Herald,* began a definite
campaign to arouse the white people, presenting the facts in his
paper and hoping they would be repeated by other journalists. His
hopes were justified and opinion was stirred across the country.

Thomas Henry Tibbles had had a varied career—circuit preacher,
army scout, manager of "grasshopper relief" and then journalist. As a
young man he had lived for a time with a group of Indians, largely
half-breeds, on or near the "Half-Breed Tract." This area between the
Little and the Great Nemaha Rivers had been set up under the treaty
of 1830. In this way, he had some acquaintance with and felt an
interest in the Indians. He was thirty-nine years old, married and the
father of two small daughters. He had been on Omaha newspapers
about five years. Tibbles was a crusader by temperament and a confirmed supporter of the underdog. His sympathies were stirred by the
Ponca predicament and he threw himself completely into their cause,
resigning from the newspaper and giving it his full time.

He took the initiative in obtaining a writ of *habeas corpus.* The
legal form stated that Standing Bear demanded his freedom from
General Crook. Tibbles and W. L. Carpenter, the officer who had
brought the Poncas from the Reservation to the Fort, signed as
witnesses. J. M. Poppleton and John L. Webster, able and highly
respected attorneys of Omaha, offered to contribute their services.
Newspapers remarked editorially that this meant fighting the "Indian
Ring" and was not to be lightly undertaken. However, this did not
deter them and at least Webster began to take a continued interest in
the Omaha. He was a helpful and true friend to the La Flesche
family for many years.

When the case came to trial the government maintained that
Indians could not appear in court or make use of the writ for "an
Indian is not a person." The arguments were presented before Judge
Elmer Dundy who decided against the government and ordered the
prisoners released, for, he said, under the law the "Indian is a
person" and entitled to its protection. The government immediately
appealed; it became apparent that at least three trials would be required before the Ponca tribe would be resettled and reimbursed.

Each trial would require more information and more money.

Tibbles went among the Ponca on the Niobrara to get their story and Joseph, Susette and John Webster went to the Indian Territory to talk with those of the tribe there. They went by railway to Wichita and then four days by stage to the Ponca location. They found the tribe housed in tents or the poorest of shanties, all spaced some distance from each other, since the Agent feared any concerted action. As a result the news of illness or even the death of near relatives frequently did not reach families for several days.[2]

Joseph explained to his brother, White Swan, and to the head chief, White Eagle, what the court decision had meant and that while matters were not concluded, at last white men were trying to help them. He would send news of developments within the next few months. Now, Susette had added reasons for helping the Indians. She knew these things and she could talk to the powerful white people. With her first appearance on a public platform she entered history— the first American Indian woman to become a public speaker.

After some weeks on the Niobrara, Tibbles went East to solicit funds from philanthropically minded friends and organizations. He called on Bishop Huntington of Syracuse, New York and Rev. Joseph Cook of Boston. He spoke to a called meeting of the *Society for Propagating the Gospel among the Indians and Others in North America.* He received some money and the assurance of greater interest and assistance if, in some way, the Ponca could more directly present their own case.

Tibbles was determined that those in the East should *see* Standing Bear, but how could they get his story directly? An interpreter was required and Susette was proving to be the best available. She made one speech in a church in Omaha and the Omaha Committee felt that she, herself, was an effective message, besides the moving story which she could tell. Tibbles could visualize the plan of large eastern meetings. Standing Bear would be the central figure as the Symbol of Injustice. The Ponca leader was a man of erect posture; in his blanket, long hair decorated with a single eagle feather, wearing a necklace of bear's claws, he was a commanding and imposing figure. While he was accustomed to "citizens' clothes" (as the Commissioners' reports always called them), these native clothes were his finest and were to be worn on special occasions just as an Army officer would wear his dress uniform. Standing Bear felt that he could speak for the tribe only when he was dressed as their leader. The white committee readily saw the dramatic effect of the blanket, the feather ornament and the great necklace.

Did this set a pattern or would drama always have weighed the balance? Even in the latter part of the twentieth century no one presents an American Indian without reaching for a warbonnet. Frequently, though, the "Indian" who wears it may be seven-eighths white and the significant feathers may have been last worn in a ceremony by his great-great-grandfather. The Indian must look like a tourist thinks he should look.

Standing Bear could act as a symbol and present a picture. The men of the Omaha Committee felt Susette should be the interpreter. Besides her skill with the languages, she had lived in the East and might open the way for the whole group. Certainly they were aware of another asset—she was beautiful. With fine, regular features, she had a general air of modest dignity and moved with an enchanting grace.

If Two Crows had objected to her teaching in Oklahoma, certainly objections were raised now. It must have taken a great deal of thought and discussion before an Indian girl started out to travel with a group of men. Probably her father's constant efforts toward the white ways was an influence; certainly this was a crucial situation and must be met with daring methods. It was decided that her brother Frank would also be included as an interpreter, and at the same time he would represent the protecting male portion of the family.

What could be more striking than the emotionally charged but incomprehensible words of the chief—the translation by the earnest young Indian with long hair who wore white men's clothes. And last, the impassioned but quiet speech by the lovely Indian girl speaking perfect English and wearing the proper dress for a white "lady." Tibbles could explain the legal complications, the objections they had met and the need to finance the coming trials. He had real skill with words and, as a friend said long afterwards, "could draw a long bow" when it was effective and it would make "a good story better."

The tour started with several days in Chicago where they were more cordially received than might have been expected for the Ute tribe in the Rocky Mountain area had just raided an Indian Agency, killed the Agent and captured his wife and children. It did not seem a propitious time to ask for sympathy for the Indians. But Standing Bear's drama, Susette's beauty and earnestness and the very appearance of Frank and Susette proving that all Indians did not spend their days on the warpath won the day. The newspapers gave them many columns and often Susette was asked for interviews. Boston papers announced in advance, "Standing Bear and Bright Eyes Are Coming East."*

Before they reached Boston, Tibbles received a message saying that his wife had died. After some indecision he continued on the journey while kind friends in Omaha cared for his little daughters. At first under Bishop Clarkson's charge, they were put in a boarding school and then later went to their mother's sister. Chief Standing Bear, too, received tragic news from his family. His brother had been shot down by a white soldier when he had not immediately obeyed an order. But the chief went on with the public appearances and the whole group remained in the East well into 1880.

They spent several weeks in New England and Susette spoke in the great Music Hall in Boston, at Mechanics Hall and addressed a crowded noon meeting in historic Fancuil Hall, where women did not usually appear. Bostonians had long thought of Faneuil Hall as almost synonymous with "liberty." One of the opening speakers said, "Faneuil Hall once more opens *her* doors to an oppressed people." (Italics by the author.)

The Governor and the Mayor with an imposing list of leading citizens entertained them at a reception. Susette spoke simply but with a sincerity which left a deep impression. She was quoted in Lucy Stone's *Woman's Journal* as saying:

> You never hear but one side: we have no newspapers to tell our story. The soldiers do things to prisoners or the dead as horrible as any Indian could think of. Your people are nearly always the aggressors. One young man with no provocation shot an Indian because when he went home to the East he would like to say he had killed an Indian.[3]

The important literary lights of the day all wished to meet Susette. They entertained her, showered her with gifts and wrote their best wishes and their famous names in the autograph album she had used during the Ponca trial in Omaha. The height of attention came when Henry Wadsworth Longfellow met her. He looked keenly at her; then turned to others present and said, "This is Minnehaha." When this was related in large public meetings it brought forth prolonged applause.

In fact, a tradition grew out of this incident, like many about other famous people. It has been repeated in different ways, changed, forgotten and then revived and enlarged until it was sometimes said that Susette (usually "Bright Eyes") was the inspiration of

Boston Daily Advertiser. Oct. 24, 1879.

Minnehaha, of Longfellow's poem "Hiawatha." This version has existed for years and a profusely illustrated story appeared in an Omaha paper, thirty-five years after Susette's death. The feature writer must have mislaid his reference books, for the poem was published in 1855, when Susette was a baby. The figure of Minnehaha must have taken form in the poet's imagination before she was born. Longfellow could hardly have known about Susette La Flesche before the autumn of 1879.

The populartiy of the poem, however, helped open doors to Susette. Well schooled in the idealism of the poem the public accepted her as the embodiment of Minnehaha and she became the Symbol of the "Beautiful Indian Maiden." This symbol endured longer than that of Standing Bear as "Injustice to the Red Man." Indeed, Susette was never able to establish herself before the public as a separate entity apart from the Indian Maid.

The humanitarian, philanthropically inclined people of New England who had worked for abolition, for the Freedmen, for the extension of public education, for better care for paupers and the insane were genuinely moved by the speeches of Standing Bear and Susette. They responded generously with gifts and even more generously with sincere and consistent interest and service. An equal response came from the Philadelphia area led by the peace-loving Society of Friends. Here, too, Susette was near the families and relatives of former mission workers and her teachers at Elizabeth. Funds large and small were established to assist Indian Schools and the individual Indians. A Boston Committee for the Protection of the Ponca was active for several years, keeping in close touch with Tibbles and Susette. Organizations dedicated to the Indians still carry on the work inspired by Iron Eye's daughter Susette in 1879 and in later speaking tours.

The publicity about the Indians and the meetings in and around Boston caught the attention of a serious woman anthropologist in Cambridge. Alice C. Fletcher, a private pupil of Frederic W. Putnam, the director of the Peabody Museum at Harvard, was eager to make actual field studies of Indian tribal life. Because of the New England interest in the Ponca she came to the Omaha Reservation and lived in the houses, lodges and tipis with the Indian families.

During these years of the Ponca troubles, a bold experiment in the treatment of the Indians had developed. After protracted tribal conflict in the Indian Territory the government had rounded up apparent trouble makers and had shipped them in chains to Ft.

Marion in Florida. The young Army Captain placed in charge was able, for some inexplicable reason, to see the human beings in these desperate, dirty, disheveled wild Indians, who sang their weird death songs through all the long uncomfortable journey. Unable to converse with them, he was still determined that they should not be treated as animals but as men. He had them cleaned and fed and their chains removed. He had their hair cut and put them into decently fitting, clean clothes resembling a uniform. Little by little, he gave them liberty and began to teach them. In three years he changed these savages (savage in their desperation and bewilderment) into respectable persons with a fair command of English and a rudimentary knowledge of the white man's skills and manner of living. This was Capt. Richard Pratt, who came to be called "The Red Man's Moses." Aggressive and firm, he could still be gentle. He seemed to have an uncanny sense of the proper approach for a given time. His ideas might have brought about greater advances, but his approach to the Indian Bureau and the philanthropic societies lacked the skill he showed with the Indian boys and girls. He almost always disagreed emphatically with the Bureau and his ideas were seldom followed.

When the prisoners at Ft. Marion were granted their liberty, they were told they might go back to their tribes or, if they were willing, they might stay in the East and teach other Indians who would be brought to them. One group volunteered to go to Hampton, Virginia to the Agricultural and Normal Institute. This had been established for the freed slaves after the Civil War, but would now enroll Indians as well. Pratt went to Hampton with this group and, after a time, when the Government daringly decided to extend this experiment, he opened the Carlisle Indian School at Carlisle, Pennsylvania. Carlisle had a far-reaching influence, touching most of the Indian tribes in the United States. This new approach to Indian education brought changes and opened up new experiences for the La Flesche family. With the exception of Susette, Rosalie and Frank, they all attended Hampton.

There is no record of any trip home for Marguerite and Susan during their stay at the Elizabeth Institute. They probably spent summers with friends of the school. The family of Rev. R. J. Burtt, who had been at the Mission in the '60's, wrote their names in Marguerite's autograph album in June and July of 1880, at Marksboro, New Jersey. The son, John, wrote "Nebraska, the home of our childhood, to it may we ever be faithful, is the wish of one, who once on its prairies has rambled."

Susette and Frank had returned by late in June 1880 when Rosalie, the second La Flesche daughter, took a long step toward white living and was married to Edward Farley. The wedding, like others in the family, took place at the Mission and Father Hamilton officiated. Hamilton, who was the first Protestant missionary to stay long with the Omaha, was given the title of the Catholic priests who came earlier. He was and still is spoken of as "Father Hamilton." Susette signed the certificate as one of four witnesses. The bride was nineteen and the groom thirty.[4]

Edward Farley came from an Irish immigrant family that had settled in Indiana in the 1850's, possibly a part of the Irish emigration after the potato famine. He had left home as a young fellow and evidently knocked about from job to job. For months at a time the famiy would not know where he was. In 1876 he wrote home from Falls City, Nebraska saying he had worked at North Platte for six weeks and then had "brought the teams to this place in twelve days"—a distance of about three hundred miles. Apparently later he moved north to the vicinity of Decatur and still later to the Omaha Agency and in some way came to know Rosalie La Flesche, slender, erect and with shining eyes.

Thirteen months later in July of 1881, Susette and T. H. Tibbles were married at the Mission by the Rev. S. N. D. Martin from Winnebago.[5] The choice of minister was probably affected by the fact that Father Hamilton and the La Flesche family were just then in one of their waves of disagreement which came every few years.

A month earlier Frank had received an appointment as a copyist in the Office of Indian Affairs through the auspices of Senator S. J. Kirkwood of Iowa, formerly of the Senate Committee of Indian Affairs, who had recently become Secretary of the Interior. Frank may have left before the wedding on the 23rd which would have been much to his wishes. The younger brother who had traveled with the speakers on their tour in 1879 had not been pleased with Tibbles' attitude toward his sister. He told Rosalie that Tibbles had shown too great attention and affection toward Susette even while his wife was living.

Such intimate matters are never fully known or understood by outsiders, but the affection obviously grew and apparently there developed a happy marriage with marked devotion on both sides. The Indians were accustomed to older men marrying much younger women and fifteen years difference in ages would have caused no comment. The Tibbles devoted themselves to the Indian cause for many years, with periods of writing in Nebraska; then when their treasury was low, they would go off lecturing again. From 1881 until 1900 they were away from the Reservation more than they were on it.

Since Rosalie remained at hand and since she spoke good English but was also familiar with tribal ways, her house became the focal point for both Indians and whites. The tribe came steadily—for help and for sympathy. The philanthropists and educators whom Susette met in the East often came to visit the Mission, the different schools and members of the tribe who had been away at school. They always came to see Rosalie and many formed close friendships with her.

Alice Fletcher, the ethnologist, was taken to see Rosalie when she first came to study the Omaha tribe in the fall of 1881 and the two women came to love and depend on each other. On Alice Fletcher's arrival Susette took Joseph and Mary to Rosalie's to meet this unusual white woman who traveled alone and who wished to live in the homes of the Indians. This meeting is not dated but in many ways it marks a turning point for the La Flesche family and for the Omaha tribe. From this time on Alice Fletcher gave them a sincere interest which grew into devotion. To Rosalie she became "my dear friend" and in Rosalie's family the name "Fletcher" was continued for several generations.

This eager student was a product of city life and private schools, by no means acquainted with the frontier. In appearance she was short and plumpish, all soft curves and gentleness, inexplicably mixed with dignity. Her close friends called her "Her Majesty," from her likeness to Queen Victoria and possibly because she could firmly dominate a situation. Her general appearance and sympathetic disposition belied her energy, her utter devotion to a cause, her dogged persistence and fearlessness before opposition.

Susette, Tibbles and Wajapa took Alice Fletcher out through the reservation and on north and west to visit other tribes. They traveled by wagon and teams, with tents for living quarters. Wajapa was delighted at her ability to live on the move and in a tent, to face all the discomforts—even the thunder storms. He gave her an Indian name, "Mashahathe," which described the high circling of the eagle at early morning, because, he said, her coming was like the dawning of a new day. Tibbles made a shortened translation and called her "High-flyer." Others, however, cherished the Indian name and years afterwards, Susette's younger sisters and their friends talked with pleasure of their friendship with "Mashahathe."

As Alice Fletcher moved about the Reservation and talked to the people through Susette's interpreting she "found every household shadowed by the fear of compulsory removal." She could not limit her own concern only to "the myths, customs and ancient rites" when she was confronted by the "trouble that lay at the heart of every man and woman."

> So putting aside one set of note-books, I took up another and made a canvass of the tribe, ascertaining what they desired and sent a unique little petition to Congress. I knew very little, indeed, in those days of political matters. I heard nothing of that petition in which the Omaha had asked to have their homes secured to them. When the spring came. . .I started for Washington with a great faith. . .it was time to go and do something for the people. So. . .I carried the war into the homes of the people in Washington, for it was a question of homes.7

She appealed to the public as Tibbles and Susette had done. Following shortly after the impression they had made, she pressed steadily toward one thing—greater security for the Omaha tribe. Senator Dawes of Massachusetts had seriously studied the Indian problem and had asked the most penetrating questions offered in the Congressional hearings on the Standing Bear case. Now, impressed by Alice Fletcher's efforts he was largely responsible for the passage of a law granting lands in severalty to the Omaha.8

After accompanying Alice Fletcher on her first trip among the Indians, Tibbles and Susette again went East on a speaking tour and to Congressional hearings. Tibbles was prone to give himself completely to one thing, but after a time, something else captured his attention and moved him to eloquence in writing and speaking. His newspaper experience led to an interest in politics and economics. In a few years his enthusiasm embraced bimetallism and the Populist Party* and he edited newspapers promoting these causes. Susette loyally followed his movements. She attended political conventions and used her own skill in writing for these newspapers. Writing and speaking became Susette's life.

She had a story in the January 1881 issue of *St. Nicholas*. It was called "Nedawi (An Indian Story from Real Life)" and was signed "Bright Eyes." Apparently she named the child in her story for her own great-great-grandmother, Nedawin, Nicomi's grandmother. However, varying forms of "Nedawi" were common names for little

*T. H. Tibbles was the candidate for Vice-President on the National Populist ticket in 1904.

Omaha girls. The story describes a little Indian girl taking care of her baby brother—and forgetting about him—playing with other little girls at preparing a meal, being interrupted by a gang of inquisitive small boys and going out with the whole tribe to meet the men coming in from a successful hunt. By the close, the reader has learned about tribal organization, the living arrangements in a tipi, about food and clothing, and even a little about a few ceremonies.

It is all simple and human and Nedawi, her family and playmates seem like real people who might appear in any race. Some incidents in this story appear elsewhere as Susette's own experiences, thus proving their reality. She gave such charming pictures only a few times, and it may be that most of her writing is lost in the unsigned columns of newspapers. It remained for her brother, Frank, to write more about Indian children in his own book *The Middle Five*.[9]

Tibbles brought out one book in 1880 and two in 1881. Susette wrote prefaces for the first two. These grew out of the Ponca case and made a joint effort to enlighten the American public on the plight of the Indians.

The first book, unsigned, was called *Ploughed Under, the Story of an Indian Chief*.[10] In place of a signature the cover added "Told by Himself." Plainly it is not told by an Indian but it is told in the first person in an effort to give that impression. It compresses the wrongs of many tribes and of many individuals into one story. Probably Susette assisted by furnishing much of the material. It is loosely held together by a romantic love interest, awkwardly contrived. In an effort to cover identities it produces confusion and contributes motives and philosophies to the principal characters which are obviously transplants from white civilization. No doubt it aroused indignation and a desire to right certain wrongs, but it does not give dependable information on any single incident.

In her introduction Susette clearly pointed out the diverse and distorted images white people have held of the Indian. She made a plea for the recognition of the Indian as a human being. She insisted the book did not exaggerate the cases cited—to this extent it may be informative. The introduction closed with an effective use of the metaphor in the title:

> ...the huge plow of the "Indian system" has run for a hundred years, beam down, turning down into the darkness of the earth every hope and aspiration which we have cherished...What sort of harvest (will)...it yield to the nation whose hand has guided the plow?

The second book is *The Ponca Chiefs: An Indian's Attempt to Appeal from the Tomahawk to the Courts.*[11] Wendell Phillips, in a bitter and scathing dedication presented this as a "specimen of the injustice, oppression and robbery which the Government called its 'Indian Policy'." He charged the government with being "incompetent, cruel, faithless, never keeping its treaties and systematically and shamelessly violating its most solemn promises."

The introduction by "Inshatheumba" ("Bright Eyes") stated that "these are the facts concerning some of my people. . .many of these things 'came under my own observation'." She expressed the hope that the white people might be "roused from their indifference." She felt that it was indifference not hatred and that in thinking of their happy homes they might give help to "a harmless race who have no spot on earth they can call their own." The author is indicated by the remarkable, coined word "Zylyff."

In a copy owned by the Nebraska State Historical Society, there is a penciled note on the reverse of the title page:

> This book was compiled from extracts made from reportorial notes in the *Omaha Herald* written when I was working sixteen hours a day and published without revision or seeing the proof. —Thomas H. Tibbles.

Might it be that Susette made the compilation? Because this book refers to and includes copies of interviews with the chiefs attested to by certificates of the interpreters and prints copies of certain legal papers in the case—it gives valuable information. Both books leave the impression which was best described much later by Dr. Edward A. Ross, the eminent sociologist. Commenting on a paper which Tibbles had sent to him for criticism, he said it had "too much denunciation and too little discrimination."[12] No doubt Tibbles accomplished a great deal by an emotional appeal for action but there are many vague or contradictory statements, and emotion frequently gets the upper hand.

The third book, a novel *Hidden Power*[13], was an exposé of the "Indian Ring." The "Indian Ring" is frequently mentioned in newspapers and personal comments of the decade although there seems no out-and-out naming of names. It was a term everyone understood, but no one wished to clarify. Obviously it centered in the Indian Bureau and Carl Schurz, Secretary of the Interior, was deeply involved.

Tibbles brought accusations, but he carefully veiled everything by changing names of people and places and by writing facts in the form of fiction. While at the time those on the "inside" and probably many on the outside understood, any clarity or sense of immediacy was soon lost. The Nebraska State Historical Society obtained a copy of *Ploughed Under* forty years after publication and the Director, Dr. A. E. Sheldon, was aware that in a few years the book would be meaningless without long research to ferret out the central facts. He wrote to Thomas Tibbles indicating that he realized this was supposed to be anonymous but he and many others knew that Tibbles was the author. Would Tibbles then be willing to make out a "key" to the book that might be available to students and researchers in the decades ahead?[14] There is no record that any such "key" was written or deposited with the Society.

The Ponca troubles stiffened the Omaha determination to be secure on their own land. They had been told it was theirs in 1854 and they had been given individual patents in 1871, but obviously other safeguards had to be found. The efforts of the Omaha committee and of Tibbles had shown that white friends could be extremely helpful, but Alice Fletcher, as a friend, was entirely different. They experienced—rather than knew her.

Here was a white person, and a woman at that, who amazingly enough came first with one of their own people, Joseph's daughter. She traveled as they did, ate what they did and lived in their homes. They made her an honored guest and were astonished to discover her deep concern over their own fear and despair. She was almost beyond belief!

After the passage of the Severalty Act in August of 1882, she returned quickly to the Reservation in order to assist with another project. She was heartily in favor of Captain Pratt's educational efforts and had confidence in Gen. S. C. Armstrong who became the director at Hampton Institute after Pratt opened the new school at Carlisle. She persuaded Armstrong and the Secretary of the Interior to accept young married couples as students. She was convinced that the development of their married life in the atmosphere of the school and in homes similar to those of white people would increase their influence on their return to the Reservation.

Of the first three such couples to go to Hampton two were from the Omaha tribe—Minnie and Philip Stabler with their small son and Lucy and Noah La Flesche. In this way Lucy, although she had not gone to the Elizabeth Institute, joined her sisters in having school life away from the tribal surroundings.

Miss Fletcher, herself, accompanied this group of pioneers to the east coast. Besides the married couples there were several Omaha boys, some for Carlisle and some for Hampton. In fact she apparently had collected too many boys. The Government had agreed to educate a number whom she would select and then, by some twist of the red tape, the Bureau would not accept six of them. Undaunted, she turned again to the public and personally raised the needed funds in less than two months. *The Woman's Journal* reported one of her last public meetings—at the Payson (Mass.) church where she was given $92.00. She had nearly reached the required amount, however, and only accepted $75.00. Accordingly, the Commissioner of Indian Affairs assured her "now you have raised the money, the Omaha boys will stay at Carlisle. The interest in Indian Education resulting will be many times more important than the money value." All thanks to private effort and private philanthropy!

The close of 1882 was an exciting time to the Omaha; their outlook had been changed. A group of young people, including married couples, were away at school, instead of only a few individuals. The tribe was reassured by Tibbles' work on the Ponca problems, there was comfort in Alice Fletcher's warm sympathy, but above all there was a new hope—hope for real titles to their land. Agent George W. Wilkinson wrote to Hiram Price, the Commissioner, that the Omaha "are a steady and reliable set of men who are trying to do what is right."

Only a slight note of misunderstanding and doubt was sounded in the general atmosphere of hope as rumors appeared that the tribe would not agree to a bill which was introduced as a companion to the Act of Severalty. It allowed for the sale of lands to furnish needed funds for the purchase of equipment. These rumors worried Rosalie and disturbed Joseph until he almost wavered in his own support—fearing again the strange ways of white men with money. He still carried heavy influence with his people, but he no longer held any recognized position. (The chiefship had been abolished by the Government in 1880 and chiefs, considered of equal standing, were chosen as the council.)

However, after an explanatory letter from Frank, Joseph sent Two Crows, Du-ba-mo-ni (Harrison MaCauley), Sin-da-ha-ha (William Hamilton) and Pa-the-na-pa-zhe to ask the Agent what these rumors meant. The Agent George Wilkinson had thought Two Crows and Joseph had had some objection and he had been strengthened in this idea by Tibbles. But he accepted Two Crows' explanation that they had only wanted to manage the money themselves, instead of having it entirely in the hands of the Commissioner.

Joseph wrote to Alice Fletcher saying that now this was understood he would see that more signatures were obtained. It also appeard that the Agency physician had been told by Thomas Tibbles that the Indians would not agree to the bill. Rosalie wrote that she got the definite impression that Susette and Tibbles did not think it best for the bill to be approved.

This seems to be the first of many differences of opinion between Tibbles and Susette and the rest of the family. Tibbles had continually met the argument that rights could not be accorded the Indians because they were not citizens. The appeals from the Ponca case had not gone well. White men repeatedly did not act in the line of Judge Dundy's decision and Tibbles came to feel that citizenship must come first before any other advances could be made. Wise Rosalie knew well enough that people did not change all their habits of thinking and acting when a law was passed and that many of the tribe were not ready to be citizens. Joseph, too, knew from personal experience that steps along the white man's path were slow and difficult; he had never seen large things accomplished quickly. They were much more in accord with Alice Fletcher's belief that broad general laws could not solve the problem but that that problem must be constantly dealt with from many different angles. Education must be rapidly increased and presented in different forms. She started night classes in English, encouraged the women to prepare handwork for sale, helped the more advanced children go away to school, assisted other organizations in special efforts and repeatedly found help for individual cases. She thought some land should be sold to white people so that the Indians would not be isolated but would mingle with the whites and learn by observation.

At this time the tribe still lived among the wooded hills in the eastern half of the Reservation disregarding the fertile valley of Logan Creek to the West. All but one allotment of 1871 had been within a few miles of the river. That one was on Omaha Creek which flows into the Missouri and is still within the eastern half of the Reservation. The Indians hesitated to leave the familiar surroundings, the wooded hills and the creeks which led to the large stream—the traveled road of their ancestors.

Forty years earlier hundreds of white men had plodded along the rich valley of the Platte, feeling ill at ease because of the flatness of the land, the great distances and the thin line of trees near the water. They pushed on, however, enduring many hardships in crossing the mountains in order to reach a more familiar landscape of trees and streams in Oregon. Change of location becomes more difficult when the general environment is unlike the home ground.

Alice Fletcher had traveled on the new railroad which ran for over twenty miles along Logan Creek where no attempt had been made for settlement. She was convinced that if the Indians obtained their patents and if they were to prosper they must abandon their little fields in the bluffs of the Missouri and begin again in this fertile valley. Accordingly she wrote to the leaders and to the Agent urging the people to select their allotments in the Western half of the Reservation.

The tribe as a whole rejoiced when Miss Fletcher was appointed Special Agent to allot the land. Soon afterwards Frank was appointed as her interpreter and assistant. The men kept coming to Rosalie and asking, "When will she come?" "Will she come soon?" "We want to see her; tell us when she comes!"

The older men consulted with each other on the best way to express their gratitude to her. Frank told about it years afterward:

> They decided to perform for her the ancient calumet cere-mony, although it was not customary to give it informally. A notice was given to the people to come, and on the day appointed many came and assembled in an earth lodge. The calumets were set up in their sacred place, and when Miss Fletcher entered as the honored guest the house became silent. Three men arose and took up the symbolic pipes (the calumets) and the lynx skin on which they rested; then standing side by side, they sang softly the opening song. At the close the three men turned and facing the people, who sat in a wide circle, sang a joyful song as they moved around the circle, waving the sacred pipes over their heads. Song after song they sang for their friend, of the joy and the happiness that would follow when men learned to live together in peace. When the evening was over they told Miss Fletcher that she was free to study this or any other of their tribal rites. 15

This was the added touch which made the evening a personal expression of thanks to Alice Fletcher. It made it possible for her to accomplish two tasks at the same time. She carried out the allotting in every detail and at the same time absorbed the attitudes, the forms, the subtle meanings of Indian life. The manner in which she combined two lines of work is symbolized by a slip of paper. On one side it is her official appointment as a Special Agent of the Indian Bureau and on the other side are the notations of a song, "made by Big Tobacco." She continued to include ethnological studies all through the months of allotting, although for many weeks she was bedridden at the Agency with inflammatory rheumatism.

At first she had received only a few half-hearted promises to move west, but when she started the actual work she pitched her tent in the Logan valley staying in one place for nearly two months. The men had to go there to see her and there she could more easily convince them that this was the most desirable location.

One day, with her assistants, she was running lines on quarter sections, determining the exact locations for each allotment. They came upon a man standing on a section mound. He looked directly at Alice Fletcher and with a sweeping movement of his out-stretched hand said, "This is my land." The surveyor gave the description by section, township and range and Miss Fletcher recorded it in her black book. Then she shook hands with the Omaha and said, "I congratulate you. I want you to build a house, a barn and granaries and cultivate this land."

Still holding her hand the man said, "We have had Agents to manage our affairs, but none have offered advice. My people are not prone to follow the advice of women, but I shall follow yours."[16] It was such straight forward friendliness that won the Omahas. Her determination was stimulating and her example in accepting a new way of living and staying on the land with them, stirred them to act upon her suggestions.

Joseph led the movement into the valley supported by Rosalie and Ed. Several others who had been in the "make believe white man's village" took their allotments near by. Homer W. Partch, Superintendent of the Mission school, was disturbed over the Omaha moving farther away from the Mission. It worried him to see that the plan of the Mission would have to be altered and feared the workers would have troubles reaching the people. Oddly enough he did not once mention whether or not the move would be of advantage to the Indians.

A new town, Bancroft, had been platted in 1881 just over the southern boundary line of the Reservation. The settlement of the La Flesche and Farley family and others who had been in Joseph's band, to the north and slightly to the east and west of the new village, stimulated its growth. For years Bancroft was the best "Indian town" in the area and the bankers and merchants thrived on the Indian trade. Regrettably certain illegitimate profits also centered in Bancroft, gained by white men taking advantage of the Indians' ignorance and inexperience in every possible transaction. Certain residents of Bancroft later labeled these people "Indian skinners." Many of them built up their own capital and contributed to the tragic movement which deprived the Indians of the land which they had longed to own.

Ed Farley selected a spot at the southern edge of the Reservation, bordering on the northwest corner of Bancroft, hoping to select adjoining lands for the children. Susan's allotment was one and one-half miles farther up the Logan and Joseph's in the next section west, just across from Susan's. Ed helped build the bridge across the Logan just north of Bancroft. Susette's allotment was a fourth of a mile north of the bridge and only about a mile east of Rosalie's home.

It has been frequently stated that during this time, T. H. Tibbles took out a homestead and built a sod house. But his name does not appear in the lists of homesteaders under the Act of 1862. The story probably relates to a sod house that was on Susette's allotment. One of Susette's nieces found a picture of a frontier house with a central frame structure of two stories, extended on either side by one story portions made of sod. Tibbles is seated in the yard and Susette is posed at an upper window. Two young ladies dressed in the elaborate fashion of the late 1880's (evidently the Tibbles' daughters) are seated, one at the door and one in the yard. The central portion of the house appears to be a part of the house where Tibbles and Susette lived off and on for nearly twenty years. The sod portions were gone before the memory of anyone living in the 1960's. One of Rosalie's daughters lived there in the 1920's and 1930's and the farm is still known as the "Tibbles' place" although the land records at the Agency show it was in Susette's name.

After their marriage Susette and Tibbles first stayed in the Mission; then they were in Omaha for several months, probably during one of his more concentrated periods of writing. Then taking his daughters, Eda and Mae, they went up on the Reservation, first to occupy part of a double house at the Agency, and for a time place the girls in the Mission school. Then, presumably, they moved to the new sod house. Fifty years later, Mae Tibbles Barris wrote to Marguerite recounting memories of the 1880's. She revealed something of the poignacy, the elements of tragedy in the strangely assorted group of people trying to become a family in surroundings strange to most of them.

Susette had been living among white people most of the time for fourteen or fifteen years. In spite of her anxiety for her people, under it and along with it had come pleasure and eager acceptance of this new way of living. She had enjoyed being with people who read, who liked music and painting, for which she herself had real ability. The New Englanders had sensed her appreciation and she received many gifts of books, doubling or tripling the small collection she had brought home from Elizabeth. Now she was housekeeper with meager equipment and the responsibility for two strange children, who she felt were resentful of her. Mae remarked that it had been many years before she, herself, realized Susette's difficult position. They had been living for a year with their mother's favorite sister who could deny nothing to "dear Amelia's girls" and as a result she had spoiled them badly.

Mae remembered, however, that when she, herself, had been especially unruly and Susette would become angry the atmosphere was cleared by the intervention of Mary, Susette's mother. Although Mary did not speak English, by little murmurs and gestures, by the tone of her voice as she spoke to them both, Mae felt she was saying, "Don't mind. She is tired, it will all be all right, we all love you." In some way Mary made her feel she was loved and wanted. The recollection of Mary's understanding led Mae to recognize how much the girls had both learned from Susette: to love good literature and to discard the sensational and crude; to love little things, little stones, little flowers and to love the great things of nature, the rolling hills and the magnificent sunsets.

Tibbles, himself, was out of his element. Idealistic and given to large generalities which he visualized in dramatic situations, he had always responded to the stimulus of a crowd. A wife, even an adoring wife, and two daughters hardly made up an audience. Farming was a steady daily grind and starting a farm on unbroken prairie supplied little drama. But the qualities which helped him see the sweep of events and the color of action helped meet one problem of his daughter's in a sensitive and effective manner, after he became aware that they had acquired a one-sided view of the life around them.

They were always hearing about injustice to the Indians, about the Indians' high mystical concept of life and nature, their pride of race and the glories of their past. The girls began to feel there was something wrong with them. They had nothing to be proud of, white people were always prejudiced, cruel and unfair. Eda and Mae began to wish they had been born Indian. They felt more than a little guilty over being white. When their father realized this he gave them a long discussion on Western man, of his development and achievements and restored to them a sense of pride in their own race. Later as they learned more, they were proud of their own mother's English heritage.

For years Mae had held the thought of her father's suffering at this time. Having been accustomed to large, important affairs and to mingling with large groups of people, she was sure it had been a tragic experience to "spend his days following a plow up and down." He spent much less time following the plow than his daughter imagined, for out of the first four or five years they were resident on the farm, Tibbles and Susette were away for months at a time. Later in the '90's, when Tibbles had definite newspaper connections, someone else did the farming.

It was a come-and-go existence financially as well as by residence. Tibbles obviously preferred the lectures and the cultivation of friends for the Indians but it was costly. Long waits between engagements often used up much that had been gained in fees. His books brought in small amounts, and farm income was only possible in the distant future. He tried stock raising but sold out to try something else before he had taken in more than his initial expenditure.

Susette continued to draw audiences. Her simple beauty and sincerity, coupled with her pitiful story made a deep impression. She kept in touch with the Boston Committee and similar groups in Hartford and Philadelphia, winning a great deal of assistance from these groups in money and in friendship for the Omaha. Mr. and Mrs. Joshua Davis of Boston, active on the Committee, furnished the scholarship which sent Marguerite to Hampton, when she and Susan with eleven-year-old Carey joined Lucy and Noah there in 1884.

These successful appearances and acquaintance with influential persons who supplied them with letters of introduction led Tibbles and Susette to a lecture tour in the British Isles. They were most cordially received and appeared for many months in different cities of England and Scotland. Readers in art and literature added their names to Susette's autograph album even as had the great of Boston and Cambridge. In Europe, she became the best known American woman from west of the Mississippi and was referred to as "Princess Bright Eyes." This annoyed her but she could not persuade them that the Omaha had no system comparable to European royal position by inheritance.

No letters from Susette to her family during this time have come to light. Were they saved in some other place or were they at some time separated from the other letters Rosalie had saved or were there none? Susan and Marguerite were in Philadelphia and Hampton and wrote home saying they had heard of Susette through someone else, usually one of their new white friends and that they wished she would write to them. Even mention of her return apparently came through one of Tibbles' daughters. But so far no first-hand account of Susette's European sojourn has been found.

More and more after 1882, when plans evolved for the tribe, Tibbles advocated action which Joseph and Frank, Ed and Rosalie and usually Alice Fletcher did not think was for the best interest of the Omaha. Having appeared before several Congressional sessions, on a number of other occasions Tibbles offered to go with a delegation from the tribe to present an appeal to the Commissioner of Indian Affairs. Frequently Omaha leaders would come to Rosalie fearing what such a delegation might do, and once or twice a second delegation was sent.

Mr. and Mrs. Davis of Boston visited the Tibbleses and Rosalie invited them to dinner. Susette and T. H. gave the impression that they could not spare time for the family when their eastern guests were there. Rosalie told Alice Fletcher, "We did not have a chance to get acquainted with them. They came to dinner, but Mr. T. H. was in a terrible hurry to get off, so we didn't have much time...Mr. T. H. wasn't still a minute they were here." On another occasion Susette was to bring guests to Rosalie's for dinner, but they never came. The family—and the meal—waited for hours and at last the Farleys sat down to warmed over food. At times the Boston Committee weighed heavily on the tribe. Noah explained it, "I'm sorry we disappoint the Committee. They think we are all as smart as Susette."

The atmosphere of general optimism which prevailed among the Omaha at the time of the allotment, culminated in two major efforts by the tribe, neither of which produced the results that were desired or expected. The tribe entered into a sort of cooperative grazing project and a little later talked of becoming independent of the government and managing their own affairs. The common pasture came to be, with Ed and Rosalie taking the lead and developing the project into a large business operation. It survived for many years, going through losses, successes, criticism, skepticism and hope; no small part of the confusion came from the Government constantly remaking the rules. The long and loud debate on "to lease or not to lease" and on what and how to lease, was complicated by white men's desire to possess the pasture lands for their own agricultural use. It brought years of anxiety to Rosalie and a succession of legal battles. In the long run, the habit of leasing resulted in loss of lands for the Indians and general disaster to the Omaha pattern of living.

Self-government was tried for a time but it was too soon, at least too soon for the Omaha, to withstand the schemes and contrary advice offered by their white neighbors. Under the experimental plan the Reservation was divided into three districts each with three trustees, a constable, a roadmaster and a commissioner. The three commissioners from the three districts were to make up the over-all governing body. Officers were to be elected and their duties were defined; taxes were to be imposed and justice administered.[17] It was not a plan set up by federal law but a voluntary effort by the tribe as a period of learning or probation with a certain amount of guidance. The decision to even submit the idea to the Commissioner was debated seriously and heatedly. The Omaha had been under the firm, frequently dictatorial, rule of the Agents for over thirty years. During this time the impact of the white culture had broken down their own tribal system which had once met their needs. It was extremely difficult to make such a decision, when they had no experience in the methods they were expected to use and little idea of what might be accomplished.

Men of influence in the Indian Office were delighted that the Omaha showed such initiative but they could not bring about special treatment for one tribe. General rules were made and general rules were to be administered. For several years Inspectors and visiting officials spoke encouragingly of the Omaha government, but the Office in actual operation discontinued all services except the school, buildings were taken down and instead of a period of training it became one of abandonment with different groups of white people offering different advice to different groups of Indians.

Tibbles and Susette were firmly opposed to the common pasture and the plan of self-government. They were convinced that citizenship must come first, that only when the Indians were citizens would it be possible to work on fundamental problems. They did everything they could to bring about citizenship as rapidly as possible and this created more irritation in the family. The matter of self-government must have been the final issue. Early in 1886 the disagreement reached the point of explosion. Three letters left Nebraska in one day, each indicating the position held by the writers. Joseph La Flesche to Alice C. Fletcher: February 23, 1886

It seems we can do much if we adopt self-government; it will teach us how to be strong in ourselves and the responsibility of becoming citizens. We are not capable now but can be fixing for it. White men are trying to get our lands. Because the foolish ones will spend foolishly is no reason the sensible should be kept from the benefit of this money. Money for the young people at school can be kept for them.

Rosalie to Alice C. Fletcher: February 23, 1886

I read the letters to the men, I think they understand the plan.,. . . What do you think of Mr. Tibbles? Do you think what he is doing will be best for the people? He stopped in Omaha for a few days. . .a long piece in the Omaha Herald (says) "Mr. Tibbles again in the city and Agitation has been renewed. . .a farmer-husband of Bright Eyes who is a granddaughter of Standing Bear." News to me; didn't know we were grandchildren of Standing Bear. If Father knew this he would be angry. I have not told him. . .

Ed Farley to Alice C. Fletcher   February 23, 1886

We talked of your plan. Tibbles has been in Bancroft, Pender, talking to white people, telling them if they'd raise $50.00 to take him to Washington he would have Congress make the Omahas citizens so that the whites could go and lease their lands and live among them. He raised $60.00. He told Father, Wajapa and Two Crows he would get the Secretary to grant them the right to lease their lands for farming. Gave them the idea they would build a house, set out trees, land all broken and give them money too and have them made citizens.

He has told this to the whites and the whites have the idea if the Indians are citizens they will get cheap farms.

A month later a delegation of the Omaha, accompanied by Ed Farley was in Washington to discuss matters with the Commissioner. Frank reported to Rosalie that they had put everything carefully into writing and each man would have a copy so that it would be understood. They were concerned about the Winnebago stealing their horses, about an annuity which was not paid in full, about intruders on the Reservation as well as the plan of self-government.

It may have been Ed's arrival with the Omaha that brought family matters to a climax; for just as the men left, Rosalie wrote to Alice Fletcher saying she was "sorry you are brought into this disgraceful family affair."

Alice Fletcher replied:

The men are here. Mr. Davis has told the Indians he has changed his mind on some of the things they discussed. The Indians had thought that Mr. Davis (agreed) with Tibbles. . .People are so delighted that the Omaha want to be self-governing that they are inclined to go too fast and I must try and hold them back.

At a meeting of Mission Boards and the Indian Rights Association in January of 1887, Susette was present when Alice Fletcher was asked to tell of her work making the allotment. Then the chairman remarked that Mrs. Tibbles was present and asked her to speak, "since she lives in that section of the country." Just what the chairman was thinking is a matter of speculation. Why did he not say, rather, that Mrs. Tibbles was a member of the Omaha tribe and it would be interesting to learn her ideas on allotments? He must have known she had, or was eligible to have an allotment. Why speak as though she were a visiting club woman from Sioux City or Omaha? It is typical of attitudes which set Susette off to one side, or put her on a higher level as the Symbol. The public looked intently at the Symbol and could not see that her burning desire to serve her people was constantly being adjusted to the ideas held by her husband.

Susette responded that she would be glad to answer questions. The chairman asked what she felt would bring the most rapid advancement to the Omaha. Of course, she replied citizenship, which must come before any other changes. She felt great evil had resulted from the removal of the Agent and at that moment the Omaha had no government and were helpless and half-starved. Although Miss Fletcher had said she recognized certain dangers in leasing land, Susette insisted the majority of the tribe was opposed, yet there was "a cattle ranch there. . .my brother-in-law is in charge; no one knows. . .what the expenses are. . .or anything about it."

Apparently no one replied to these statements although certainly Alice Fletcher knew that Susette was not distinguishing between allotted land and tribal land. At that time only tribal land was leased for grazing. Alice Fletcher knew and Susette could easily have known that Ed had made an accounting to the Omaha each year with several hundred dollars paid to the tribe.

As the grazing project had gotten well underway bringing added funds to the tribe and self-government was feebly starting, an additional "severalty act" was passed by Congress in February 1887. It applied to more land on the Reservation and one clause declared that "allotted Indians" were citizens. The members of the Omaha tribe now were citizens, and there was great rejoicing. The Act of 1882 had placed the tribe and the Reservation under the laws of the State of Nebraska, but the Agent had continued to control and for all intents and purposes the State paid no attention. This Act of 1887 reiterated that the Omaha Indians were to live under the civil and criminal laws of the State. Their start at self-government was entirely unnecessary, and it was said to be impossible to organize "a state within a state." Still the State took no action to establish administrators or courts or any of the facilities for the enforcement of the law, until several years later when Thurston County was organized.

In another year T. H., as all the family called him, decided he had been a farmer long enough, or he was able to get a paying newspaper job. He rented the farm and went back to the *Herald* in Omaha. He probably also felt that he and Susette had completed their self-appointed task; their goal had been reached—the Omaha were citizens.

CHAPTER V

ROSALIE: THE FAMILY AND THE PASTURE

Rosalie had no formal education beyond the Mission School, but she mastered the tools of learning and never stopped using them. Every book she read and every visitor she entertained brought material for her eager mind to explore and remember. In this she was far beyond Ed for his few remaining letters show his education had been extremely limited. Rosalie wrote his letters just as she wrote those for her father and others of the tribe. But Ed had energy, a capacity for hard work and persistent effort, good judgment, business ability and a working familiarity with frontier life. To a large extent he was what Wallace Stegner has called the "multi-purpose man of the nineteenth century."[1] A member of the tribe wrote to Washington saying, "Edward Farley is one of us and we trust him," and a woman from New England remarked that he had "such lots of common sense." He became an effective liaison between Joseph's family and the white world. He was always doing countless errands and completing important commissions for the family and for the tribe.

Early in 1881, both Ed and Rosalie were teaching at the newly reopened Mission School. Ed was the Industrial Teacher, which meant he trained the boys in the farm tasks for the time; the sowing and cultivation of crops, the care of domestic animals, the use of a few tools and simple carpentry. By late February they left the Mission and established themselves in a little house near the Agency. Here their first baby was born, a boy, Caryl Edward. He presented a problem to the superintendent of the Mission, for Rosalie was a valuable worker. Superintendent Partch wrote to headquarters explaining (almost complaining) that the baby kept Mrs. Farley from regular attendance at church and that her absence hampered his organization of the Sabbath School. Rosalie and Frank had been the mainstays of the Sabbath School, teaching the smaller boys and girls and those who knew the least English. They used the Catechism as a text and on it built a combined study of language and religion. Frank also was an elder in the church and Partch spoke highly of them both as teachers.

82

When Caryl was only a few months old, Frank received his appointment to the Indian Bureau and Partch was left, not only short of teachers, but without an interpreter for the Sunday service. Moreover, if a law for severalty was passed, the Farley's expected to move on to the land allotted them and would, no doubt, be even farther away. Homer Partch was not an ordained minister and he liked to have Father Hamilton take a complete service at regular intervals, but he did not wish to impose on him for the weekly task of translation. The situation became so critical by the end of the year that, faced with a shortage of help in other areas, Partch made what he felt was a most fortunate arrangement.

Ed was to have charge of the little boys outside of school hours, to have the supervision of all work around the outside buildings and all work on the farm and garden. Then in order to secure Rosalie as interpreter, she was to be given fifty cents a week and "board at the Mission." It is hoped this meant "room," too, for she also was to allow the Mission the use of her sewing machine and her organ and was to "make herself generally useful."[2]

This arrangement was to last for four months, probably through March or into part of April. Almost no letters written from the Mission in 1882 have been found. Rosalie's own letters do not start for another two years, so the location of the Edward Farley's for the next year is indefinite. Whether they remained at the Mission longer than the expected four months or whether they returned to the house at the Agency, is a question. But quite unquestioned is the arrival in July 1882 of twin boys, John Francis and Joseph. Joseph died as an infant but John grew to be a vigorous child, soon known to everyone as "Jack."

When Jack died in his fifty-fourth year, the local newspaper said that he had been born at the Mission which would indicate that Rosalie and Ed had remained longer than planned at first. However, their son-in-law, Charles Conn,[3] who had been associated with Jack in business even before his many years as a member of the family, said that all ten of the Farley children were born in that same little house.

Just before the allotment was made, Rosalie wrote to Alice Fletcher that Ed was going to build a little house on their land so they could live on it. It was going to be "on the edge of the settlement, right among the whites." Charley Conn said that it was the same house moved from the Agency to the new allotment with two more rooms added. Even with the possible exception of it not having sheltered all the births, the house had a memorable history. It survived still other moves, and many remodelings and additions and remained the center for the Farley-La Flesche families for over eighty years. While Rosalie, herself, lived in the house only about twenty years, her children and grandchildren lived in it. Ed, after building a larger house, came back to it for his later years and the great grandchildren have returned to it.

Ed and Rosalie and the babies, and probably the house, moved on to the farm in the summer of 1884 after the attotment was completed. In September Rosalie had requested a change in the allotment planned for Caryl so that it would be a fractional quarter-section crossed by the railroad and adjoining her land to the south. Here in the little house on her allotment, Rosalie spent the rest of her life and here she met the constant demands which filled her days— the family (both Joseph's family and her own), the Tribe and the Farley pasture.

As Joseph had been the first to build his own frame house in 1857, he was again the first of the tribe to build west of Logan Creek. His land was a quarter section in which, at the extreme north-west corner, the Logan made a deep bend.[4] The Agent told him this would not be farm land but it would make an excellent mill site. Joseph agreed but reminded the Agent that he had no capital and could not build a mill. The last twenty years, after losing the position as trader, had brought Joseph barely enough to care for his family with no possibility of putting money aside although he had the largest farming operation in the tribe. He would be glad to have a mill on his land if someone else could supply the money.

He moved his family into the new house before March of 1886, after Ed and Rosalie were settled. The family at that time still included Marguerite and Susan, since they had returned from New Jersey in August 1882, about the time Lucy and her husband, Noah, left for Hampton. And then there was Carey, now almost eleven years old. Marguerite immediately applied to teach at the Agency school and the next year Susan was at the Mission. First, she was tried as a seamstress, but she was none too satisfactory, so she taught the smallest children. Both of the girls and Carey, too, went to Hampton late in the summer of 1884.[5]

Mary's mother, Nicomi, had been granted land near the Mission in 1871, and a map of 1862 showed that in the first years on the Reservation she had had her own house a few miles north of Decatur. However, there is nothing to indicate that she or her half-sister,

Madeline Wolfe, ever lived on their allotments, as of 1883-1884. Letters indicate they both spent their last days with Mary.

When Alice Fletcher was appointed allotting agent by the Office of Indian Affairs, she was expected to recognize those allotments of 1869 and 1871. In a few cases, men wished to retain the land which they had come to feel was theirs. Miss Fletcher tried to ascertain the desire of each person. Frank was serving as her interpreter and this extended period of work made it possible for her to become better acquainted with the rest of Joseph's family. An unforeseen twist of circumstances brought her into daily contact with Susan.

Alice Fletcher had thrown herself into the work of assigning land with the same absorption and self-forgetful earnestness she had shown in collecting data on the Omaha attitude toward land-ownership. Living in a tent in the Logan valley, paying no attention to regular meals and making use of the long hours of summer daylight, she worked to the point of exhaustion. One day after being thoroughly drenched in a thunder shower, she had a severe chill. Since she could not change to dry clothing she went on working, but it was soon seen that she was ill. Within a comparatively few hours she could not walk and was in constant pain. Frank lifted her on a cot, then onto a wagon box and drove as quickly as possible to the Mission—the Omaha haven.

Susan came to help care for her and Frank went back and forth trying to carry out part of the work under Miss Fletcher's instructions. Could this experience have influenced Susan when she thought of Medical School? Tradition has liked to say that Susan was influenced to choose a medical career by her grandmother, Nicomi, remembering Dr. John Gale. Susan's letters filled with descriptions of her work, always included affectionate messages to Nicomi, but never addressed the work description to her grandmother. This did give Susan an opportunity to watch an ailing body and observe the treatment and care given by a physician professionally trained. The doctor at the Agency came to the Mission.

Later, Miss Fletcher was moved to the Agency buildings at Winnebago and spent most of the winter there, practically immobile. She depended on an "invalid chair," whatever that may have been. Whether it was something of a reclining lounge or a wheeled chair is not clear. Here early in 1884, she received word that Rosalie had a little daughter, Mary Rosalie,[6] to be called Mary. Often the name was affectionately changed into "Maidie" or even to "Little Witch" by the family. She soon learned to have her way and to be the queen with her two brothers. She exercised her prerogatives over two more brothers, Louis born in 1885, and Fletcher in 1888, before she had feminine competition in Marguerite who arrived in 1890.

Louis' birth had come after a long and agonizing labor which came nearer to breaking Rosalie's courage than any of the many severe tests life brought to her. It no doubt set the family in a determination to follow the white man's medicine. Joseph's leg had been cared for by the pioneer doctors nearly thirty years before. Added work had been done on it in New York City, under probably the best care to be found. But many people of a primitive or semi-primitive culture have held child birth in a separate category to be cared for by the women, usually the nearest of kin. At first they "sent for Mother" but when over a day had passed and nothing Mary knew could bring about the birth, they sent for Dr. H. W. Francis of Bancroft. Through the years Dr. Francis looked after the Farley's. Later of course when Aunt Sue was a doctor, she cared for them all. But she, herself, frequently called on Dr. Francis and Dr. W. L. Hildreth of Lyons for assistance, and they in turn called on her.

Little Marguerite was greatly welcomed in 1890, for a baby girl had died at birth in 1887. Marguerite grew up with a better "give and take" relationship with her brothers than Mary ever achieved; indeed, Marguerite showed most of the best qualities of her parents and grandparents. No person in the large, extended family is still spoken of with such affection as is Marguerite. She seemed to reach out toward others and yet draw them to her; she never showed resentment and had an amazing ability to forgive. She was followed by two more boys—the genial, dashing La Flesche in 1892, and Eddie, Jr., a favorite in the family and community, in 1897. La Flesche was two years Marguerite's junior and Eddie seven years younger, but she was called "Baby" or "Babe" even after she had babies of her own.[7]

By spring in 1884, Alice Fletcher was up again, moving about the Reservation and completing her work by July. She must have exercised too strenuously and too soon, for she strained weakened muscles and was lame the rest of her life. In the next forty years, several Indian tribes came to know her as a short, plump, limping figure, negotiating sharp inclines with crutch or cane, while whatever pain it may have cost was hidden by a friendly, gentle smile.

But in 1884 she was thinking about the thousands of acres of lush grassland still untouched by her work or by the grants of 1871. Her eager mind kept searching for means by which the Omaha could earn money in their new economic existence. These undivided lands were to be held in common and were to provide a slow advance of cultivation, as well as provide land for future children. This land, however, was rapidly being pre-empted by white squatters. They swarmed in ahead of surveying crews and staked out their own claims, whether in the public domain or on an Indian Reservation. What difference did it make? These were only savages and they, themselves, wanted land! James C. Olson, in his *History of Nebraska,* says the settlers disregarded tribal claims in "sublime defiance of federal law."

The Omaha had long told the story that many, many years before the birth of men living at the time of the allotment, Big Elk had told the tribe:

> A great flood is coming, will soon be here. I am old and near the grave, I may be gone before it comes but I am sure it will come. The wild animals which God has given us for sustenance will disappear even the birds will find no resting place; some of you may not understand my meaning but if you do, prepare yourselves, take what steps would be best for the people.[8]

Never before had so many Omahas realized what Big Elk had meant. Surely it looked as though the flood was upon them.

White men were allowed to put cattle on the Reservation, on paying a fee to the Agent. Beyond this the government assumed no responsibility. The cattle often were not herded, but roamed at will over grass or planted fields and vegetable gardens. The cattle industry had existed in Nebraska since the late 1860's, from the time Texas herds were first driven north to the new railroads. The immense area once called the Great American Desert was finally recognized as embracing the finest grazing land men had ever known and the cattlemen thrived on the open range. Because northeastern Nebraska was Indian land, the industry had not entered, although by the last of the 1870's, it had come to the Reservation borders and now was spilling over them.

Alice Fletcher suggested that the Indians fence in their crops; but fencing was a strange idea to men who less than a dozen years before had hunted buffalo over this area, unobstructed by fences or farmsteads. The Indians were not alone in being slow to fence; the prairie country presented a fencing problem which American agriculture had never known. There were no stones for walls and no trees for rail fences; barbed wire was only beginning to appear. The grass was there and the cattle (other men's cattle) were there; crops could be grown and the government expected the Indians to support themselves by raising grain as well as stock.

So the eastern city woman, the trained anthropologist, had an idea which no one else had pointed out to the Omaha. Instead of fencing in the crops, why not fence in the cattle? She spoke to the Agent and a few leaders of the tribe suggesting that the unallotted lands be fenced and that the Council appoint a committee to manage a co-operative grazing program, but she had no part in further plans. It developed that the Indians might put in their few cattle at no cost; outsiders who wanted to use the grass would put in their herds at a definite fee. A manager should be found to lease the land, put up the fence and manage the cattle. At the end of the year, he would deduct his expenses, pay rent to the tribe and divide the profits equally between himself and the tribe. At the same time, the Indians' crops would be protected.

Ed Farley took this suggestion with enthusiasm and in July 1884 he applied for a twenty-year lease on 18,000 acres of unallotted lands at an annual rate of $.04 an acre. The first payment was to be made in advance on January 1 for the year of 1885.[9] The Agent, George Wilkinson, warmly recommended that this request be granted. He explained the need for fencing, declaring that the destruction of crops by white men's cattle had caused many irritating complications which would steadily increase if no change were made. He felt that "Mr. Farley's proposition" would bring greater income to the tribe than they had formerly received from all of their lands.

From the letters it would seem this particular angle constituted a new approach. Ed, through the Agent was dealing directly with the Commissioner and Congress was not concerned; but at the same time, he was a partner of the tribe. The committee was set up, the lease was granted and the machinery had barely started to function when the first of many obstacles was presented by the government.

Prior to 1884, the Office of Indian Affairs had made a few grazing leases, but each case had been handled by itself and there was no general policy on leasing Indian lands. Just as Ed was well launched into the first season, the President proclaimed that the leases previously made to the Arapaho and Cheyenne were null and void. Later, the United States Attorney General, going back to 1837 for his authority, gave an opinion that Indians could not lease land for grazing without the consent of the United States Government, which he interpreted as meaning consent by an Act of Congress.[10] Since this ruled out Ed's agreement with the Commissioner, it came as a thunderbolt—with the fences built on borrowed money!

It was doubly hard on Joseph. He had worked for over thirty years to secure land for the Omaha where they might do as they thought best. He had believed this was accomplished at three different times and now again they were told that they could not manage the land but must submit to a higher authority.

He said:

> ...the Agent told us he's heard from Washington that we had no right to lease land...We feel the unallotted land is ours, we wish to have it...We were going to use the money for machinery...It is like torture in the fire...like a stroke of lightening...when I was called from ploughing on my farm to hear the words...

Adjustments were made, however, and the lease was not cancelled, although no Congressional Act was passed and no definite policy was formed on leasing or grazing. The Farleys and the Omaha continued to do business on a special basis which existed in no other tribe. The Commissioner of Indian Affairs frequently mentioned this unusual practice in his annual report to the Secretary of the Interior.

However, this action by the government was only the first of many troubles connected with the pasture. Ed's management had two strikes against it from the start. Public opinion was inflexibly set in an attitude of condemnation for any man who had extended business dealings with the Indians. No doubt there were honest men among the earliest traders, but there had been so much crooked dealing that by mid-nineteenth century such a position as Ed had assumed was taken to be unquestioned proof of his dishonesty. Before this, Ed had been held in high regard by the outstanding, able and upright men of the whole community and had a reputation for the utmost integrity. Now the generally accepted prejudice led many to pass on the evil tales originated by a few jealous men who envied him the possibilities of the new position. Sadly, these tales were believed by a few white people who had been close to the family and who would have been expected to distinguish truth from falsehood.

The long standing factions and quarrels within the tribe made the unexperienced, easily influenced Indians ready tools for the clever manipulators. The pasture became big business; but, through the years, it was beset by controversy, envy, intrigue and underhanded dealings which almost led to a small scale civil war. It meant success to the Farleys but it was dearly bought as balanced against the labor, the misunderstandings, the slander and suffering it brought to Rosalie and Ed.

Family tradition speaks of Rosalie making several trips to Washington on tribal business, but only one (possibly two) such instances can be actually dated. Late in 1887, the Omaha were disturbed over the results of the Dawes' Act which gave them citizenship. Many were confused as to what citizenship might mean, others were wondering what might happen to their efforts toward self-government. The Council decided to send a delegation to Washington. They had wished Joseph to go but Mary had been very ill and he said he had no one to care for the stock. A few men set off for Washington by themselves to ask about citizenship. Since an authorized group was to go later, the tribe generally did not like this and efforts were made for Ed to follow these independent travelers. At last there were plans that Rosalie would go and speak for the tribe. It was one of the first times when she publicly filled her father's place.

The decision must have been made quickly after the first group had left, for Rosalie reported the Indian's departure to Frank on January 4, 1888, saying, ". . .how I wish I were going with Ed." On the 9th, Alice Fletcher wrote from Winnebago where she was working on that tribe's allotment, "I hope you will go. . .hope Ed will wire Francis so I can reserve a room for you at the Temple Hotel." She went on to say that Rosalie could get a prettier and cheaper dress in Washington if she did not have time to get one in Omaha. On February 3, Alice Fletcher wrote to Rosalie from the Winnebago Agency:

> So you are expected back today. I trust you had a splendid time and come home happy. Hope you found all the little ones well and that Ed found all right on the farm. Hope you found Francis well. I've not heard from him for weeks. . .and Susan,11 how is the dear girl? Did you meet her friends? Did you go to Hampton? Write and tell me how you like the great big world. No place like home I am sure you will say.

Winnebago is, relatively speaking, less than twenty miles from the Farley farm in the 1960's, but it was probably almost twice as far in 1888 and such a drive was not lightly undertaken in February and a letter was probably written to take the place of a visit they would both have enjoyed. If Rosalie wrote, the letter was not saved and those first impressions are still unknown.

In 1887 the Indians had better crops than did the white men in the neighborhood; a fact which added to the general determination to get hold of the Indian lands. Although 1889 was not a good year, it did not completely destroy the self-confidence of the Omaha. They found the pasture could bring an income to the tribe, more young people went to school and at first, the "hard times" of the nineties did not obliterate their hope.

For the Farleys the pasture became the center of all activity, although by 1890, there were six children all under ten years of age. Rosalie's busiest years with her family were those of greatest controversy over leases of grazing land. Little by little rules were set up on the length of a lease, the amount of rent and the land which might be rented. A member of the tribe was given preference and allowed to rent for a longer period than were outsiders. Most of the time, therefore, the Farley negotiations stood in Rosalie's name with Ed designated as her agent. Tradition throughout the community and intimate stories within the family testify that Rosalie's part was far from nominal. She had a natural ability to grasp large enterprises, to bring them into orderly arrangement and to attend to endless details. Through her life she kept the accounts and cared for all the correspondence—by long hand, of course, in a beautiful, even script.

Since the business operated through the tribe, Rosalie handled still greater responsibility for she made all the contacts with the men of the Council and the Committee. The Tribe had confidence in Ed, but many of the leaders did not speak English and Rosalie was their interpreter in more than just language. The transactions with the tribe increased when it was made possible to lease allotted lands, and many Omahas found it easier to rent their land instead of developing it themselves. A great deal of allotted land was rented before it was legal to do so. White men could easily persuade a less progressive Indian that it was quite proper to rent; and having no experience with money, even small amounts of cash seemed enormous to the Indians and they went on in good faith. Ed tried to give the younger men work, but they found it less effort to live on the rents. Certain of the "young men's party" (by this time men in their sixties) tried to follow Joseph's example to learn new ways themselves and inspire others, but too often, the younger generation ignored them.

At the same time, it became easier for white men and halfbreeds to enter the Reservation, put up a fence and declare that they had leased the land. In 1891 Congress established the rule that leases must be made through the Agent. However, two years later, in 1893, it was estimated that there were 50,000 acres under illegal leases.

Other pastures developed, with several managed by white men and within ten years a dozen or more members of the tribe had smaller areas. Since Ed and Rosalie started first, made a profit and increased their acreage, stories sprang up exaggerating the profits and the whole operation was looked on with envy. Ed usually reinvested much of his own share and in 1888 spoke of having "5,000 head on the range." He bought better strains of cattle, built a yard near the railroad and started to feed cattle through the winter. The stories grew larger and larger and tales of his mismanagement, and of his putting more than his share in his own pocket became more insistent. The Office of Indian Affairs sent out Robert S. Gardner, an experienced inspector, to look into the matter. Gardner found everything in good order, but since Frank had been detailed as the interpreter for the work, the dissident elements who wished to injure the Farleys extended their enmity to Frank.

There were at least two groups of speculators who operated in the newly organized Thurston County, which included the Winnebago Reservation and most of the Omaha. One group concentrated more particularly on the land of the Winnebago and leased a large area at $.10 an acre and then re-leased to actual farmers at $1.00 an acre.[12] Another group of men concerned with Omaha land was more or less led by William E. Peebles who desired to be appointed Agent, relying on his record as a supporter of Senator Thurston and his belief that he could talk the tribe into whatever plan he might promote.

In December 1890, this group made a new effort to gain control of Indian lands just as Rosalie was preparing to make a new lease. Since the leases always read that any area of tribal lands would be withdrawn if the lands should be allotted, it was to the white men's advantage to promote further allotment. In fact they frequently stirred up the Indians by telling them that allotments were to be made immediately. The old men would tell Rosalie that the Agent had already left Washington and would be on the spot to allot almost any day; when, of course, no legislation had been passed for further land distribution.

The tribe had appointed a delegation, however, to go to Washington and talk over allotments with the Indian Office. Peebles decided it would be well for him to go along and apparently to be the guide and mentor for the group. He prepared a paper saying that because the Council was sending this delegation, they further requested that William E. Peebles accompany them to assist them in obtaining their rights. He sent this paper to the clerk at the Agency asking that he have the "principal Indians sign...have them make their mark as I have the names written" and cautioning the clerk to be careful to "not soil" the enclosed paper.

Ed and Rosalie learned that this had been done, and went to

the Agency to confront the Clerk with their knowledge. He became panicky and started to throw the papers in the fire. Rosalie wrote to Frank "...we managed to get them." Get them they did, for these papers were found sixty years later among the letters Rosalie had saved. Pebbles' effort was unique in manner of presentation. Typewritten on a piece of cheap white satin was the statement:

The Omaha Indians
reposing the utmost confidence in
William E. Peebles
request him to accompany our delegation to Washington...

Pasted on the bottom of the Satin was a piece of paper with the Indian names written and a place indicated for each "mark." The names were Fire Chief, White Horse, Wajapa, Two Crows, Sindehaha and Prairie Chicken, but there were no marks. The best laid plans had gone wrong. Most of these men were real friends to Joseph and Rosalie and they had known nothing of this paper. The press in Omaha reported that Peebles had joined the Omaha delegation in that city and gone on to Washington with them.

Although it was several weeks before the time Rosalie usually met with the tribe's representatives to go over the leases, the men sent for her to come and meet with them. They were determined that the tribal land should be taken care of while the delegation and Peebles were away, fearing what might be accomplished. The lease was signed the last day of 1890 and Rosalie promptly took it to Pender, the county seat, to be recorded.

Failure to obtain the Indian signatures recommending his company to Washington did not in any way discourage William Peebles, who with others saw possibility of quick returns if they could manipulate Indian lands. In the spring of 1892, acting under the new law which placed leasing in the Agent's hands, Agent Robert Ashley made a lease for Rosalie with the properly delegated representatives of the tribe. This was for 2,632.18 acres of land for five years, to be renewed each year for $.25 an acre. The length of the lease had changed from twenty to five years; the price from $.04 to $.25 an acre in less than ten years. But the Indians said that Peebles told them he could arrange to have it for seven to eight years at $.50 an acre, if the land were used for agricultural purposes.

In less than a year, a suit was brought against Rosalie in the Federal District Court charging that this lease was fraudulent; that the Omahas signing as the committee had not authorized Ashley to enter into the agreement; that the lease was delaying allotment and thus injuring the tribe.[13] It was not difficult to see that behind the complainants, "Fire Chief, White Horse, et al" were actually Peebles and his associates. Rosalie met White Horse in town one day and he was as affable and friendly as ever. She soon learned that once again the names of the Indians had been used without their knowledge. The added excuse that all the Council had not been present when the lease was authorized was a flimsy one, as all had fully understood the terms by which a lease was to be granted.

The excited Tribe was aroused to decisive action. A meeting was called at Daniel Webster's and Ashley was amazed at the crowd that gathered. Nearly everyone denounced the few men who had been used as tools; in fact, the accusations became so vehement that Rosalie almost felt sorry for the culprits. When one tried to defend himself an older man turned to him and said, ". . .go and sit down and speak if you have something to say. . .you are like the wind."

The meeting declared that the tribe would assume no expenses for any trial which would result; they were not involved. The men who had brought it about would have to attend to the cost. By fall the Tribe had another meeting, this time at Wajapa's, and elected a new Council. Old Two Crows, sturdy leader for many years, who had not been present at the meeting to authorize Ashley, was the only one of the former council retained.

Squatters constantly moved in on the pasture and there was reason to believe they were aided and abetted by "the Pender ring." Accordingly, Rosalie brought a counter suit for an injunction since her attorneys found evidence that these men had boasted that they would break up the Farley pasture. The first three defendants, William E. Peebles, D. N. Wheeler and George Chittenden were accused of "having maliciously meddled with the affairs of the tribe" and to have counseled members of the tribe "in violation of the rules" to make selections of allotted lands.[14] Six other defendants were "squatters," most of them mixed-bloods who had not been considered members of the Omaha tribe but who now made claims to land on the grounds that they possessed some Omaha blood. They were charged with having broken down fences, plowed and ruined grass lands. The United States District Court granted an injunction to be in force for the term of the lease.

Then the leading defendants turned to another tactic. They had a large circular printed and widely distributed saying that the land in the Farley pasture was soon to be allotted and any cattle placed there would have to be removed. This brought real damage to

Rosalie, for stockmen did not bring their herds. A few even took out cattle already there. She was faced with rent to pay and no income. This, of course, was not covered by the injunction and to meet this move Rosalie brought a suit for conspiracy against Peebles, Wheeler, Chittenden, A.C. Abbott and Harry Swanson.

This case came to trial late in 1893 and was conducted in a strangely partisan fashion. The Judge consistently sustained the motions of the defendants, denying any position claimed by Rosalie's attorneys. As each juror was questioned, the attorneys asked if the fact that Mrs. Farley was an Indian would in any way affect their decision. Everyone declared that they were completely unbiased and that this would not influence them. Then when the defense attorney made his summation and plea to the jury, he pulled out all the stops in impassioned oratory, relating all the Indian atrocites committed against white people throughout American history.

The jury was out seventeen hours and could not reach an agreement. They asked to be discharged, but did not specify any one point of disagreement and did not ask for any instructions. The judge refused to discharge them and, as one listener said, proceeded to make a "stump speech" to them. They returned shortly with a verdict against Rosalie; no conspiracy had been proven. A month later the Court overruled a motion for a new trial and Rosalie's attorneys immediately appealed to the Supreme Court of Nebraska, citing thirty-six irregularities in the proceedings.

One ray of comfort came when the members of the tribe withdrew the case, charging that the lease was fraudulent; the Agent withdrew the lease from the Indian Office and made a new one. Three years later, the Supreme Court reviewed the conspiracy case and reversed the decision, asserting that conspiracy had been proven and the plaintiff's business had been injured. It completely refuted the basic premise on which the lower court had rested its verdict.[15]

Those three years were years of uncertainty and concern, but Rosalie could not have spent much time harboring anxiety—too many other things happened. Members of Nebraska's delegation to Congress, led by Senators John M. Thurston and William Allen, came, they said, to get the opinion of the Indians on leases and allotments. Rosalie wrote to Frank that the Indians they talked to were the ones rounded-up by the land company men. Wajapa, Silas Wood and a few other friends of Joseph and Two Crows were not even allowed to get into the room, although ostensibly a tribal meeting had been called. She felt that only Senator Allen showed any understanding of the

Indian's situation.

Several times Senator Thurston reprimanded Captain Beck, the Agent, until Beck asked point-blank if this were an authorized investigation and the Senator admitted it was not. Yet the Commissioner of Indian Affairs acknowledged a communication from these men in his annual report, suggesting a compromise favoring the land companies and intimating that the Agency should be investigated.[16]

Stories are told within the Farley family of Rosalie meeting Senator Thurston at what amounted to a debate on the legal aspect of Indian Affairs and that she had figuratively driven the Senator into a corner, showing much greater knowledge of the law and its application than he did. This is usually spoken of as having taken place in Washington, but it would appear this might have been the occasion. Rosalie's letter mentioned that ". . .nearly all last week we were attending the so-called Congressional investigation," but she said nothing of crossing verbal swords with the Senator.

The courts had ordered the squatters to move, but they stayed on. The Agent and the Indian police finally carried out several evictions and the excitement throughout the neighborhood reached fever heat. The newspapers fought the battle on paper while the lease holders, land companies and settlers contended with each other. Each "side" secured injunctions against the other and then a higher court reversed the grant of an injunction. The sheriff arrested the police and the police arrested the sheriff.[17] Additions were made to the police force, more rifles and ammunition were issued and Capt. Beck asked the Governor for troops. Rumors were afloat that men from Pender were in Omaha buying arms.

Only then did all parties try to come to a compromise. In the meantime, other events influenced the controversy. Several key positions in the Indian Office were changed; Capt. Beck was ordered to return to his Regiment; the demand for farm lands increased and more Indians found it desirable to lease; and more became vocal in demanding allotments. Rosalie continued to renew leases and expand her operations, but the stock business began to depend more on the feed lot than on the open pasture. The big pastures became smaller and the number of farms increased.

These new developments were appearing at the time of Rosalie's death in 1900. Without his interpreter and with less need to deal with the tribe, Ed made business arrangements with other white men and later with his sons. Still later "Farley Brothers" engaged in buying and selling livestock and dealing in real estate with offices in Bancroft and Walthill, Nebraska, Sioux City, Iowa, and Rapid City, South Dakota.

CHAPTER VI

ROSALIE AND SUSETTE:
THE TRIBE AND THE FAMILY, WHICH WAY?

The older generation, those men most closely associated with Joseph, were passing out of the picture during the earliest days of the pasture. The absence of their counsel and the increased influence of less stable men made many of the Omaha more easily influenced by the less desirable white men around them. This added pressure, together with the continued crop failures through the early 1890's, led to bad habits and a breakdown of standards within the tribe.

If in the new century the children ever thought back over the years and placed events in time, they must have been glad that their father did not live to see the extent to which, as Wajapa said, the Omaha had "fallen victim to the vices of the white man, while they have not made his virtues their own."[1] Late in September 1888 Joseph suffered a few days of fever and died. Up to the last he was still trying to set the Omaha on the path of the white man, on the path followed by the best and finest white men he knew. At a Fourth of July picnic a year or so earlier he had talked eloquently about the need of sending the children to school.

His last act before becoming ill was to assist Frank and Alice Fletcher in putting down the words of tribal rituals. The three of them sat in Joseph's house in the Logan Valley with old Shudenahze, Yellow Smoke. Shudenahze was the last of the tribe to know the sacred story, to be able to repeat the old, old words of a certain ceremony. He consented to give the words and sing the songs only after Joseph had said that if it were a wrong thing to do, he, himself, would accept any penalty.[2] Yellow Smoke probably always felt that this was the reason that Joseph soon became ill and died. To the last, Joseph was the leader, assisting his people in putting away the past that they might walk into the future.

This last act for the tribe was followed by honors shown to Joseph by the white men, for both white and red men joined in a service when he was buried. It was said to be the largest funeral known in the area. The gravestone later placed in the Bancroft Cemetery is marked:

INSTAMAZA

Iron Eye

Joseph La Flesche

Died Sept. 24, 1888
Aged 67 years

Last Chief of Omaha Tribe

Joseph's death was the second one in the immediate family, for Nicomi had died the spring before. Rosalie now gave extra attention and thought to the house up the valley where Mary and old Madeline Wolfe lived. One of her tasks was discontinued, however, since she no longer had letters and letters to write trying to collect the annual payment that was to come to Nicomi from Peter Sarpy. He had left his property to relatives in St. Louis but had stipulated that two hundred dollars should be paid to Nicomi each year. As time passed, the heirs in St. Louis resented this and regularly resisted sending the money. Rosalie at last had to rely on a lawyer in St. Louis who reported:

> . . .receipt for annuity. . .from Sarpy estate was duly received, as usual have only been able to get the money after using all kinds of threats and persuasions. Mr. Noonan, the agent of the heirs and the heirs themselves all seem to think "Necoma" has long since survived her usefulness and at least their patience. . . Would suggest you procure as witness some public official.[3]

Two Crows died only a few years after Joseph. They were both sorely missed. Two Crows had a habit of waiting to speak until the latter part of a Council Meeting and then, with a pithy statement or an allegorical story, he could point out errors and quiet the arguing Indians. On one occasion the long debated question of Half-Breed rights on the Reservation was discussed and many took the stand that white men who settled on the Reservation with their Omaha wives had no place there. Some even ventured the idea that it was wrong to marry outside of the tribe; the land should belong only to those who were pure-blood Omaha. Two Crows rose and said:

> My friends, I agree with you. . .you have said it wisely and well. None but pure blood Omaha have a right to this land. All others should move off at once. Now you know that my family and Wajapa's family are the only two families of pure Omaha blood in the tribe. All the rest of you have a little Ponca blood, a little Sioux blood, a little Ioway blood mixed in. . . Now all of you move off. . .and Wajapa and I will keep it for the pure Omaha.[4]

The loss of such men brought responsibility and leadership to Rosalie, a leadership tacitly accepted but never openly acknowledged.

During the distressing days before and during the conspiracy case, one of the men of Joseph's party, who never quite understood the extend of the changes taking place and whom Joseph had always had to keep pushing in the right direction, became deeply involved with the white schemers. He had been flattered into taking step after step into a tangled web of circumstances until the trial was near. It suddenly dawned upon him that he was repudiating all that a dear friend had taught him.

He said to Rosalie, "I have thought of your father all day. I know if he were here he would have told me to stop before I had gone so far."

The month of December 1890 had been quite taken up with the question of rival delegations, the prospect of allotments and the matter of the pasture lease, as far as the Omaha and the Farley family were concerned. But for the country as a whole it was a time of climax in the relationship between the white men and the Indians. Earlier in the year a Paiute Indian in Western Nevada had declared himself to be a Messiah come to save the Indians from their enemies, the white men. His preaching centered in the ceremony of the Ghost Dance, which swept through the country like fire over dry prairie grass. It particularly appealed to the Sioux who had been in almost continuous struggle with the white men for thirty years. Nothing had stopped the white men; why try this? The excitement engendered by the Messiah and the Ghost Dance came to a climax among the Sioux of the Pine Ridge Agency in December 1890 and in the battle of Wounded Knee, the last pitched battle (or massacre) on the Plains.[5]

Thomas H. Tibbles, accompanied by Susette, went to north western Nebraska as a correspondent for the Omaha *Herald* and for a Chicago paper. During the days of skirmishing, they were at the Agency buildings and after the one-sided battle, Susette helped care for the wounded who were carried into the little Episcopal church still decked in festoons of Christmas greens.

Excitement had been widespread; the State of Nebraska had called out its militia and was prepared to make a stand along its northern boundary only a few miles south of Wounded Knee Creek. But the combination of many deaths, a superior military force and a severe blizzard stopped the comparatively few hostile Indians and the long revolt of the Plains tribes came to an end. The correspondents soon drifted back to their papers and their tasks.

Shortly after this the Tibbles were back on the farm and T. H.

was taking a keen interest in the case of the Half-Breeds who were
demanding allotments on the Reservation, often on unallotted land
leased to Rosalie. He was also making connections with members of
the Populist or Peoples' Independent Party. He frequently mentioned
his associations with William Jennings Bryan, who was then representing Nebraska in Congress.

Although 1892 and 1893 were hard times in Nebraska with
drought and bank failures, many Nebraskans found the means to
travel to Chicago to the Columbia Exposition. Even Rosalie went
unexpectedly and at the last minute. For months the family had been
helping Frank and Alice Fletcher collect materials for an Indian
exhibit and Rosalie had kept her eye on the railway fares. By late
summer they came down and down and down as the railroads tried
to lure the last possible passenger. "It is tantalizing that the fare gets
cheaper and I can't see the wonderful fair." She could no longer
count on Mother. Marguerite and Susan were on a short vacation
from their duties at the Agency. Moreover, this was the summer the
law suits began and it did look impossible.

Then Frank sent Rosalie $18.00 and in October she planned to
go to Chicago with Sue, taking Mary and the baby, La Flesche. But
at the last minute Sue changed her mind and Ed went in her place.
Rosalie said:

> If I'd gone alone I would have taken the next train for home. I'd
> have been as helpless as a child in the crowd...after I got used to
> the noise and the people I was all right. Everyone was so
> kind...I told Ed we could work a little harder to make up for
> the money we spent...We found our way to see if Miss Fletcher
> could help us find a room...got a nice one on the ground floor
> so my fear of fire left me. Miss F. took us to the Fair...and
> suggested how we proceed. We first left Mary with La Flesche and
> visited the Art Gallery, then went through Midway...felt we must
> go there again with Mary; so the next day we took the children.
> Mary was such a help, could find her way better than I
> could...La Flesche was as good as could be...the view of the
> Colonade was beautiful.

This letter reporting to Frank (with many thanks) added, "I'm
so glad I saw what I did—it is so pleasant to look back upon." It
went on to tell about Mother being ill and how Mother had made a
bead belt for Frank; then discussed problems of the pasture.

The hard times had strengthened the Populist Party and T. H.
Tibbles had found a new crusade. With Susette he went to Chicago in
July to spend several days at the Exposition and an equal length of
time at a meeting of the Bimetallic League. It was understood that

T. H. would edit a newspaper for the League. Rosalie hoped this might be the time they would "get hold of something and make it pay." An opening came to serve several Populist journals that wished to have direct reports from Washington. The Tibbles' spent the next two years in the Capital acting as correspondents for a number of papers, mouthpieces of different groups of the People's or Independent Party. Susette did much writing for these papers and probably some for magazines. She greatly enjoyed the cosmopolitan city and took advantage of its many offerings. She had the opportunity of seeing the art which she loved, but it is doubtful that she had much time for her own painting. She found time at some period in her life, however, although few pictures can be located today. They were scattered, possibly not identified or may have fallen into hands where the signature may not have been recognized.

Rosalie's diaries and letters speak eloquently of her effort to guide and direct and of the difficulties of the task. The Connecticut Women's Indian Association carried on extensive work in assisting Indians to build houses and get equipment. Sara T. Kinney (Mrs. John C. Kinney) of Hartford was in charge for many years and became a dear friend of Rosalie's and a staunch support to many individuals of the tribe. When Phillip and Minnie Stabler returned from Hampton they moved into the first house built by the Connecticut women, which was called "Connecticut Cottage." Phillip was more advanced than most of the tribe, but Rosalie had a great deal to do in explaining a loan, a mortgage, interest payments and insurance costs. Even the letter to Alice Fletcher about Louis' difficult birth and her own fear turned quickly to business matters.[6]

> . . . it has made a coward of me to think I may have to pass through it again if it is God's will . . . Minnie has a boy, too. Mrs. Kinney [wrote] about the cost of the house . . . Ed thinks $420, a house of three rooms without a cellar . . . [including a well] . . . I will tell Phillip how Minnie should write to the ladies . . . Mrs. K. wanted to know if she could send some things for house-keeping . . . I'll tell her sheets, pillow cases, towels, two table cloths will help.

After the Stabler's moved in and Minnie had written her thank-you note, she mentioned she had hoped for a rocking chair. Mrs. Kinney turned the purchase over to Rosalie:

> Rocking chairs are not exactly among the necessities of life, still I can easily see how comfortable Minnie would find one to be . . . there is no money available through the Association . . . It must go out of my pocket . . . but I have a soft spot in my heart for anyone who enjoys a rocking chair . . . I'll send two dollars, no

doubt you can get something ... a fair rocking chair here is $1.50.

There was always need to help, to teach, to lead, to warn and direct:

> Yesterday several Poncas came in on the train ... six parties to dance on six Omahas for ponies. I asked one which Omaha he was going to pipe-dance on and he said Phillip Stabler. I told him Phillip had gone East to School ... I thought he had taken up white men's ways and put away his old customs ... might not let him dance.

> I am provoked at Big Elk for writing for his boys to come home (from Carlisle) to help harvest.

> I told Noah you would be better pleased if he would write himself ... he promised to next time ...

> I must see about Badger's affair and find out if Big Elk will assume a debt ... Phillip has not bought the cow yet ... I must see Sindahaha about the bills for lumber ...

> Julia Baptiste came up and had me write to a harness maker for a set of harness, $15.00 to be paid Oct. 1st; balance out of annuity payment or April payment next year.

At times the help Rosalie needed to give was distressing and made it difficult for her to carry on the duties at home:

> Christmas and the day after I had some horrid interpreting to do. Simpson Stabler you know is a hard drinker of anything. He threatened to whip his wife and fearing him she stole out of the wagon and walked up to Mother's where she staid all night. Mother took her to Noah's and he sent her home, Ha-she-mon-ne and wife to go with her ... when they left he gave her a terrible beating ... On Christmas morning during the worst blizzard we have had all winter, she got away and started for Noah's ... when she reached there she and the child were almost frozen. In a few minutes in came two of her little ones ... almost dead as they had nothing around them but calico slips. That afternoon Noah and Phillip brought her and the children over and had me go (into town) and ask the lawyer's advice. ... The woman was afraid to go across the creek and stayed all night ... she was terribly bruised about the face. The little girl, as old as my Mary ... had her hands swollen from the cold. I did what I could for her. ... The next day Noah and Phillip had the lawyer make out papers for arrest of Simpson ... the woman was afraid to go back to him ... Simpson pled guilty and asked to be punished, but at the last the woman would not appear against him ... so he was fined $5.00 and costs. ... Marguerite said some of the Indian women told her they had not slept in their homes for months, for fear of the men ... it is so distressing.

Frank and Alice Fletcher were always asking help on their ethnological work:

> I send measurements for two pair of moccasins.
>
> Tell father the mink skins are very nice. He has not sent me the two duck's heads yet . . .
>
> Mother has not been here since Tuesday, but I will see her Sunday and ask her the questions you want . . .
>
> Tell father that when he sends the tobacco pouch made of bladder he must fill it with Kinnikenick.
>
> If any old fashioned Indians come to the House ask about old Indian pack-saddles and tail pieces . . . I shall want one.
>
> I want the feathers of an owl—a big one—all the largest feathers.
>
> Joseph wrote to Frank: You wanted beaver made into a quiver—it is too small and they never use it for that purpose. It is round and has no tail. Otter skins is used for quivers. . . . I will make you the leggins, send the deer hides and we can tan them here. Two big ones will make what you want. The bonnet you want I will see about. The Winnebago used to have them. I haven't seen them lately.

Mrs. Kinney, Miss Fletcher and Frank all depended upon Rosalie to carry out transactions with individuals, which required many letters and much bookkeeping. Several individuals, as well as organizations, sent funds and Rosalie kept different accounts:

> Tell father to hurry the other men up about paying for the threshing machine. It is nearly three months since the money was due . . . it is only $15.15 apiece and only two men have partly paid.
>
> Tell Ed I have the money for Andrew Johnson, that he may buy a horse . . . sending the money to Uriah.
>
> Wajapa gave me $13.00 to send to Mrs. Kinney and $12.00 for Miss Fletcher . . .
>
> Edward Esau sent out his son-in-law to have me write . . . he wishes help in buying a set of harness. . . . Albert Pappan, Lettie's husband, wants help . . . he has a good team, but no harness.
>
> I sent you a draft for the following sums . . . $10.00 from John Webster on his old accout, $12.00 from Wajapa . . . will you please send receipts to John Webster and Wajapa so as to keep it straight . . . the two men trusted me with it and I want to show them you received it . . . have sent word to Sindahaha that he must bring some money and make a payment as I have written so

> many times to Mrs. Kinney that he would pay and that I could not write another letter. . . . I could not go on *forever* making excuses for them. . . . I have to go over and see Tae-on-haha and poke him up. Dear me if they don't do any better what are we going to do with them?

Mahawatha had me write for him about his hay land.

The money by which the Omahas met these many loans came from the government payments. Frequently an Indian's debts, a bit here and a bit there, amounted to more than his check. The merchants in Bancroft as well as various money-lenders operated on a credit basis and then were careful to be on hand when the checks were given out, in order to get their money. Rosalie became the banker, the go-between, the chief financial officer for the tribe. She kept all the separate accounts owed by different Omahas and regularly went to the payments to see that the money was honestly divided. This often took several days and she would pack up the children and move into the Agency until matters were settled—as far as they could be settled.

In 1890 Frank was at home for a payment day and she took him with her into "the room where the payment was going on and had him lecture Two Crows and Sindahaha." She reported to Alice Fletcher who had arranged for many loans:

> I collected only $45.00 on the notes you left with me; $25.00 from Schyler Wells . . . $10.00 still due, which must come from his crops . . . $10.00 from Albert Pappan on his $37.00. Little Heel $10.00 the balance on his $20.00, Migazhega had to pay on a horse so could do nothing but would chop wood this winter to earn money.

Time for the affairs of the Farley family must have been hard to find, although they had hired help inside the house as well as on the farm and pasture. There was a second house on the place for a hired couple; the wife was to help Rosalie and feed the extra "hands." But the diaries are full of the tasks of housekeeping and the frequently inefficient "help."

> Ironed seven shirts for the boys. Killed three chickens. Baked and made doughnuts.

> Plum butter nine quarts. Ironed three shirts and mopped.

> Swept out bedroom and cleaned outside of couch. Ironed all afternoon.

> Young Jordan came around with cherries which we pitted this

afternoon. Ed took me down to Presser's to see about making black calico dress and the plaid and the check.

Eddie is better from the fever. Washed his clothes and baked. Sewed on curtains.

Cloudy and put off washing. Covered the couch.

But she could find time to make things pretty:

Wrote to advertisers for flower seeds.

Set out plants. —Put out rest of pansies. Hung the pictures in the living room.

Ed brought two rolls of paper for dining room. Papered this afternoon. Ed put up climbers for vines. Two yellow ramblers came.

The effort for pretty things was largely made for the daughters, by the time Mary was fifteen and Marguerite eight years old, as shown by a few days from Rosalie's diary of 1898.

March 1. March came in like a lion, flurries of snow. Cut out Mary's white dress and sewed on it. . . . Carey was here for dinner. Ed gave him a pig.

March 2. Sewed on Mary's dress all my spare time. Mary still sick. Mahawatha and Webster were here.

March 3. Cut out Marguerite's blue dress and sewed on it. John took me to town and we got some all over embroidery.—and some lace, 40¢.

March 4. Mary went to school. Mrs. Sedig came to wash; finished at 3. . . . Sewed almost all night on girls' dresses and coughed a great deal.

March 5. Sewed on girls' dresses as soon as the work was done up and finished at 3. Mary and Marguerite went down to practice. Mother was down, spent afternoon and had supper with us. Ed took the girls down (into Bancroft). Caryl staid home with me, I coughed all day. Entertainment was a success. Am told Marguerite did well. Both my girls looked very pretty.

— — — — — — —

March 15. Windy again. Sewed on Mary's dress.

March 16. Caryl and John staid out of school to help put in wheat. Boys drove up to Pender to attend concert.

March 17. Boys returned at 1 a.m. Mother and Marguerite came down and spent the day. Mother washed out some garments for me. Baked. Sewed on Mary's red skirt. Cleaned three chickens for supper tomorrow night.

March 18. A dark nasty day. Got chicken on at 12. Caryl, Mary and Louis went to the supper, also Ed and John. Had supper for the children. Folks got home at 9. Brought up our supper.

— — — — — — —

May 30. Ed went to range. Made Mary's collar this a.m., finished it this p.m. John came in (from the range).

May 31. Cut out Mary's white dress. Susan and Mother were down.

June 1. Sent T. H. Tibbles check for pony sold for Susette. Went down this evening to Mary's room exercises in school house. Eddie has a heavy cold. Did not go to bed till one.

June 2. Eddie very sick, high fever, sent Louie up to Sue's for medicine; near noon sent him back to tell Sue to come. Came and worked over him all afternoon. Lung fever. Did not go to bed till one. Finished Mary's white dress.

June 3. Eddie much better, no fever. Last day of school, couldn't get to hear Marguerite who took part in exercises. Ed went to range. Marguerite wore white.

Besides the tribe and the children, Rosalie constantly had visitors who brought her great satisfaction. Moreover her hospitality was extended to the families and friends of these visitors. For many years the most eagerly welcomed was Alice Fletcher and then with her, E. Jane Gay who was a whole company in herself. A school girl acquaintance of Alice Fletcher's Jane Gay was horrified when she found how utterly her friend disregarded her own health and strength. Finding that Alice Fletcher was to go on an extended assignment to the Nez Perces Indians in Idaho, she was convinced Alice could not be trusted to go alone. Therefore, she acquainted herself with the art of photography and got herself appointed as photographer on the expedition. She furnished all her own equipment, however, and actually felt her most important task was to be the cook and to see that Alice Fletcher had properly planned and regular meals.[7] Miss Gay lived with Alice Fletcher in Washington for a time and on a number of occasions visited the Farleys.

Mrs. Kinney of the Connecticut Women's Indian Association came, so that she might know Phillip and Minnie, Noah and Lucy and above all to know Rosalie and Ed on whom she depended for help. Rosalie had been drawn to Sara Kinney from her first letters in 1885. Mrs. Kinney apparently had met Susette, and had become interested in the Omaha. She was at work on building plans for

Omaha village about 1860 with both earth lodges and tipis as dwellings,
probably within the first five years on the Reservation.
(Bureau of American Ethnology)

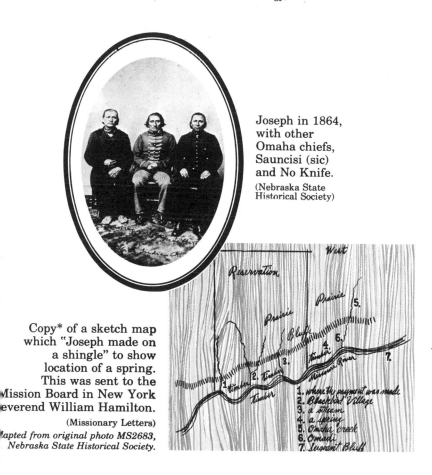

Joseph in 1864,
with other
Omaha chiefs,
Sauncisi (sic)
and No Knife.
(Nebraska State
Historical Society)

Copy* of a sketch map
which "Joseph made on
a shingle" to show
location of a spring.
This was sent to the
Mission Board in New York
everend William Hamilton.

(Missionary Letters)

*apted from original photo MS2683,
Nebraska State Historical Society.

1. where the payment was made
2. Blackbird Village
3. a stream
4. a spring
5. Omaha Creek
6. Omadi
7. Sergeant Bluff

Joseph La Flesche, Iron Eye
1822-1889

son of Joseph La Flesche,
Franchman and Wa-tun-na.
Sources disagree over
her tribe; either Ponca
or Omaha.

Mary Gale
1826-1909
daughter of Ni-co-mi and
Dr. John Gale with the
United States Army at
Fort Atkinson.

ravestone in
ancroft, Nebraska
metery, giving
e Indian names of
ary and Joseph.

children of joseph and mary

Susette "Bright Eyes"
1854-1903
Mrs. Thomas H. Tibbles

Louis
1848-1860

NO
PHOTOGRAPH
AVAILABLE

Rosalie
1861-1900
Mrs. Edward Farley

Marguerite
1862-1945
(Mrs. Chas. Picotte)
Mrs. Walter Diddock

Susan, M.D.
1865-1915
Mrs. Henry Picotte

children of joseph and ta-in-ne (elizabeth esau.)

NO PHOTOGRAPH AVAILABLE FOR ELIZABETH ESAU.

Francis
1857-1932

Lucy
1865-1923
Mrs. Noah La Flesche

NO PHOTOGRAPH
AVAILABLE

Carey
1872-1952

Susan and
Marguerite
at school in
Elizabeth, N.J.

Susette and Frank
in Washington, D.C. in 1881
when traveling with
the Ponca Chief,
Standing Bear.

1890-1915

The sod and frame house, said to
have been on "the Tibbles place,"
which was Susette's allotment,
as a member of the tribe. Susette
is in the second floor window;
T. H. Tibbles at the left. The other
figures must be his daughters.

Four granddaughters of Joseph;
daughter of Rosalie holds the
daughter of Marguerite.
This child's sister to the
left, in front; on the right
is the daughter of Carey.

Lucy's husband, Noah
stands by the second house
he built for her.

Susan's "tall house"
in Walthill.

Carey's house, southwest of the Agency.
The house where Frank died.

This sketch of an unstrung bow with an arrow was drawn by Susette La Flesche for Fannie Reed Giffin's book *Oo-ma-ha Ta-wa-tha*. It appears twice. Each time it is at the close of a chapter which tells of a funeral or death. In more permanent form it marks the end of another life, for it is carved on the gravestone of Susette La Flesche Tibbles in the Bancroft, Nebraska cemetery.

It is an appropriate accompaniment for the La Flesche story, since "la flesche" is French for "arrow." Early reports of Europeans meeting the Omaha spell the name in several ways. The family came, however, to use for their name the correct French spelling of the common noun.

returned students even before she was aware of Rosalie's identity. The earliest letter from Mrs. Kinney in the La Flesche papers asks if the sister Rosalie had mentioned might be Bright Eyes and continues by saying "... then you are also the sister of Mr. Francis La Flesche whom I met last winter." The friendship grew by correspondence and by working on a common project. Then Rosalie, not wishing to appear in a false light, and no doubt wondering what a born and bred Puritanical New Englander might think, must have broached the subject of multiple marriages and her own family situation. Sara Kinney passed the test with the breadth of view and fine tolerance which she frequently showed. She wrote that she was not shocked at what Rosalie had told her of Joseph, that "good and wise men as well as bad ones usually go on in the ways of their forefathers until taught wise and better ways ... as you truly say it is a blessed thing for a man to have one wife."

Sara Kinney's first visit to Nebraska apparently was in 1891, probably in the fall, for she and her husband, the editor of the highly esteemed *Hartford Courant,* usually attended the conference of Friends of the Indians at Lake Mohonk; but she was represented at the 1891 meeting by a letter which was read to the conference and included in their report.

> At Bancroft I was met by my Indian hostess, taken to her home, a cottage one mile from the village where she lives with her husband, six children and one or two servants (not Indians). A canary swung in its cage on the outer porch, a hammock under the trees, filled with one little, two little, three little, four little, five little, even six little Injuns ... [later] a little chap of nine years asked if I would step out to supper ... we were seated to a delicious meal of prairie chicken ... the same little boy [had] asked the blessing with as much ease and reverence as a member of the Hartford theological fraternity.... In the evening we discussed the Indian problem but ... other topics of general interest ... at one end of the room in a prettily drapped bay window was a table with magazines, *Harpers, Century, Youth's Companion* and the *Agriculturist.* You say my hostess is not an average Indian. True, far from the average, no more like the average white woman. She is a sweet, gentle, modest, wise, far-sighted, quick-witted, refined Christian woman, yet an Indian, has never been in any school but a reservation school and (seldom) more than fifty miles from home ...

Mrs. Amelia S. Quinton, president of the Women's Indian Association and an ardent Presbyterian, contributed to establishing work of the church away from the original Mission building. She, too, came to visit and became a friend of the La Flesche and Farley families. Miss Heritage, a friend Susan had made in Philadelphia came to see Susan and stayed with both Susette and Rosalie, but most of the time with Rosalie. Rosalie wrote to Alice Fletcher, ". . . she wished to pay for her board, but we told her we would not take anything, . . . we could not when she was Susie's guest and we all liked her from the very first day."

The final appealing touch from Rosalie was Miss Heritage's attitude toward the children. She and Susan went to Sioux City for overnight and took nine-year-old Caryl with them. He came home with such tales to relate to the younger children, about the elevator at the hotel, and that he had had a towel all to himself! The guest had filled a small trunk with gifts for everyone, including winter suits for Caryl and Jack. She had left some of her own dresses with Rosalie, suggesting the material could be used for the children, but they fit Rosalie and she put them away for the next summer, rejoicing in their pretty materials and better style.

Alice Fletcher's book on Omaha songs and music published in the middle 1890's also brought friends to Rosalie. The collaborator on the music was John C. Fillmore, a widely recognized musician. In the fall of 1891, he sent his young son John to Nebraska to recuperate after an illness. The lad spent two months with the Farleys, nearly six weeks of that time out on the range, cooking for the men. Rosalie reported on the experience:

> I did his washing and ironing and made him as comfortable as possible. We paid him $22.00. I like him—he did not make it a bit hard about the eating as he was always hungry. I can't see how he managed to stay so long on the range with those big rough men. Ed showed him about the cooking and he borrowed a cook book—did pretty well. He was going to learn how to cook things besides coffee, potatoes and meat if he was home this winter.

True to the universal Indian rule of hospitality and open house for all relatives, there were guests from kindred tribes, for Indian relationships are extensive. A tipi was frequently pitched in the Farley yard. The Indians were still accustomed to bringing their house with them, but certainly the eastern friends did not and yet Rosalie seemed to manage. Only one letter telling of guests said something about getting the children home again. Probably they also went to relatives.

White Swan, Joseph's brother Frank, remained with the Poncas in Indian Territory even after Standing Bear's group had been resettled in Nebraska. He frequently came visiting the Omaha before going on to the Ponca on the Niobrara. The children noted how much he resembled Joseph and enjoyed the occasion of a Fourth of July celebration when, "a great many beeves [were] killed" and there were to be "several pipe dances" and Uncle Frank was invited to "wave the pipes." At times his daughter, another Rosalie, would come and there were also visiting relatives of Mary's from among the Otoe.

Ed and Rosalie, busy themselves, were leading a busy family, for with repeated contacts with a world beyond the Reservation, a mother who was always reading and studying, a father busy with wider and wider operations, the children soon were busy too. The fact that on the trip to Chicago, Mary, not quite ten, had been helpful and capable of caring for fifteen months old La Flesche by herself, was just one example of the way the Farley children grew up. Caryl and Jack were doing the work of men when they were barely ten years old. In fact, the summer after Caryl's tenth birthday, when Jack was not yet nine, they went to the range with their father for they "knew every head, how old it is and where it came from." They had done enough work through the spring that Ed had dispensed with hiring one more hand for the season. At fifteen Jack was a full time herder in charge of two pastures and the same summer, Louis, twelve, and Fletcher, nine, helped milk and were responsible for driving the milk wagon into the creamery. They "celebrated the Fourth by putting La Flesche into pants." In the nineties small boys wore "frocks" until nearly five, so that was an occasion worthy of celebration.

Indeed, besides the children's growing up, by the mid-nineties many other things had happened. Marguerite had had a brief, rather tragic marriage to Charles Picotte, a French-Sioux whom she had met at Hampton. He was never strong, was ill for months and died after four years of marriage. Susan had finished medical school, was the physician of the tribe, then worn out, she withdrew and devoted herself to her mother. Later she married Charles' brother Henry.

After two years in Washington the Tibbles' came back to Nebraska in the Summer of 1895. At first they were at Rosalie's and it was understood a new editorial job was soon to develop. But for some reason it did not materialize and at last they went to housekeeping in their own house, in which they had reserved three rooms, although the farm and the house had been rented. At last the opening came when a group of men who were publishing the *Weekly Independent,* a Populist paper in the capital city, Lincoln, asked

T. H. to be the editor. Later this became the *Lincoln Independent* and the official organ of the Populist Party.

They moved to Lincoln early in October with Susette assuming most of the responsibility, for T. H. threw himself into the current political campaign and spent the next month making speeches in support of the Populist ticket throughout the north central part of the state.[8] By mid-November he had returned and they were able to become more permanently settled. They maintained a home in Lincoln for the next five years although they frequently spent time on the farm north of Bancroft.

They lived in two different houses; both in a pleasant neighborhood east of the capitol building. The "den" or, it may have been only one corner of the "parlor" was completely decorated with Indian handicrafts. A picture shows Susette seated on a couch which is covered with a buffalo robe and blankets; woven fabrics, leather bags or pouches and bead work are to be seen. Another picture shows a reed organ in a corner. The top of the organ, the music rack and the walls on both sides are covered with numerous pictures. This was the fashion and Susette loved pictures. There were prints of famous paintings, several paintings of people and scenes, some of which must have been her own and many other pictures that cannot be distinguished in a small photograph.

At one end of the music rack is a picture of Rosalie and on the center the most familiar picture of Henry Wadsworth Longfellow, the venerable poet with white, white hair and beard. Was this Susette's tribute, a grateful recognition of the man who had acknowledged her as the embodiment, the living illustration of his imagined Indian Maiden? Her recognition of his compliment apparently did not extend to a frequent perusal of his poetry or even of "Hiawatha," for her copy of his selected poems, given to her by the publisher, Harcourt, in 1879, was pristinely fresh and unused through the twenty-five years it was in her library.

Susette was too passionately absorbed in the trials and the troubles of actual Indians to spend time on imagined ones of another day. The advancement of her people was of paramount interest and for many years she was pulled in two directions: following her husband's interests, his causes, her enjoyment of the city life led by educated white people, and at the same time feeling a compassion for her own family and tribe and a yearning for the rolling prairie hills and the high bluffs along the river. The one editorial signed with her name in the first few months that she directed the *Weekly Indepen-*

dent has a tone of militant sarcasm that is not found in her passionate appeals for justice in Indian policy. It would seem that the direct election of Senators and the cause of free silver espoused by the Populists did not engage her as completely as did the Indian's need for recognition as an individual.

Changes had come to the tribe as they more and more disregarded the words of Joseph, Two Crows and others. Where in the 1860's and 1870's Joseph's police had kept order and the Agents wrote of never seeing a drunken Omaha, constant drinking became more and more common and frequently resulted in death. Wajapa tried to organize a Temperance Society and there was a Law and Order Committee on the Reservation which, for a short time, had some effect when white men who supplied the whiskey were brought before the courts and heavily fined. Too often, no one would bring charges against the bootleggers or, having gained the habit, the Indians protected the white men. An Eastern visitor said that if the Indians failed to establish themselves it would be because of the white man's gift to the red man—whiskey."

Even Ed slipped for a time in the days of the early pasture, much to the disdain of the teachers at the Mission and to Frank's horror. Rosalie met the problem directly and sternly, as her father had, not cringing from open expression of her scorn and disgust and her own superior strength. Ed braced up, "took the cure" and trod the path of the teetotaler from then on. Before the days of the law suits, Rosalie would write to Alice Fletcher, "Ed is the same dear old fellow we used to know, he has done so well and worked so hard." She told Frank that "ever since that night when you and I had that talk," she had watched Ed carefully and was sure that Ed never went to a saloon and she was happy he was again "steady and hard-working."

Ed showed his appreciation and affection, performing many added and extra little jobs that would help her. When he shipped stock to Sioux City or Omaha he always brought back gifts for Rosalie. She loved pretty things and would write of her pleasure over an attrative calico print or dress pattern, a soft silk scarf "which feels good around my neck," the glowing color of materials for curtains, or the new carpet for the sitting room. Food for her mind was equally welcome—thanks sent for magazines; "Ed brought me a dictionary which I've wanted so long and, extravagant fellow, a whole set of Dickens' works." Ed's trip took him near better markets and he frequently returned with the larger clothing purchases for a season, an astonishing number of shirts, stockings, coats, shoes and yards and yards of material, or needed equipment, "Ed brought me a new sewing machine."

Matters of leasing were changed for the better in some unexplained manner in 1896, for one letter indicates one day in that year as red letter day for the business. Obviously the future looked better with more opportunity to save and plan for the children.

The next two years were interesting for many reasons. Caryl would be going away to school; Ed talked of building a larger more comfortable house and everyone was anticipating the Trans-Mississippi Exposition to be held in Omaha in the summer of 1898. There would be an Indian department with displays from many tribes and, if possible, an encampment where each tribe would live and cook, worship and celebrate according to their own fashion. Alice Fletcher was largely responsible for the Indian exhibit and most of the adults of the La Flesche family aided in gathering material and information.

The same summer Alice Fletcher was working on a paper about the Indian earth lodges. By 1898 there was not a lodge left that was entirely of native construction. There were one or two on the Reservation which had a few basic features combined with newer materials and techniques. Only a few older women could tell exactly how the old lodges had been built. Alice Fletcher wrote questions to Rosalie and she and Susan spent many hours with Mary, relaying the questions or asking more when some step in the process was not clear. Mary made a small model and also drew a circle on the dirt of her own dooryard and with sticks and bits of bark, demonstrated the method. She said their father had had two lodges; she had worked on the first one and watched the building of the second. However, Rosalie and Susan had no recollection of the underlying structure or the general arrangement of a lodge.

Three long letters with measurements, diagrams and detailed directions are among Alice Fletcher's papers in the Bureau of American Ethnology. The letters and the measurements of Fire Chief's lodge which Miss Fletcher had measured in 1884 were sent to E. Jane Gay. Miss Gay made a model to scale which was added to the permanent Omaha exhibit at the Peabody Museum of Harvard. In her transmitting letter, Alice Fletcher gave full recognition to Mary and Rosalie:

> . . . I reviewed data with some of the old women of the tribe, who had . . . worked on these buildings. Mary, widow of Joseph La

Flesche, about 80 years old, active and sound in mind, gave me much help. . . . During the time of Miss Gay's work, I was in correspondence with (her) through her daughter, Rosalie Farley. Their help was invaluable.9

In Lincoln Susette and T. H. were working with Fannie Reed Giffen on a book to be published during the Exposition. This was *Oo-ma-ha Ta-wa-tha* (Omaha City) to tell the story of the lusty young city, which required the story of the Omaha tribe as introduction. This small pocket size book with only ninety-four pages represents the work of several persons. John Webster wrote the preface, dedicating the book to the Omaha tribe, and mentioning Mrs. Giffen's long knowledge of the Omaha since she remembered when chiefs of several tribes were welcome at her father's home.

The book contains folk tales told by Joseph and by Mary, put into English by Susan—and probably Susette—a message from Frank, the story of Big Elk, of the two La Flesche men helping take the prisoner to St. Louis, of the little brother Louis with the drawing made by the traveling artist. Of real importance is the full text of the treaty with a sketch of each of the signators and pictures except for Village Maker who never would accommodate himself to that strange custom of the white man. Rather typically Rosalie's name does not appear but through the letters we know she helped gather material and that Mrs. Giffen made at least one trip to the Reservation during her work.

The greatest beauty of the book lies in the illustrations by Susette—delicate little sketches of Indian life and artifacts by the initial letters and at the close of chapters and two full page pictures in color, one of a chief in war-bonnet and one of a young Omaha girl. These are among the few precious examples of Susette's work that survive. This is considered the first book to be illustrated by an American Indian—another *first* for Susette!

Early in 1897 Susette had been seriously ill and T. H. had brought her to Rosalie. The newspapers said she was exhausted from working too hard on her husband's newspaper. However, it was more than physical fatigue, since for several years she had had an increasing tendency to become irritable and at times extremely angry. Old friends like Wajapa were hurt and puzzled and the family was deeply concerned for this was quite unlike the controlled person they had always known. Now, after weeks of Rosalie's solicitous care she even turned against this nearest sister. During the work on *Oo-ma-ha Ta-wa-tha,* T. H. went back and forth from Lincoln collecting the material. Probably Susette was happier in Lincoln—with her painting.

Most of the family got to the Fair. Rosalie went in July when Frank, Alice Fletcher and John C. Fillmore had a day at the Musical Congress on their studies of Omaha music. Illustrations for the talks were given by professional artists on orchestral instruments but also by six members of the Omaha tribe, who gave several traditional songs.[10] Rosalie made this trip by "going to bed at three and (getting) up before five to take the 6:45 train." She took Marguerite and Eddie with her and one day of sight-seeing at the exposition compelled her to "get a roller chair to go down to our stopping place." The third day she was home again, coming in on a late train and finding that Mary had gone to a neighboring town with a girl friend of her own age. As Mary reached the time when she might have carried larger responsibilities, she frequently failed to assume them and as soon as she could she began to clerk in the stores in Bancroft.

Early in August Ed took Mary, Louis and Fletcher to Omaha for three days. Since Mary and Louis each had a special chum with them it amounted to quite a conducted party. Indian Day was the great attraction with a parade downtown, one on the Midway at the Fairgrounds and Indian sports and dances in the afternoon. The newspapers remarked that this was the last time the public would see "reservation Indians," for plans just being put into operation would do away with reservations and old Indian customs in a few short years. They also said that the promoters of the Indian Encampment were disappointed, for few people took the pains to observe the differences between the tribes, they were only seeking amusement.[11]

Rosalie's diary for those three days, speaks eloquently of her absorption in her children and deep seated habit of dealing with many people:

> August 1. Ed and children took the 9K* train for Omaha. Did up a.m. work and got dinner. Very lonely. Took a nap this afternoon. Exceedingly lonely. Had Supper early and went out with the children to wait for Caryl. He came in after 9 (from the range).

> August. Drizzled all day. Cleaned kitchen. Caryl did not go to the range. Saw no one all day.

> August 3. Caryl killed two chickens. Cleaned them and put them on and washed out some garments. Made the beds upstairs and swept out lower rooms. Had supper when Ed and children got home on 8K train. So glad to see them.

*K was Rosalie's shortened version of "o'clock."

She had had no thought that she might welcome a quieter day, she had made little of the luxuary of a nap and she was *lonley* even with her two biggest boys and two smallest ones at home.

Mary went again to the Fair to sing with another group from the tribe. Near the closing date in October, Rosalie and Ed, again taking Marguerite and Eddie spent two days in Omaha. It was a most special occasion because Caryl came up from Lincoln to spend the time with them. He was there preparing to enter the State University and was one of the first of the tribe to venture beyond Hampton and Carlisle. Evidently Rosalie and Ed sought a different kind of education for their children. Hampton and Carlisle academically covered little more (if as much) as the three-year High School in Bancroft, but placed emphasis on vocational training and the experience of living part of the time in the homes of white people.

All of the Farley's, except Jack, completed the High School, and by the time La Flesche and Eddie were in the school it was a four year course. But since Caryl had only had the three years he was not ready for entrance into the University. The lack of one year was not his only handicap for there are few entries in Rosalie's diaries that do not begin: "Caryl (or John or Louis) staid out to help." Even a mother always learning and reading to the children could hardly make up for such irregular attendance. Caryl went for one year to the Wallace Preparatory School which was located near the University campus.

He was by no means alone in this need for added preparation. There were many three-year high schools in the State at that time and indeed, ever since it had opened, the University of Nebraska had maintained a preparatory department or had fostered one near by. This was a good school and Charles Wallace, who conducted it, was later on the University faculty in the English department. He became famous for having discovered one of the few known authentic signatures of Shakespeare.

At first Caryl had gone to live at "Auntie's"—Susette's. She had cordially asked this and for several weeks it was a most satisfactory arrangement. He helped about the house and kitchen as he always did at home and Susette seemed to enjoy him. T. H. told him that Susette seemed easier than she had been for some weeks, but the usual explosion of anger came and Caryl left to find a room nearer the University. The moments of anger always passed and apparently left no permanent impression, so cordial relations continued and Rosalie often wrote that in case of any need or if he ran short of money he should "go to Auntie."

Rosalie sorely missed Caryl, her oldest and her most dependable
helper. There must have been many mornings when, with the older
ones in school, Eddie could not keep her from being "exceedingly
lonely." Like all mothers her fostering care still reached out to
include this one bird that had left the nest. Like all mothers the habit
of giving directions built up through seventeen years still controlled
her and she wrote:

> Be sure and go to church Sunday—don't fail. It would be well not
> to pay a great deal of attention to young ladies as you need all your
> time for work. I know the companionship of good girls will not
> hurt you . . . it is the time I'm thinking of. I am anxious that all
> shall go well with you.

After Frank had sent Caryl a Christmas gift of a book she
wrote: ". . . be sure and write a nice letter to Uncle Frank, spell
correctly and thank him."

The next fall Jack, too, went to Lincoln to take a short course
at a business school and Caryl did register in the University with the
class of 1903. Jack had never stayed long with books and even con-
centrating on business methods did not suit him. He needed action
and felt he could trust his own shrewd sense in handling money and
could understand figures better in the terms of a horse trade or the
sale of a carload of cattle. Before long he was begging to come home.
He had done so poorly that he would need to repeat several courses
and Ed felt he was only wasting time.

Rosalie was extremely disappointed saying, "I cannot agree
with the conclusion you and Papa have reached. I certainly expected
you to finish. If you come home, you must try and be helpful and
get along with Papa."

Rosalie had not been well for years. The letters and diaries
never have a word of complaint or self-pity and the reader is compelled to read and check the dates before realizing how often the
mere statement of illness appears.

> Had a sick headache all day.

> My face was swollen this morning.

> I was sick when we got to Blue Lake.

> I've not been able to stand for several weeks.

> I don't know what I would have done without Miss Fletcher's
> invalid chair.

I was sick Saturday night and not up at all yesterday.

My eyes hurt all the time.

My foot is sore again.

My fingers have been badly swollen.

I have had a bad cold.

It can also be noted that by the fall of 1899, Ed was handling more of the small Indian accounts and paying money to the merchants and talking to the individual Indians about their planning.

Rosalie's letters to Caryl and Jack, to Alice Fletcher and to Frank, so frequent through the years, came to an end in February of 1900. Shortly afterward Jack was home working at the herding and in the feed yard as usual, but making quick money with horse trading, writing Caryl for permission to sell his horse, talking of hunting, going to town and staying late at night and planning for a baseball team in the summer.

His letters to Caryl and one or two from Mary and Marguerite sent the home news for a few months. Rosalie at last was spending most of her days in bed. The swollen feet that had covered so many miles all within the little house and the hands that had performed so many useful and helpful acts were quiet. She would lie by the window and during the last week of April enjoy the purple plumes of the lilacs waving outside and look up toward the knoll where the new house was to go up in the summer.

The house for Rosalie was destined to be like the school entertainments, the lodge suppers, the church services that Rosalie had planned and worked for but never attended because some other person claimed her time and attention. The house was still only a plan on paper when on May 9, Jack wired to Frank, "Mama died this morning. Come at once. Answer at once." The supports were gone from Ed and eighteen-year-old Jack had to take over. Usually so sure of himself, he probably needed some support himself as he said to Frank, "Come at once."

The whole community, Indians and whites, united in sorrow. The Modern Brotherhood of America Lodge to which Rosalie and Ed belonged, passed resolutions lamenting the loss of one who was "a loving wife, an exemplary mother and a faithful friend." The tribe began to realize what her strength, assistance and advice had meant to them all. The younger sisters mourned and Frank felt the loss of understanding and sympathy, the tie that kept him always belonging in the old family circle.

The Omaha Bee, the paper farthest away, expressed her life most forcefully. Could it have been the hand of John Webster or the lawyer Breckenridge?

> Mrs. Farley never severed her relations to the tribe . . . was one of its most influential personages. Old Iron Eye was a keen, strong man and although he left . . . other children, his mantle fell on his daughter Rosalie. She was a woman of rare business qualifications . . . conducted large enterprises successfully. . . . But her influence among the Omaha was not due to her sagacity, she was an earnest Christian woman who . . . persistently and unselfishly sought to induce the tribe to accept the benefits of education and Christianity. She was the resource of the poor, the sick and the improvident, her life was a benediction, truly she was one of the most remarkable women of the state.

Ed struggled on, the house began to rise. Marguerite and Susan, with families of their own, tried to help out. One or the other would come for a few days in between the short trials of inefficient "hired girls." They came a little longer in the fall and helped with the moving into the new house, with its two stories, cellar and attic and wide steps leading up to an inviting front porch. Caryl, with John, went back for his third year in Lincoln for another attempt at school and Ed would write to him in desperation asking if he could not find a housekeeper there. Ed too urged them to go to church saying it would be well "if Jack thought a bit more about God."

Frank tried to help from a distance urging the girls to try and carry some of their mother's load; keeping them reminded of the dreams Rosalie had had for them. He would say of the new house, "the rooms ought to be pretty . . . and the furniture kept tidy all the time." He would compliment Louis on having a good garden. He urged Mary to learn to sew; warned her that she must not let other girls her age go further in their studies for she would need an education in many ways. He explained to her how to start a letter and how to address the envelope, "I tell you these things because I want you to know them as well as your Mother knew them."

Although Mary did not carry on as most of them felt she should, she was the one who unsuspectingly found the solution to their common problem. Because she worked in Bancroft she knew several other young women who worked in the different places of business. The next spring after Rosalie died a Miss Winnie Wood, a milliner, had come to assist Miss Graff the local provider of feminine headgear. By early summer the millinery season was over and Miss Wood was looking about for some other position. Mary had come to know her and suggested that since the Farley's were for the moment without a housekeeper maybe she would be willing to come and help them between seasons.

The arrangement extended beyond seasons as Winnie brought order and comfort and a new spirit into the household. Tall and slender, Winnie had a brisk manner, a sharp wit and great love of children. In less than two years she and Ed were married and the whole extended family took Winnie in as one of them. Long, long afterward, after the children were all gone from home, indeed, when all the Farley's had died, someone suggested to Winnie that she must have fallen in love with the children. Winnie had answered, "Well, Eddie was so sweet." Eddie who had been under three when his mother died became Winnie's son beyond a doubt. When he died at thirty-five the papers spoke of him being the son of Mr. and Mrs. Edward Farley with no mention of Rosalie.

Indeed they all became Winnie's family; the fact that she was only nine years older than Caryl seemed to make no difference. While she was "Winnie" to the older ones, she became Mother and then Grandma Winnie to the next generation. She, herself, more than sixty years later was laid to rest by her six "grandsons," the sons of Caryl, Marguerite and La Flesche.

About the time Winnie had taken over, the Tibbles' definitely moved back to the farm. Susette was not well and T. H. managed to edit the *Independent* by mail with frequent trips to Lincoln. Susette was much happier back in the Logan Valley, near to the river bluffs where she could enjoy the trees, the small animals and the changing sky -its dawn, its glowing sunsets and the stars at night. They usually had someone with them to care for the farm and for a year or so this was another Ed Farley, Ed's nephew, about Jack's age. He remembered T. H. as always writing, but he did not remember Susette painting. It may be that the pictures for *Oo-ma-ha Ta-wa-tha* were among her last. The farm became a favorite spot for the young families growing up. The children, Joseph's great-grandchildren, remembered picnic suppers in the yard and Uncle T. H. playing with them and taking them in a wagon for rides about the farm. There are pictures of such family parties with Susette looking quiet and motherly in an enveloping apron, the same fine straight features as when she was a girl, unspoiled by an increase in her weight.

It was a beautiful calm time before the end, for she became

more ill, plainly very ill, till Susan lost hope. Late in May 1903, Susan knew Susette might slip away any time. Preparing to spend the night with her sister she asked Winnie, the young woman, the recent addition to the family, to come and be with her. Mary the mother was there, too, and T. H. Winnie told of that night a few years before her own death and said T. H. was in "the front room" and wasn't to be blamed for it was a hard thing to expect him to see his "Bright Eyes" go.

Susette's mind wandered as she talked incoherently and disjointly of many things. Then at times she would say something perfectly clear and intelligent. Once she looked up at Winnie and said something in Omaha and then quickly apologized saying she had forgotten that Winnie did not speak Omaha. Later Susan translated and told Winnie that Susette had said, "Don't let Mary get you down." Plainly Susette had been aware of many overtones in the family life around her. She asked, over and over and almost at the last, for "the boys"—meaning Caryl and Jack. Winnie tried to quiet her and said Jack had gone to the Agency but she thought he might come by any time.

In a short time Susette breathed her last and Mary, her mother, who had seen so many others go and watched so much tragedy during her life, broke into a wild weeping—weeping mingled with the Indian mourning wail. Neither Susan nor Winnie could quiet her and Winnie in desperation stepped outside into the dark night. She used to say afterward that she didn't see why she did it but at the time it seemed perfectly natural. Standing in the dooryard, looking up at a few faint stars, she called, "Jack! Jack!" as loudly as she could.

In a few minutes Jack walked in the back door. A sister-in-law remarked that this was exactly like Jack, to appear at just the crucial moment; he always turned up at the exact time that something was happening. His appearance was not always helpful but somehow he was there! He was helpful that night, however, and although later he frequently troubled Winnie, she always gratefully remembered that night. He went over to his grandmother, sunken in her grief, and, amazingly, the young man only a little more than twenty, picked up his grandmother as tenderly as a woman would pick up a hurt child. He carried her to a rocking chair and sat down and rocked her, talking and singing to her in Omaha until she became quiet.

Winnie was further drawn into the family circle by being requested to serve the dinner on the day of the funeral. She was a bit nonplussed but Ed told her all she needed to do was be sure and have plenty of meat for there would be many Indians and they always liked meat. She knew that people had come from Lincoln and Omaha for Susette's funeral but she was so occupied that she never had a clear idea as to their identity.

The cemetery is on the opposite side of Bancroft from the farm and it must have been a long trip with horse-drawn vehicles. At last Susette was laid beside Joseph, Nicomi and the "Oldest grandma," the granddaughter of Chief Blackbird, the first of the Omaha chiefs known to white men, making the connecting link between times past and the present. Later a marker was placed there which reads, "She did all she could to make the world happier and better." Rosalie's stone says, "The nobility and strength of two races were blended in her life of Christian love and duty."

Two sisters, whose lives had started in the tribal circle but in moving out from it had taken widely different paths. Yet they both maintained a loyalty to their origin and proved that they could learn new ways, that they could walk a goodly distance along the white man's road beckoning to their people to follow.

CHAPTER VII

MARGUERITE AND SUSAN

Susette had broken the trail toward further education when she had gone to the Elizabeth Institute in 1869. Her efforts and her experiences made the same journey much easier for Marguerite and Susan when they followed her almost exactly ten years later.

It had been a memorable ten years. When the Omaha were pressured into giving up part of their Reserve for the Winnebago tribe, they had been promised individual land grants. Such promises had been made in 1854, then in 1865, but the papers designating each man's land did not arrive until 1871. These delays and the arbitrary settlement of the Winnebago regardless of the Omaha objections had aroused suspicion. If the treaty that had solemnly promised them the land for "as long as the waters shall run"[1] could be repudiated, could these land patents also be brushed aside? In 1874 the United States asked the Omaha to grant an additional tract for the Winnebago. Close on the heels of this demand came the Ponca trouble increasing their suspicions. Fear was added to suspicion when the Government used military force to move the Ponca.

Here, again, Susette had been the pioneer, traveling with her father, serving as an interpreter, stirring white men to action and then preparing to carry the Ponca story to the metropolitan areas in the East. Marguerite and Susan had been welcomed at Hampton as the sisters of the former brilliant pupil, Lucy La Flesche. Soon they were pointed out as the sisters of the eloquent public speaker, the beautiful "Bright Eyes." Susette took the center of the stage and to a great extent has always remained there as story after story repeated the contemporary accounts written when she was the only La Flesche sister in the public eye.

The first connection with the Elizabeth Institute had come through the Mission and the missionary families. Marguerite and Susan both worked at the Mission and maintained the friendships formed there more intimately than did Susette. Her close friends came to be the New Englanders who worked for the Indians and, near the end of her life, certain figures in politics and journalism.

The girls were at Elizabeth for three years and, as Marguerite summed it up in a letter of application, they had studied the "common branches" most thoroughly until she felt she was ready to teach them to little children. But beyond the "common branches" (usually considered arithmetic, reading, and writing which included spelling and composition) they had studied philosophy, physiology and literature. The term philosophy covered a wide field in that day and it would be difficult to know just what this course may have included. However, it must have been in the class in physiology that Susan started on the study of medicine, and in literature that Marguerite established her life-long habit of reading.

They returned to the Reservation in the late summer of 1882, a fortnight or so after the allotment act had been passed by Congress. They found a different atmosphere than the uncertainty caused by the Poncas' woes which had colored everything when they had left. Now there was a lively interest in the allotment and discussion of possible movement toward the Logan Creek Valley. Much about the tribe had changed; 119 frame houses were occupied by Omaha families and among the 1,193 members of the tribe 250 habitually used English and still others could read it but hesitated to speak, fearing they would make mistakes.[2] The family too had changed, had increased in size, since the older sisters were married; Susette had two step-daughters not much younger than Susan, and Rosalie had two babies, the oldest nearly eighteen months.

Marguerite immediately applied to teach in the government school near the Agency, but the next year taught at the Mission. Susan must have busied herself at home, probably Marguerite did, too; for later Sue wrote about the way they frequently piled into a wagon and drove to Rosalie's to spend the day. Certainly Nicomi and "the oldest grandma" (Madeline Wolfe, Nicomi's sister) could not have carried as large a share of household tasks as they had three years earlier. It seems probable that Ta-in-ne, or Lizzie, may not have been there for she died only a few months later. The next summer Susan helped care for Alice Fletcher during her illness at the Mission.

The Presbyterian Mission School had been closed for nearly ten years after the Government had withdrawn support from the different denominations and emphasized the advantages of the day schools. A Mission had been maintained, however, and under Father Hamilton who had stayed on in the neighborhood, a small Presbyterian Church had been organized by the Christian Indians and the few white people in the area. It was here that Frank was an Elder and both Frank and Rosalie had taught Sunday School and interpreted the Sunday service.

The school had re-opened in 1879 under the temporary leadership of Rev. Irwin. Then in 1880 Homer W. Partch had come as Superintendent. There were many difficulties; the physical plant had deteriorated after thirty years facing the weather and ten years of limited use. It was only three or four miles from the Agency school and faced competition not experienced in its more active days. Its control was soon shifted from the Board of Foreign Missions of the Church to the supervising Home Missions. (Since Nebraska was now a state it must have become "home" and no longer fitted the category "foreign".) The change meant that certain devoted leaders at headquarters who had personally known the school, its setting and its members were replaced by men and women less well informed and less intimately acquainted.

As the tribe moved away from the banks of the Missouri and out on to the prairies, the old building was too far away from the people. By 1890 the Church was granted two pieces of land. On one, at the edge of the Agency property, a chapel was built; the other plot, a few miles south and west at almost the exact center of the tribal population (in 1887), was for a house, the residence of a church lay worker. As these changes were being planned and developed the Mission school in the old building on the Missouri River became a boarding school for girls only. Under Mrs. Margaret Copley Wade this became a good school and a strong influence in the community. The first lay worker was Mrs. Wade's brother John. He later was ordained and served both of these new centers as superintendent and minister.[3]

These church workers were the niece and nephew of Mrs. William Thaw (Mary Copley) of Pittsburg. The Thaws were people of wealth and of marked generosity and they consistently contributed to philanthropic causes. Mr. Thaw carried most of the cost of the residence-community center and they contributed largely to the chapel built at the Agency. These were but the first of the gifts to the Omaha. The largest and the one of most lasting value was the "Thaw Fellowship" granted to the Peabody Museum of Harvard University. This was a grant of $30,000 for a Fellowship to be held by Alice Fletcher to assist in her Indian studies and for the publication of her findings. Marguerite and Susan worked at the Mission school most of the time from 1882 until 1884 when again they started off together on a new educational adventure—this time to Hampton, Virginia.

The Hampton Normal and Agricultural Institute had opened shortly after the Civil War as a school for freed slaves. There had been fifteen young Negro students and two teachers to carry this long name in 1868, but less than a dozen years later it had a fairly adequate plant and faculty and nearly 300 students. Then Hampton was unexpectedly called upon to offer its services to the Indians. Capt. Richard Pratt's experiment with the Indian prisoners at Ft. Marion, Florida had proved that Indians could be educated. The change brought about in these men in a short time under Pratt's direction was widely publicized. To be sure individual Indians, here and there, had demonstrated that they could learn, but this instance involved a large number in one place. They had all, according to the white man's view, been especially "savage". The effect was impressive and appeared after several years of warfare between the whites and the Indians on the Western plains.

The continued unrest among the western Indians and the fact that Individuals of these same tribes had responded to both education and contact with white communities brought a change in Indian policy. It had been argued that the Indians were a dying race, to be tolerated for only fifty to eighty years, during which time they could be pushed back across the Mississippi—or the Missouri—or the Rocky Mountains and controlled by a small military force. But by 1880 the politicians and leaders were forced to admit that the race was not dying and was not being controlled by any small military force. It was hard to believe that Indians could ever conduct their own affairs, but it might be well to try Pratt's system—it might be cheaper to educate them than to fight them.

Because Hampton was a non-white school it was selected for this experiment although there were grave doubts about the wisdom of mixing the two races. General Samuel Armstrong, Superintendent at Hampton, reported after a year that the "colored and Indians mingle pleasantly, there is no fracas". Others remarked that the Negroes derived a certain pleasure from discovering another minority was oppressed by the white people. Since the Negroes were familiar with the pattern of white living and most of them spoke fairly good English they were of real assistance to the Indians.[4] Many Indians knew no English and had never seen a white settlement. The officials often mentioned the help given by the Negroes but the Indians seldom, if ever, mentioned it.

Personal accounts by Indians who attended Hampton Institute intimate that the "mingling" was kept to a minimum of certain special and carefully selected occasions. In many letters written by and to the members of the La Flesche family there is almost no mention of the Negroes. An uninformed reader might assume the school was entirely for Indians although actually the ratio was three or four Negroes to one Indian. Susan's letters mention the "colored girls" a few times and once, when she had been away, she related with obvious pleasure that she was welcomed back by "both the colored and the Indian girls."

When the Indians first came to Hampton the girls were housed in two corridors of Virginia Hall with the Negro girls. When Winona Hall was given as a dormitory for Indian girls, it also housed the married Indian couples until separate houses were built for them.[5] Lucy and Noah La Flesche lived in Winona Hall at first, but had moved into one of the cottages by the time Marguerite and Susan and Carey came. Carey was in the Wigwam with the other Indian boys. The fact that four of the La Flesche family had lived in Winona was a pleasant tie in the family. Winona Hall became a symbol of friendship among the educated Indians of many tribes, standing as the reminder of a fortunate entrance into a new world.

The school operated on a study-work program—in school for half a day and in the laundry, sewing room, shops or fields for the remainder. There were two definite lines or courses, two paths of progression that rested on proficiency in English. If newly arrived students spoke, read and wrote understandable English they were placed in the Normal course, where they proceeded academically as they were able, while in the "work" part of the day they might be grouped with others of quite different ability as they all were trained in the skills required in homes and on farms in the nineteenth century. The study half of the day for the Indian speaking boys and girls was largely concentrated on learning English until they had mastered enough to move into the Normal course.

The La Flesche girls, Lucy, Marguerite and Susan all went into the Normal course and all graduated from it. Noah spent most of his time in the Indian school but did not graduate; for, after allotments were made, he wanted to get to work on his own land. He said he was "afraid he would mistake" but several readable and interesting letters of his have survived the years. The girls all entered into the life of the Indian groups with enthusiasm, enjoying the contact with other tribes and helping in the activities of a small church in Hampton. They taught Sunday School in country Negro churches and Lucy wrote that "often Susie and I on Sunday afternoons go read aloud to some old colored people".

Hampton published a small monthly paper called *The Southern Workman,* indicating it had first been addressed to former slaves. After the addition of the Indian students it added a small "Indian Department." This column became a page as the number of Indians increased. The first year the La Flesche girls were there this was the work of Elaine Goodale of the teaching staff. Later as Inspector of Indian Schools she was present at the Pine Ridge Agency when Susette and Tibbles reported the fighting at Wounded Knee. She, too, wrote for newspapers in the East. It was at Pine Ridge that she met Charles Eastman, M.D., a Sioux, a graduate of Cornell University, who later became her husband.

The Southern Workman gives a more balanced view of the biracial school, showing that the races were in classes together and, of course, in assemblies and programs of various kinds. Each race, however, had its own clubs and literary societies; for the leaders considered there was a difference in their social situations and requirements. If graduates, or nongraduates continued to subscribe to this paper they were supplied with a fine tool for further education. It did not stop with reporting the school events or the personal items concerning students and graduates but also offered poetry, articles and pictures of wide interest. A glance over the issues of one year showed matters of world-wide interest occupying the front page, such as a discussion of positions taken by different parties in the British parliament. Frequently space was given to items of classical lore, the orations of Cicero or the work of Aristotle. There were certainly many white households in the United States with less material of broad general interest than this paper brought to Indian and Negro homes.

Marguerite was out of school and at home for a year, between her two years at Hampton—during 1885-1886. Sue after two years and Lucy after four graduated the same day, May 20, 1886. (Lucy had not had the opportunity of study at the Elizabeth Institute.) Noah had gone home a month or two earlier in order to get his crops planted. It was a wonderful day for the La Flesch family and for Hampton—its 18th Anniversary; also a great day for the Indians for Susan gathered in more honors for the race. She was the Salutatorian and made the opening address, "My Childhood and Womanhood." They had all expected the Valedictorian would be a young man and it was Martin Woodlin of Philadelphia, presumably a Negro since no tribe is designated.[6] Then Susan was presented a prized gold medal given by Mrs. J. W. Demorest of New York. It was awarded by the faculty to the senior passing the best examination "in the Junior studies."

There were over a thousand people present that day. *The Woman's Journal* reported the audience was of "every shade and color and from every circumstance of life"[7]—the sort of democratic gathering greatly approved by that paper. They heard Susan talk and gave "thundering applause" when she received the medal, standing with downcast eyes before General Cutchem who made the presentation. He said:

> This is for the excellence with which you have laid a founda-
> tion . . . you will become a part of the foundation work of your
> people. It is a great thing to be one of the first women of your
> race to lay this foundation. . . . I charge you to regard it as your
> duty to live for your people. To devote yourself to them.

Later the girls asked her if she heard what the General had said and she replied "as in a dream." But dream or not she must have remembered the words many times in the years ahead as her life followed that charge. Alice Fletcher had gone down from Washington on the boat with many notable people and she wrote all about the commencement to Rosalie who took the letter up the road to Father's and told the household there about their child. To help them visualize it their friend had added, "I wish you could have seen the girls, both dressed in striped dresses, wash goods, simple but neat and pretty. Susan's face was very lovely."

It was an exciting day for the advocates of Indian education for Susan had decided to study medicine and was being considered for the women's Medical College of Pennsylvania. Less than two years earlier, Alice Fletcher had been quoted as saying she thought it would take another generation before an American Indian could go into one of the learned professions.[8] Now one of her own friends was taking that step, years ahead of that expected schedule.

Both Susan and Marguerite became involved in one of the side effects of Hampton's plan for education, the extremely different atmosphere into which they came because Hampton was co-educational. If eyebrows had been raised, questions asked and doubts expressed over the mixing of the two races, it was nothing compared to the criticism aroused by placing both sexes in one school.

Coeducation was still in the experimental stage and many educators and parents believed it was ill-advised, even dangerous. It was more disturbing to Indians, for only a few understood what the white men meant by education and still fewer thought it might concern girls. Among the Indians the sexes were more or less kept apart during adolescence and young girls never appeared alone in public, but were guarded by strict chaperonage. The idea of sending their boys and girls of marriageable age away from home for several years was startling, but a plan that put them in the same school was almost beyond belief.

Wajapa was worried about his thirteen year old Nettie, for he had heard that at Hampton the boys and girls wrote notes to each other and he certainly did not want Nettie doing things like that. The distance, the length of their absence and coeducation altogether made Chazaminga say, "Indians afraid sent children to school."

The leaders at Hampton, with other liberals of their day had new attitudes toward men and women in society. They believed that in this new Western world men and women would meet on a more equitable basis then in Europe. Higher education for women and coeducation ranked high in importance in their philosophy of society. If the Indians were to be a part of American life, they should be introduced at this highest level.

General Armstrong in a report, written in September 1886, expressed these ideas and explained the manner in which Hampton worked to bring about a complete change in behavior patterns that had been followed for generations. He fully recognized it was not easy to unlearn Indian etiquette and establish freer, more familiar relations between young men and women. It could only be done by giving them considerable freedom and frequent opportunities to meet together. This, he acknowledged, required "strict over-sight" but it could produce a habit of "guarded but natural and pleasant intercourse."

Accordingly the Indians at Hampton had more social life than in other schools. It centered in Winona Hall, which took the place of a girl's home, with the teachers there in the position of mother, aunt or grandmother, her natural chaperons. If they wished to, the boys came there for a meal on Sunday, on Saturday evening and on important holidays. As a rule the boys were expected to leave thirty minutes after the close of dinner but Saturday night, twice a month, was social night. Then the evening was spent in "games, conversation, marching and literary and musical exercises . . . good practice and good fun." The annual all-Indian picnic was a joyful occasion.

The concept of boys calling on girls in what served as their home was one of the ideas to be learned in the new etiquette for it was entirely a white concept. Indian young people met only at tribal ceremonies and large gatherings; formerly in the movement of the tribe on journeys or the hunt. It was part of the established custom that a young man might "accidentally" be along the path where a girl, with a sister or friend would daily pass on some household duty,[9] but open "calling" was not done.

At Hampton plans were made by which young people came together for a definite purpose. There were seven organized societies among the Indian students, friendships often produced parties and gay times. Both boys and girls led their own prayer meetings and Armstrong was proud of the fact that boys in the Helping Hand Society (largely Sioux) had, of their own accord, contributed to a fund to help an Omaha whose home had been destroyed by a tornado. They had said they lived in a new day and must disregard old enmities.

Armstrong felt that the Indians were able to make surprising and far-reaching changes in custom because, "an Indian is a ceremonious being . . . an instinctive gentleman . . . he adapts himself with ease to strange manners . . . is seldom awkward or embarrassed in society." He went on to refute the implications of a recent Congressional investigation that had insisted Hampton students completely reverted to tribal ways on returning home. He said they had careful reports which showed over half of their students had done well, four fifths had done fairly well. In six years 203 Indians had returned to their homes from Hampton.[10]

The La Flesche girls entered eagerly into the social side of school life. Susan's letters are full of club meetings, group singing, of games. She explained the patterns of a grand march with obvious relish and retold many jokes. There is much on what this boy said and what this girl did, frequent mention of other Omaha students who had come in the same group—Josephine Barnaby, Nettie Freemont (Wajapa's daughter), David Wells, known as Catching Thunder, George Ramsey and Susan Burt.

More of Susan's letters are available than are Marguerite's and life at Hampton is viewed through her eyes. She would write:

> I had a letter from Logan yesterday, a funny letter.

> . . . he told Josie (Barnaby) and Josie told me so Sunday evening I told him how it was and you should have seen how jolly he was,—not hurt. He walked with M. and Nettie to prayers . . . and I know not where I found Sam walking beside me. . . . Sam is very nice. . . . Walter is helping me learn to skate. . . .

The girls tease me unmercifully about Ashley.

Miss R. would like me to see more of Charles D.

It was a trifle ironical, or possibly prophetic, that both Marguerite and Susan, daughters of the Omaha, became interested in young men of the Sioux, their tribe's ancient enemy. This may have been another expression of the attitude of the Helping Hand Society, "We are living in a new day."

Marguerite was extremely pretty, with soft curves and beautiful dark eyes. She must have attracted many boys, but within a few months she was returning the interest of Charles Felix Picotte from the Yankton Agency. Susan wrote:

> Mag and her Felix have a mutual admiration society. He says, "Daisy is so good to me; life could not be without her." She says, "Charles is so good to me. I don't think it would be possible to quarrel."

Susan added her own approval, saying, "He is one of the gentlest men I ever have seen."

Charles Picotte's grandfather was a Frenchman, one of several by that name who figured in the history of the fur trade and early settlement. His father, Charles Felix, Sr., a half-blood had been interpreter at the Yankton Agency for many years. Charles, Jr. had come to Hampton in 1879 when he was only fifteen and had stayed until the spring of 1884.[11] Then after a summer of farm work at home, he knew he wanted more study and came back to Hampton with a party of new students.[12] This was shortly after Marguerite, Susan and Carey with other Omahas had come with Alice Fletcher.

Charles graduated when Lucy and Susan did; then returned again to Hampton in the fall to repeat certain Junior studies. He wanted to study law but the teachers discouraged him. He was not strong and the teachers, always under pressure, saw more teachers as the best contribution to solving the Indian problem. Charles was a part of a second commencement, when Marguerite graduated in 1887. Her senior composition had won special honors and she read it, "Customs of the Omaha" as part of the exercises.

In a few weeks they were both back on the Plains and teaching. They were both disturbed and unsettled. The separation was hard and the next step seemed uncertain. The church approached Marguerite to become a missionary, to receive $500.00 a year besides having a furnished house. Charlie was following his teachers' advice rather than his own wishes. Everyone had ideas for them; the only points of

similarity were that Marguerite wished to be near home for a time
and Charles wished to earn for their home. It may be that Joseph's
death in September 1888 influenced or set the time for their next
decisive move.

Here was Joseph's farm, fairly well developed, the allotments of
Nicomi (now Mary's) and those granted to Mary, herself, to
Marguerite, to Carey and to Susan and no one to take charge. Noah
had an interest in his father's land, his own and Lucy's to care for.
Frank was definitely settled in Washington, Ed Farley almost too
busy with the tribe on the pasture, Carey was still under twenty and
back at Hampton and the family had little confidence in Tibbles.
Marguerite and Charles Picotte were married late in 1888 and he
assumed the responsibility for much of the family land.[13] Marguerite
continued to teach at the government school.

Charles was one of the many in his generation whose health
suffered during the trying transitional period. The shifts in food,
housing and clothing and in the whole pattern of living proved too
great a burden to hundreds of American Indians. He had never been
strong but he must have worked hard and steadily on the land for he
was considered one of the best farmers on the Reservation, having a
record crop in 1890.[14]

Because of his knowledge of the language and the people he
went to Pine Ridge with Tibbles and Susette in the winter of 1890
and 1891 as they reported the troubles aroused by the Ghost Dance
which culminated at Wounded Knee.

The only exact dates of Marguerite's short marriage to Charles
Picotte are found in Rosalie's letters to Alice Fletcher and to Frank.

> Jan. 7, 1891. T. H. and Susette are still north. Chas. wrote M. he
> was coming home and she thinks he is disgusted with the way T.
> H. is going on pitching into the Eastern schools and everybody in
> general.

> Jan. 18, 1891. Chas. is home and seems to have had enough of
> our brother-in-law for awhile.

> May 3, 1891. Charlie is going to Detroit to go into a hospital.
> The Miss Jennings whom you saw here last summer made the
> arrangements.

> May 4, 1891. Charlie has been looking as if he could not last
> much longer, he has just started to Detroit to a hospital.

> June 24, 1891. Charlie has just come home. I am afraid is not
> much better.

Jan. 28, 1892. Marguerite has had a leave of absence to care for her husband, who cannot get out of bed.

Susan sent for Dr. Hildreth of Lyons, but he gave them no hope and they sent to Yankton for Charlie's father. During his last few weeks Charles wrote to the teachers at Hampton, expressing his appreciation of the advantages the school had given him. He felt this was his last letter and wrote to assure them that as one of the first Indian students he regretted he could not continue to work for his people. In spite of all the disappointments he felt he had been fortunate. Hampton closed the account of Charles Felix Picotte, Jr. saying he left only friends in his own tribe and that of his adoption and that "in his life, dress and bearing he (was) ever above reproach."

Susan's Hampton romance was a very different story, indicative of Susan's place in the late nineteenth century as an Indian girl and also as that new person of the century—the Career Woman. She wrote home about many boys at school and did not particularly mention Thomas Ikinicapi, full-blooded Sioux from the Dakota Agency, until the early part of her second year when he was writing to her from his home in Dakota Territory. He was the son of Tall Prairie Chicken and the nephew of Little No Heart, a man of considerable influence among his people.[15] He had had little schooling and after four years at Hampton did not speak or write English easily; certainly his letters must have been limited. But unquestionably he was deeply interested in Susan.

After she was in Philadelphia at Medical School her letters home included much Hampton news as she received it from Marguerite. The letters at first had almost as much about Hampton as about her medical studies. As early as October she was talking about going to Hampton for the Christmas vacation.

> ... had a letter from dear old Miggs. ... She said Ikinicapi was coming back. ... I dreamt about the dear chap last night ... that he was glad to see me and talked better English. ... I have dreamt this before. ... I told Miss Patterson, an old Hampton teacher that T. I. was coming back. She said, "He was a handsome rascal."

Miss Patterson and others watched Susan's affair with trepidation. They did not want to lose a promising leader to a man of poor physique and meager ability and potential.

But Susan had a mind of her own:

> They want me to have a Platonic friendship. ... I like Ikinicapi. ... Perhaps he won't come back, or come as a married couple ... it won't break my heart for "I ain't made that way." I

should like to see him. He is *without exception* the handsomest
Indian I ever saw.

She would at times ask Rosalie to tell her frankly just what she
thought about the situation and she would remark with an obvious
effort to be casual that "Carey and T. I. seem to think a great deal
of each other." On the other hand, her sense of dedication was
strong, her determination to be part of a good foundation for her
people. She thought her father had been disappointed over
Marguerite's desire to marry, for she knew how intensely he wished
his children to advance the tribe. So she made her final pledge to
serve through medicine and wrote:

> Friendship is all it can be.... I shall be the dear little old
> maid ... come and dose you all. Won't it be fun?.... I'm cut out
> for an old maid, Dr. Sue, how fine!

The Christmas vacation at Hampton was reported in minute
detail and T. I. (sometimes "Ik") figured largely in it all. He was at
her side for every game, every walk, for the Christmas service, the
New Year's Watch Night and everything possible, but saying very
little. If by chance some other fellow got the cherished position first,
he stood at one side following her every movement with mournful
eyes. They had a poignant farewell, disturbing to them both. All the
close friends watched and observed each move; Marguerite felt all
their emotion with them until she could hardly bear it. After Susan
had left, the Indians had all gone to chapel; Marguerite was trying to
steel herself against not seeing Sue again for months and months,
when Josie called her attention to T. I. He was sitting with his
handkerchief covering his face and poor Miggs dissolved into tears.

Susan had entered Medical School with the most glowing
recommendations. General Armstrong had said, "I have no hesitation
in speaking of her as a young woman of unusual ability, integrity,
fixedness of purpose." Did he really know how fixed that purpose
was? She was to receive $167.00 a year from the Congressional Indian
appropriations and the Connecticut Indian Association, appealing to the
people of the State, assumed the responsibility for all other expenses.
Mrs. Sara Kinney was head of the women's part of this group and they
added this project to the one of providing homes for students returning to Reservations. Mrs. Kinney in asking for the proper blanks
for a contract with the government said, "She is of exceptionally
good character and mental ability." She enclosed a letter from
General Armstrong expressing his hope that the Indian Association

would see Susan through this new venture; for, he said, "I regard her as about the finest, strongest Indian character we have had at this school. She is a level-headed, earnest, capable Christian woman, quite equal to medical studies. . . . She is independent, naturally a deep but not a sentimental woman." One of the teachers was quoted as saying, "gentle, consciencious (she is) a rare character for any walk of life . . . she would minister not only to physical needs, but to the deeper wants."[16]

The Women's Medical College confirmed these opinions. Sue graduated in 1889, at the head of a class of thirty-three women, many of whom had prepared at universities of higher standing—the first American Indian woman to become a Doctor of Medicine. After graduation she was one of the six from the class chosen to have added training and experience in the hospitals of Philadelphia, before she went home under government appointment as the physician to the Omaha Indian School.

The recommendation which said Susan was a "rare person" almost expressed the center of Susan's personality but did not explain clearly or completely. In fact, it is an extremely difficult thing to explain—something elusive, vivid, yet indescribable. Her superior mental ability was linked with the utmost gentleness and unusual discernment. These qualities were undergirded by integrity, firmness and dedication. She had a devotion, a vivid reaching out toward life and people which resembled radiation. This quality continued and pierced through the accumulation of emotions, thoughts, associations and experiences built up by years, until long after her death, people spoke of her with glowing warmth.

One woman tried to describe the first time she had seen Susan, "this charmer." She herself had been but a small child, four or five years old. Susan had had difficulty with her horse-drawn buggy and had asked for help at a near by farm. The man of the house saw it was a task too extended to be handled before night and went in to tell his wife she would have a guest, saying they had better keep "the Indian woman doctor" over night. He went to invite Susan in and the child—speaking long afterward as a woman, said, "—and there she stood that—that—that *wonderful woman*"; her own expression spelled out the words in glowing capital letters. The child had recognized immediately that quality of personality which made Susan "a rare person."

The vividness, joy, eagerness for life shows even in a picture taken at Elizabeth when Susan was little more than fourteen. It shows in her letters from Philadelphia, her pleasure in the sights of the town, in her studies, the people she met and in dozens of experiences as she absorbed new ways of living, new attitudes toward life. It shows in the number of times she said, "it was splendid," "everyone is so kind," "I like them so much," "we had a wonderful talk," "it was beautiful," "I am so happy."

At Elizabeth and at Hampton, Susan had been in supervised homes or dormitories, but Mrs. Talcott, chairman of the business committee of the Connecticut group had come to Philadelphia and found a boarding house for Susan. Here she was one of many young students and business people all part of the huge city, with its rich and its poor sections, its beautiful parks, its historical landmarks and its offerings in education, in music and the arts. Because she was in this atmosphere she met many kinds of people. Besides those at the boarding house table, she was introduced to the best of Philadelphia by the Connecticut women, by Alice Fletcher, the missionary families and all the philanthropists interested in the Indians.

She had an innate good taste which selected the fine and the distinctive from the many impressions which crowded upon her. What an experience it was for a young girl coming from meager surroundings beside the wide Missouri to hear Mme. Pattie sing, see "the Jersey lily" (Lily Langtry) on the stage, to hear *The Mikado,* to hear Frances Willard, great scientists and great orchestras! Omaha and Sioux City had metropolitan aspects by the late 1880's but the Reservation was "Indian country" comparatively unchanged from virgin prairie for all its few better farms and villages. Indians, moreover, could seldom travel to these few cities or spend the money to see and hear what might be offered. In Philadelphia Susan went to the Academy of Fine Arts, heard concerts, and looked at Benjamin West's pictures. With passes several students went to Girard College to see the drill "quite as good as West Point, they say" and she described one building as "pure Greek architecture."

Frank came for a New Year's visit. they were entertained by her new friends and they went to the Opera. On New Year's Day they watched the Masqueraders' Parade and decided those dressed as Indians looked "pretty well." Sight seeing became reversed, when, in Independence Hall they realized everyone was looking at *them.* They left and outside had a good laugh over people thinking *they* were something to be observed and studied.

During vacations with other students she explored the city and the country round about, visiting Franklin's grave, going down the

Delaware to see the Old Swede's Church and with another girl going to Fairmont Park and sitting to talk on a rock by the Schuylkill Bridge. Every special beauty she saw, every bit of interesting history she touched were described to the family at home and stored within herself.

George Armstrong was right when he said she was "equal to medical studies." The subject matter of each course was eagerly seized upon, examined, studied and made her own—often discussed in detail with Rosalie. Susan insisted that Rosalie should have been a doctor, she was exactly the right sort of person. Often in lectures as the professors described and discussed the body, its functions and malfunctions, Susan would say to herself, "Why, I remember, Rosalie told me that." She began to grasp the necessity of good health habits and to shudder when she realized they were too often absent in the life of the Indians. She realized, too, that much of this lack came from the sudden change in a whole manner of living and the few facilities for teaching new habits. It was more difficult to learn new health habits than a new language or new forms of etiquette.

She sent advice to the family at home:

> I think Mother doesn't have the right food or her foot would be better.

> It's not unusual, Ro, for women in your condition to have trouble with their teeth.

> Tell Ed Dr. Sue prescribes less quinine and more time for his meals.

She saw to ordering a new artificial leg for Joseph. She rejoiced that Rosalie and Ed had a good couple in the extra house, "Ro won't work so hard." She asked Rosalie to send "all the cases" she could, meaning Rosalie should describe the ailments she observed in the tribe, so Sue could try and diagnose the trouble.

She liked everything—studying bones in the Museum, "even the tiny holes have names," watching operations and telling about them. Not minding the dissecting room in the least but amazed when on the first experience a young man had fainted, "none of the girls did"; she found it fascinating to discover the arteries and all their branches." "Tell Ed I'm going to wield the knife tonight, but not the scalping knife." She was saddened over the suffering she saw among women—the difficult births—but most of all she ached for those who could not know the joy of their own children. Then she rejoiced again in Rosalie and the wealth she possessed in her children.

New experiences, new people, the fascination of her work never blotted out the family or the home landscape. She was homesick for the bluffs, the hills and the creek valleys, counting the time until she could be at home—as did La Flesche when far away. Three years from now will be Paradise when we can all be together"; "Twelve weeks more and I'll arrive, bag and baggage. Hurrah!" "Tell Father and Mother I'm coming"; "Wish I could have been there for the mingga hung."[17] The whole circle of the family was included in her thoughts and love, "Give my love to Grandma and the oldest Grandma"; "Wish I could cuddle Maidie right now"; "Give my love to sister Lucy and ask why she has forgotten me,—remember me to Noah"; "Kiss the children."

Only by implication do the letters reflect the life at home. It is plain in Susan's concern over food and clothing that at times they had not had enough of either. "Tell Father and Mother my boarding house is fine. I have such good things to eat. I am never hungry here." When Mrs. Talcott bought her wardrobe for the winter she wrote, "I have more clothing than I need and I put them down with a sigh because I can't pass them on to you as Mother or Grandmother."

Besides providing for her school supplies and her clothing, Mrs. Talcott gave Susan one dollar for spending money, to use just as she wished. Surprised to find at the opening reception that nearly all the faculty ladies and the students wore kid gloves, she thought of buying some. But she had a good time, everyone was kind to her even though she was gloveless, so she put the dollar away "to buy a few little things for the children for Christmas." Then she became concerned over her mother's health and thought she would send the dollar "to buy meat for Mother, maybe chicken." But before she acted on this plan, the word came that Mary was critically ill and Susan quickly sent the dollar to Rosalie so that if Mother grew worse, Rosalie could telegraph, if Mother were better she was to keep the dollar and get some meat.

The time in Philadelphia brought her intimately into beautifully appointed homes, where, after generations the routine of everyday life had become formal in a simple, taken-for-granted gracious manner. The Omahas, the Indian Agents and the Office of Indian Affairs had been proud of the Omahas' first frame houses. They were always listed as a mark of progress. At the first these houses were furnished as the earth lodges had been, with robes, skins, beds made with hand-hewn posts and interwoven strips of willow branches tied by the willow bark. One minister described a three-room house in the middle 1890's as having no floor covering, one table and a few chairs, with clothing hanging from pegs on the walls.

The family had eaten, at first, seated on the floor probably in a circle as formerly around the central fire. The only formality lay in the order in which the individual bowls were filled and the fact that no one ate until the father lifted high a bit of food and murmured a prayer—not too different from the white man's habit before eating. The houses looked like white men's houses but the life inside changed slowly and most of the changes had come in Susan's own twenty-odd years.

She loved the beautiful furniture, the carpets and curtains, the formalities at the table in the Philadelphia homes. She loved the daintier ways of personal care which were impossible at home, where large families lived in three or four rooms and water was carried from a spring or a well fifty to one hundred feet from the house. She wrote, "I wash my feet often and my face, neck and ears every morning. I wish I could live like this at home." One Christmas Mrs. Kinney sent her "a *white* comb and brush and a *nail brush* and a bottle of cologne—that good kind."

She often spent the night in lovely homes and the Indian sense of ceremony helped her become a part of the new forms, new manners.

> I had a great big bedroom to myself, with an ivory comb and brush. Then at breakfast, the first course was oranges and we had finger bowls. They just dip in their fingers and wipe them on napkins. Then all was removed and we had kidney and gravy, potatoes and bread and butter and coffee. The coffee was in a great big silver urn and had a flame under it and Mrs. Ogden turned on a faucet and hot coffee came out.

She went to a church wedding and took in every detail. The order in which the families entered, the material and style of the bride's dress and the conduct of her parents. The bride's sister came back along the aisle on the arm of a young man. She carried an armful of roses and he had her white shawl over his arm; at the door he placed the shawl around her shoulders.

She described the dresses the Connecticut ladies had given her and the occasions when she wore them. At the opening reception she had worn "a pretty blue made of a sort of flannel with ruching at the neck and sleeves. My roommate wore black silk and lace and kid gloves." Later gloves became an accepted part of the La Flesche girls' wardrobes since one Christmas Susan mentioned making a glove case as a gift for Marguerite.

Susan returned to the Reservation in the fall of 1889, as physician at the Government School. A few months later, the Agent, Robert Ashley, formally asked if she might care for other members of the tribe; there were constant requests for her services, the care of the children did not fill all her time and she found many of the drugs left with the supplies were only for adults. Such permission was given and in January Susan wrote to General Thomas Morgan, the Commissioner, expressing her thanks. She was to have much more work and a great deal more responsibility, but no added salary. She wrote as though she had been given a boost in salary or an added bonus. Certainly she considered it in the light of a bonus—the broader opportunity to serve her people.

She wrote of her pleasure in still maintaining the connection with the school; she would give the children all the time they might need and she was planning a series of talks on health habits. Here was the result of her recognition while a student that new health habits were a basic need for the Indian. She was to supervise matters concerning health throughout the Reservation and she covered the area on horseback, never refusing a call, summer or winter, in snow, heat, winds and floods—a tremendous task for a slight young woman of twenty-five.

Her work expanded until in a year she ordered "a covered carriage." This was an advantage at times, but often a single horse and rider could travel the rudimentary roads and trails when a carriage would be a handicap. Others offered help in transportation. Mrs. James Allen of Pender who had been Nancy Harper of the Tekamah area had a team of good ponies and a light buggy and she often took Susan about on calls. She, herself, became interested in the individual families, particularly in the babies. At one Fourth of July celebration at Pender a bright-eyed Indian baby girl peering out from a tiny pink ruffled sunbonnet was a main attraction. Nancy Ellen had made it in token of her part in the child's birth—getting Dr. Sue to the scene. The effect was so fetching that every Indian mother there came begging Nancy to make a bonnet for her baby.

Marguerite, after Charlie's death returned to her teaching at the Government School and Sue's work centered there. Except for their own families, from this time on the sisters' lives were focused on the Reservation and the Omaha people. Their services went far beyond school teaching and medical care. In every possible way they tried to bring to the Omaha the new methods, techniques, habits, philosophies which they had gained through their wider education and the Christian church. They remembered their father had tried to direct the tribe along the white man's road. They knew it was much more complicated, much more difficult than he had thought even in his moments of deepest discouragement.

They knew a new language and a different etiquette could be learned; they believed new health habits could be learned; but the hardest part was to accept and act in accordance with completely different laws on the basis of human life—the relationship between men and women. Joseph had said, "I can tell a man to build a house and live in it and he will do so but I cannot tell him to have a good heart and know he will change." They could say, "You cannot have this until you ask for it in English" and little by little English would be learned. They could not say, "The kind of family which our grandfathers' fathers had, long before white men came up the river is wrong. You should form your families as the white men do and as is described in the laws made by the Little Grandfather (Governor) in Lincoln," and know that the custom of multiple wives would disappear. One young Omaha said, "The Omaha went to bed as Omahas and woke up as citizens."[18] Such speed cannot change age-old customs.

The environment in which their small group had lived by a combination of farming and hunting no longer existed. The old habits which had directed an orderly life were destroyed. There had been little organized or consistent effort by white men to help the Indians establish workable substitutes for these customs.

When the State was organized and later when Thurston County had been formed, the machinery of government was run by white men for white men with the Indians left to the Federal officials. Twice it had been declared that the Omaha were under the civil and criminal laws of the State of Nebraska. This meant that customs worked out through centuries of experience by a Christian society were to be imposed upon a people where a small percent had been nominal Christians for less than a score of years and where most of the people had no comprehension of the white man's law. They only knew they were men and women as there had been men and women before the Europeans had entered history.

Marguerite and Susan advised and tried to explain to both Indians and whites, encouraging the marriages by license and law and,

if possible, with the sanction of the church. When the State of
Nebraska made one of its periodic attempts to adjust laws for an
interim period, the sisters worked in every way possible to help the
races understand each other. A committee from the legislature was
invited to Susan's home and the leaders of the tribe came to meet
with them. It was not a productive meeting. The white man seemed
to have set opinions on what Indians were and what Indians thought.
Other citizens offered help; the sisters interpreted the languages but
could not interpret the thoughts. That year the bill was indefinitely
postponed when the legislature adjourned and all effort was lost.

Susan was alert to many things among the people as she went
into many homes. She and Marguerite tried persuasion on the point
whenever possible. Rev. W. A. Galt came to the Blackbird Hills
Presbyterian Church in 1893 and found the two were often the promoters and planners of weddings. He assisted them on several
occasions and wrote out sketches of Omaha life, which included
weddings manuevered by Susan and Marguerite.[19]

They had known two young people had been living together
and persuaded them to right themselves with the law and have a
church wedding. The license was secured and the minister notified;
the church was nearly filled for few Omahas of marriageable age had
ever seen a church wedding. Both bride and groom understood
English so an interpreter was not needed. Marguerite played the organ
and Susan directed the affair. Was she remembering the church
wedding in Philadelphia? She must not have anticipated all the
coaching required, for the couple refused to join their right hands
when the minister asked them to, since to an Omaha this was an
impropiety. At the close when they had been pronounced man and
wife and the blessing had been said, they did not know what to do
but stood awkwardly and self-consciously in front of the minister. He
spoke to them quietly and said, "You may go." They turned and
walked away down diverging aisles and sat down on opposite sides of
the church. It was prophetic of their future for they soon separated
and each remarried. It was all considered so extremely embarrassing
that few others ventured to have a church wedding.

In 1892 Susan was invited to be the Commencement speaker at
Hampton.[20] It was the school's twenty-fourth anniversary and was to
be a great occasion. It was a propitious time for the school to attract
attention and also honor one of its greatest graduates. It was a joyful
occasion because General Armstrong, who had been ill, was able to
be present at the exercises in a wheeled chair. His contribution to the

exercises was small but, if he were given attention then or now, it may be he made a great contribution for the future of his country when he said, "The test of the civilization of any nation is the care which it gives to its ignorant and oppressed classes."

Before Susan was to speak on "My Work as a Physician Among My People," the students gave a dramatic, symbolic interpretation of General Armstrong's thought. They had given this dramatic sketch three months earlier on Indian Citizenship Day. This annual celebration recalled the signing of the Dawes Act, when allotted Indians were declared to be citizens. Marguerite had taken part in the first spontaneous celebration in 1887, speaking on "A Woman's Thoughts"; it seemed fitting that Susan should take part in this ceremony on the sixth occasion. In 1887 the day had been called "Indian Emancipation Day," indicating the Civil War influence. Five years had shifted the emphasis to citizenship.

This dramatic effort in 1892 was used as an introduction for Susan. A figure representing Columbia was seated on a throne; at one side were famous men of colonial times, John Smith, Miles Standish, William Penn and others. The "Indian Petitioner" threw herself at Columbia's feet asking why her people were not there. Then Fame and History called in Pocahontas and other Indians who had been friends of the white men. When Columbia was flanked by famous sons and daughters of both races, the Afro-Americans filled in one side of the stage and the Indians the other.

A voice said, "But what of the future?" The Indian students came forward with the Hampton banner singing "Spirit of Peace." Columbia stood with the flag and said, "Take my banner and your place as my citizens." Then all three races sang "America." The Hampton paper, *The Southern Workman,* waxed eloquent in describing Susan's entrance:

> Then before the half circle of brilliantly costumed heroes of Two races came a dignified, erect, high-souled woman, the personification and product of the best progress of one race and the best philanthropy of the other, *La Flesche,* the Arrow; Arrow of the Future, from the bow of the Past, strained by the cord of the Present.

This seems the only time anyone used the direct translation of La Flesche to give a symbolic significance, while it might have been appropriate many times.

Susan's entire annual report for 1893 is included in the Indian Commissioner's report of that year. It indicates a slight although encouraging response to her educational efforts and gives a vivid account of general living conditions effecting health.

> Tuberculosis of the lungs seems to be on the increase in our tribe. In place of wild game, diseased meat is eaten in many cases and much pork. In place of the airy tent, (we have) close houses when often in one room, two families are found with doors and windows closed night and day, so we cannot wonder that scrofula is the result.

She closed with the comment that she had not attended as many cases during the year as she had formerly, because of her own ill health. The work was hard; she was nurse, teacher, interpreter, social worker and general advisor as well as doctor. Severe weather constantly hampered her movements. At one time, having delivered a new baby, she was caught by a storm and snowed in for a week. It was not too bad, since the new mother was an old friend, a former Hampton girl and everyone had a jolly time, not daring to think if others were needing her services. Many times she faced the blizzards when she was overtired and she constantly drove herself to long, long hours as she hunted out the widely scattered families. Rosalie wrote to Frank that "Sue's ears hurt her. . ." It was an early mention of the trouble which too swiftly brought deafness and her final illness.

She talked of resigning but the Agent would never listen—he needed her too badly. She was deeply concerned about her mother, quite alone since the death of the "oldest grandma" at the age of 105. Sue asked Marguerite to take a leave of absence and look after Mother, but Marguerite felt keenly her need to look after herself since Charley's death and she feared the red tape of returning to government service if she left it for a time. One day Sue came home (to the farm on the Logan) and found Mary critically ill. That decided the matter and knowing the Agent was away she handed in her resignation before he returned.

Early in 1893 Rosalie mentioned to Frank that Marguerite had been over from the Agency with some of the other teachers, among them the Industrial Farmer, Walter Diddock. Diddock was mentioned several times in the next few months and then, in August, "Marguerite is engaged to the Industrial Farmer, Walter Diddock. They say he is a good steady fellow and he seems to think everything of Marguerite."

Walter Diddock's family had settled near Decatur when he had been about twelve years old. In the next few years while attending school he had had charge of the town herd. Each morning he collected the milk cows from the individual owners and drove them to the common pasture. At the close of the day he brought them back for the evening milking. The first years after he was out of school Walter had herded cattle on the open range and later attended a business college in Omaha.

As a boy he had been held up as a model for others; his pictures as an adult show a handsome and engaging young man. He was self-supporting from his late teens and proved to be both resourceful and public spirited. In 1889 the Indian Agent offered him the position of Industrial Farmer at the school. Diddock extended the job to include continuing supervision of farming efforts by the boys after they left the school. In a way it was the kind of thing emphasized later by 4-H Clubs.

During Marguerite's service to the school she was, at one time, the Field Matron. She visited the Omahas in their homes wherever they were and taught whatever seemed most needed—better sanitation, care of the ill, new ways of cooking, possibly a little sewing and general care of a white man's type of house. This foreshadowed another service of the future, the Home Demonstration Agent.

Marguerite and Walter were married June 29, 1895 at the Blackbird Hills Church by the Rev. W. A. Galt who had officiated at many weddings arranged by the La Flesche sisters. In one of his little stories he mentioned one wedding when Marguerite had been the Interpreter and had brought Walter Diddock with her. The minister had been quite aware of their courtship and as he went through the familiar service he wondered what was in their minds as Marguerite translated the vows into the soft Omaha tongue.

Before Marguerite's marriage Susan had amazed everyone by announcing she was going to marry Henry Picotte, a brother of Charles. Intimate personal matters are never completely understood by even the closest family members and accounts on such matters usually differ widely, colored by the personality of the narrator. However, on the point of Susan's marriage every letter saved and every comment by personal acquaintances sound the same note. No one could understand how this marriage could come about. The historical researcher should hesitate to venture any guess if so many present at the time did not understand, but with the exception of Rosalie and Marguerite, no one of those people knew about Thomas Ikinicapi and Susan's renunciation of marriage for the sake of medicine and her dedication to the Tribe.

Ikinicapi had worked at the Yankton Agency and the Hampton teacher making her last visit spoke of his failing health and of his marked gentleness and courtesy. His death must have closely followed Charlie Picotte's. Susan had been touched by both events; the two young men had been associated with each other in her experience and she had admired them both for their manliness and gentleness.

Presumably then Henry had appeared, from the Agency where T. I. lived—and a brother of Charlie's. There is no mention of Henry having been at Hampton; family tradition says he had been with a Wild West show. These shows figured largely in the life of this first generation away from the old tribal pattern; they threw a fleeting glamour over the young Indians. They offered the chance to act out a little of the life their grandfathers had lived and had fully expected them to live.

The glamour still hangs today over these shows and influences the popular picture of the opening of the West. At the time, close friends of outstanding leaders (or owners) of the shows spoke favorably of the effect on the young Indians. But the missionaries and the educators with the closest experience never felt the experience was wholesome. Too many times the Hampton records read, "had been with a show, was restless, unreliable," "could not settle down," "ran away and would not work." Many people said "Henry was likeable," "a friendly fellow,"—he may have had some of the engaging qualities which drew people to Charlie, but he did not have the education or personal stability.

The Heritage family in Philadelphia who were related to Rev. Burtt, had become very close to Susan during her Medical College days. Mother and daughter wrote in disbelief. They expressed regret over the news and asked Rosalie if she felt Henry were the "right one" for Susan, what did Rosalie think and Ed, who was always so sensible. "We cannot think the step wise, for one thing because of her health." There was a tone of disappointment over a career forsaken, for in the nineteenth century women thought of a career *or* marriage.

A lost career did not enter into the matter with an older white woman who had been close to the family for years. She talked directly to Susan on the importance of the proper combination in marriage. Having observed many marriages where the man and woman were not well suited to each other, she begged Susan to think carefully. Sue had replied she desired to marry and she did not think any white man would wish her for a wife—a strange answer from a woman who had two sisters married to white men and another planning to be. Independent as ever, Sue might have answered only to brush an argument aside or she might have thought about the sorrowing, childless women she had known in the hospital.

The two marriages brought Marguerite and Susan closer together. They had their first babies within a period of a few months, Marguerite, a girl and Susan, a boy. In the late 1890's Walter Diddock conducted a small pasture business near the old Mission building where there was no longer a school. In fact the Diddocks lived in the building for some months. One day in 1898, when the Trans-Mississippi Exposition was on, Rosalie went "up to Mother's" to ask Mary some questions for Alice Fletcher. However, she wrote, conversation had been impossible since both Marguerite and Susan were there packing to go to the Fair in Omaha "with husbands, babies and everything."

After her marriage Susan did participate more directly in Indian life than she had done. She had always been in the position of leader or interpreter, not a participating member of the group. Shortly after they were married, Susan and Henry went for a visit to Yankton. Henry's father had sent for them for the Sioux were expecting a large annuity payment and, of course, Henry was on that roll. Thus, Joseph's younger daughter after over twenty years of acquiring white habits of living participated in a typical Indian custom, the inter-tribal visit. Henry probably took over the farming as his brother had done; there were the allotments of Joseph, Mary, of Susan to manage. The local newspaper often included items about Henry Picotte's stock or his crops. Susan later built a small house on her allotment but it is questionable if they lived there since Mary's house was the established one and Mary and Susan were always together from the time Susan abruptly broke off her connection with the Agency until Mary's death.

Part of the time Susan and Henry lived in Bancroft, in a small house across the street from the Presbyterian Church. In some way, wherever they were, even after a second boy followed the first one, even when for two years Henry required nursing attention and later when Mary was bed-ridden, still Susan continued to practice medicine. She continued to answer the calls of the sick, among both the Indians and the white people. In Bancroft and on the farm, unless she needed to be away from home at night, Susan put a lighted lantern where it shown on the doorstep to guide anxious messengers in the dark.

One rainy night, Rob Kelley, son of the merchant in Bancroft, was loafing with other young fellows around the depot telegraph room when an urgent message came from the next town, eight or nine miles down the line to find Dr. Picotte and come as quickly as possible; a woman was desperately ill in childbirth and the two local doctors needed Susan's help. One of the boys hurried to the livery stable, got a team and covered buggy and drove to find that light. Susan was ready quickly and they started off in a gathering storm for Lyons, following the section lines for much of the way where there were no real highways. They were met at the hotel and Susan went on with one of the doctors. The next morning the driver and doctors had breakfast together, knowing both mother and new baby were fine. Dr. Hildreth added, "Thanks to the skill of Dr. Susan."21

Susan threw herself into the work of the Presbyterian Church in Bancroft just as completely as she had entered into the life at Hampton and at Philadelphia. She frequently interpreted if a service involved Indians but as time went on there were not many Indians connected with that church and more went to the Blackbird Hills Church.

For years Wajapa came to the Bancroft church although he never became a member. Perhaps it was his gesture of remembrance or loyalty to Joseph and Rosalie since his English was scanty and he could not understand all the service. A tie to the family was obvious for he included Ed Farley's second wife, Winnie, in his inner circle. Winnie remembered that although he could not talk to her, he never missed coming to her after the service to shake hands and give a word of greeting. As Rosalie's successor, she, too, was one of his family.

Susan nearly always had a Sunday School class. It might be one of little girls or of young adults. She had a young adult group in 1903 and 1904 when Clyde Filley, recently graduated from the University, came to be principal of the High School. Filley came of a studious family, he had done well in college and made teaching his life work. He was on the faculty of the University of Nebraska for many years and throughout those years he was an active church worker observing and sharing in many Sunday Schools. He had said that Dr. Susan Picotte was without question the greatest Sunday School teacher he ever knew. He had often wondered where her power lay, beyond a thorough knowledge of the Biblical text. In some way she made the ancient stories alive and fraught with meaning for the moment. This class which included young people of but little formal education as well as a few college graduates was no more highly praised or remembered than the one she had for little girls.

It was but a step from the church to active work for another of her father's convictions. If Rosalie assumed his role as leader of the tribe, Susan took up the torch of his crusade against alcohol. She saw it from the medical angle: she saw the effects of drunkedness in society at large as she cared for neglected families; she saw it personally as Henry drank more and more; and with her sisters she worried over the habits of Carey's companions. She dealt with its criminal effects; she gave evidence in one trial growing out of drunkedness in which she traced and documented many incidents when members of the tribe had committed crimes or had met death because of alcohol.

She became an active temperance speaker of considerable renown. Dr. John G. Neihardt, author of *The Cycle of the West* was at that time (by his own admission) a brash young newspaper man in Bancroft. He has described Susan as one of the most remarkable and inspiring speakers he had ever heard. He felt much of her oratorical power grew out of her use of silence as a means of emphasis. She would clearly, convincingly, logically build up her thesis, come to an impressive climax and then, just before the final line which would tie together the argument and the emotional content she would stand in silence. It was a silence of some moments, when no one moved, a silence which had a force of its own. The sensitive young poet in her audience felt in some way she "vibrated," that waves of emotional and mental power passed from her to her listeners. Then when the silence seemed unbearable, as though something would break under the strain, she would quietly bring out the last sentence, clinching her argument. As an old man, a veteran of the lecture platform, who had heard hundreds of speeches, Dr. Neihardt had known no one to surpass her.

This eloquence or forcefulness was even apparent in her writing. She frequently expressed herself on public questions and would be quoted by the press. She wrote convincing arguments to the Indian Commissioner and more than once made her points before Congressional committees. The local paper remarked that Dr. Picotte had contributed "a warm" article to last week's issue. The warm article was on gambling.

Henry died in 1905 after an illness of two years and Susan faced life as a widow, possessed of a quarter section of land, schooled in a profession and with an invalid mother and two small boys dependent upon her. The pain in her head grew worse, centering in her ears but extending into her back. She had become extremely deaf and her own health and the care of her family made the practice of medicine difficult. A few months after Henry's death she moved to the Agency as missionary to the Omaha Tribe under the Presbyterian Board of Home Missions, the first American Indian to be appointed by this Board. She had housing furnished and a small salary and she was located where the Indians came and went. If her duties were expected to be more spiritual than physical, it did not greatly influence her action, the two were intricately interwoven in Susan's philosophy.

The Blackbird Hills Presbyterian Church had grown from the Indian group at the old Mission and had been located at the Agency since the late 1880's. The Agency came to be called Macy, a name coined from the words "Omaha" and "Agency," since as a post office it was officially "Omaha Agency" with the mail too often going to Omaha. George C. Maryott, who was postmaster as well as trader (by this time called merchant) suggested the new name and it was officially recognized. The Church had largely served the Indians but a few white people in the area were in the congregation. The institution had not been too active under a Reverend Stewart (or Stuart) who had recently left.

Shortly before Susan took charge the Church had been rededicated under the supervision of the Home Mission officials. She went steadily ahead to teach the Gospel story in which she devoutly believed. She was the teacher, the preacher, the field worker—everything. Little by little the work extended and she had two Indian helpers. The effectiveness of her work was shown by a newspaper account eighteen months later. Communion had been conducted by Rev. R. M. L. Braden, the minister-at-large for the Board and twenty-one children had been baptized, one white child and twenty Indian children. Also twenty adult Indians had joined the Church. At one midweek meeting five children had been baptized and ten adults united with the Church—all Indians.

The news item continued, saying this was not the result of a revival or any sudden and concentrated effort but of the steady missionary work of Dr. Susan La Flesche Picotte who gave "not only spiritual and medical advice but sympathy and the help of one Indian to her own people." It continued in a didactic vein asking if the white people of the community realized their own responsibility to these neighbors.

They see us white people who have been brought up in a
Christian community in decent society. Do we always act that
way? These Indians are our neighbors, forming new ideas,
changing very rapidly, forming character, to an extent we are
responsible.

Carey's daughter, Elizabeth, remembered hearing Aunt Sue
preach at the Blackbird Hills Church. Years later, when there was
an appointed pastor, Elizabeth would go with him and Aunt Sue as
they held church meetings at other places. Elizabeth usually had a
part in the meeting by reciting portions of scripture.

After the formation of Thurston County the Reservation lost
some of its distinctness since the area continued to develop much as
the surrounding counties. At the same time the increasing number of
white farmers began to overshadow the Indians. The railroad which had
served Bancroft had cut across the southwest portion of the country by
the time of the allotment in 1884. It was extended to Pender in the
1890's and some of the Reservation was made a part of Cuming County
and another portion was in Burt County. By 1900 it was evident that the
long east-west railway lines, widely spaced north and south could not
adequately serve the expanding agriculture in the hundreds of acres
between. The Burlington and Missouri served the southern part of
Nebraska; the Great Northern of James J. Hill and its related lines
were farther to the north. The Sioux City and Western Railroad,
sometimes called the Burlington-Great Northern, was organized to
connect these longer lines. The survey was approved by the Interior
Department in 1905 and the road was completed two years later,
cutting directly through the Omaha and Winnebago Reservations.
Two towns which might be shipping points and supply centers were
planned to be carved directly from the Omaha Reservation. Town site
companies made the necessary purchases from the Indian allotees
with the consent of the Indian office.

James J. Hill's son Walter was in charge of the construction of
this line and one of the towns was named for him—Walthill. Rosalie's
sons Caryl and Jack (later with Louis and Fletcher) had a business in
real estate and were active in promoting the second town six miles to
the south and west. At first "Farley" was suggested but there was a
town by that name on the Great Northern in Iowa. Then the name
of an official of the road, "Hodge" was mentioned but the railroad
did not accept that. Some suggested "Reedville" for Mr. and Mrs. W.
W. Reed, who had grown up in Bancroft. Soon after they had been
married the railroad was projected to pass their farm and while the
work was in that vicinity, Mrs. Reed had cooked for the workers.

This name did not gain support and it was said that "since the Farley brothers were the principal promoters" the town was named "Rosalie" for their mother.[22] This has been the only instance when a name of Joseph's family has become a place name in the area.[23]

Through Susan's efforts the Secretary of the Interior ruled that no liquor could be sold on any lot in these towns made out of the Omaha Reservation. This ruling was included in every deed for decades, but it came to mean little when automobiles could take the thirsty quickly outside the given boundaries. Fifty some years later, the residents of Walthill overwhelmingly voted to abolish the restriction.

The first lots in Walthill and Rosalie were sold in May of 1906 when one building had already been erected in Walthill. Within six months this town had more than fifty buildings and a population of over 200. Walter Diddock and Susan Picotte both bought lots on the second Walthill lot sale in November, 1906. The lots were on the corners of blocks with a street between them, up toward the end of Main Street and well up the hill which looks out over Omaha Creek, winding northeast to the Missouri River.

Here they built large comfortable houses, well planned and of solid construction. Walter teased Sue because her house was too high for its breadth and depth and before there were trees around it, it did give the impression of height more than anything else. He said this was because Sue was only sure what she wanted the living room to be and beyond that the rooms had to be piled on top. There was a long living room across the front, with windows on three sides, a dining room and kitchen behind it. She wanted a fireplace at one end and an open stairway which should have a turn giving a wide landing a few steps above the floor, putting the sweep of the stairs across the far side of the room from the entrance.

The bedroom and storage spaces had to be built above; there was to be a roomy attic. The house stands today, solid and true, a tall house crowned by the sharply pointed attic gable. The woodwork is of good solid oak with beautiful grain brought out by years of waxing and polishing. A long brass plate is fastened to the edge of the shallow mantle shelf over the fireplace. On it are these words, "East, West; Hame's Best." Susan must have come across some Scotch Presbyterians in her association with the Church, to have transplanted such a rhyme from the Highlands to the country west of the Missouri River.

The Diccock house was of a better balanced design, with

suggestions of Dutch Colonial. The sides of the roof which extended
down to the ceiling line of the first floor were shingled. Here again
was a good use of oak,[24] with living room, dining room and kitchen
on the first floor and three bedrooms above. The rooms were large
and comfortable and both houses had bathrooms. The girls who had
known the rough frame house in the "make-believe-white-man's
village" with its scanty furnishings and frequent crowding, at last had
the facilities for personal care which they had admired in New Jersey,
in Philadelphia and Boston. A series of photographs of Susan's house,
inside and out, taken soon after she had moved in, includes one of
the bath tub.

Life flowed back and forth between the two houses for the
next ten years, much in the nature of the old extended, all-inclusive
Omaha family. Eventually two girls and three boys came to the
Diddock's but the first little boy Francis lived only a year. Across the
way at Susan's house there were two boys and the grandmother.
Walter Diddock got along well with children and was a delightful
companion to his own. He was musical, as was Marguerite, and music
of some sort was a part of the family life.[25] Always helpful and
anxious to spare Marguerite it became established habit that Walter
got Sunday morning breakfast—always of pancakes. Susan would stop
over, in from a call, or appearing as one of the family. Conscious of
her role as health teacher, she would say,

"Walter, why make those doughy cakes? Can't you tell they
will lie in your stomach like leather?"

And then, "Fry me two or three!"

Grandmother Mary was in Susan's house a little over a year.
She had a fall and for much of the time after the move to Walthill
she could not leave her bed. One day Sue sent word down to
Bancroft asking Winnie to come to Walthill for a few days, that
Mother wanted her to make something. Winnie had been drawn to
Mary from her first acquaintance with the family, never feeling the
lack of a common language was a problem. Mary apparently was
equally drawn to Winnie.

Mary was sure she did not have long to live and she wanted
Winnie to make the clothes in which she would be buried. Susan had
received complete instructions and had purchased the materials, yards
of fine black crepe and black lace for trimming. Winnie sat by Mary's
bed measured the shrunken tired old body and made her plans. Then
she cut out a long smock-like robe, then often called a "dressing
sack." She stitched by hand as Mary watched and the two women,

far apart in age and experience, had an uncommunicative but understanding time of companionship. Mary lived several months longer
but was never out of bed again. Then, clad as she had wished to be,
she was taken to lie by Joseph.

The La Flesche sisters both entered into the life of the growing
community. They were both charter members of the new chapter of
Eastern Star and of the new Presbyterian Church. Susan again tought
Sunday School, although she had her responsibilities at Macy.
Marguerite's home was the meeting place for many church organiza-
tions, she was active in the Missionary Society and spoke at County
Sunday School conventions. They both addressed meetings of
Organized Agriculture held under the auspices of the Extension
Service of the State University. They served as interpreters at count-
less weddings and funerals. Walter Diddock led the choir and before
many years Margy Diddock and Caryl Picotte were being elected
officers of the Christian Endeavor Society.

Dr. Susan and the Diddock's supported all manner of
community projects: a series of lectures and concerts, special projects
for the County Fair, with Sue in charge of the Indian Department
one year. Their friend, the attorney, Harry Keefe gave space in his
Office for a station of the Nebraska Traveling Library. When it was
possible to have their own library and a local committee Mrs. Keefe
was President of the committee and Marguerite was Secretary-
Treasurer. The Library was one of Marguerite's major interests as long
as she was able to serve. Through following years both her daughters
Marguerite (Langenberg) and Rosalie (Boughn) continued this
community service.

These homes were open for all manner of events; Susan
particularly loved to entertain. A visitor from Bancroft, the guest of a
neighbor, a birthday, the presence of a musician studying Omaha
music, special occasions for Rosalie's daughters—all might be the
reason for a party. It might be a family dinner, an evening musical or
a delightful luncheon. In every way possible a party at Susan's was a
special affair. Their homes also were headquarters for scholars of
many different fields who came to study the botany, music or the
ethnology of the Omaha.

Life in Walthill followed the white pattern of living but it did
not make the La Flesche sisters unaware of the Indians around them.
Indeed, Walthill had many Indian residents who owned their
property. Many had assumed white ways as had Marguerite and
Susan, while others lived in the village for a time but always looked

toward the more Indian life around Macy. The trials growing out of the sweeping changes, the hard work of adjustment, the doubts and fears of the less educated and the suffering of the older generation brought many problems to their doors.

Sadly enough many problems came from the white man's bureaucratic control, the incessant red tape involved in every move made by an Indian and the discouragement over repeated rebuffs at the Agency. Twenty years before the Government could find no way to help the tribe make an evolution from dictatorial Agency control to the democratic machinery of an organized country. In place of searching for a method, Agency system had been re-instated.

Originally it had been assumed that twenty-five years with lands held in trust and with constant help and assistance would make the Indians ready to handle their own affairs. But the assistance given was not on the order of teaching as the outline of self-government had planned; it was a matter of the Indian Agent (or Superintendent) doing everything, controlling everything for the Indian. Naturally the Indians had not learned how to handle money or anything about business affairs.

The twenty-five years trust period was to expire in 1910, since the last allotment papers had been delivered in 1885. As the time approached a new Assistant Commissioner in the Office of Indian Affairs and many members of Congress were most aware of the backward Indians, the uneducated and the untrustworthy. Yet in 1909, 90 per cent of the Omahas under forty years spoke English, most of those between forty and sixty could speak a little; over 95 per cent of the tribe had acquired personal property.[26] Besides Susan as a physician the tribe had two lawyers, several merchants, a number in Civil Service and many teachers.

Nevertheless, the decision was made to extend the trust period for ten years and at the same time introduce a new system of supervised farming and consolidate the work of the Winnebago and the Omaha Agencies. Also an Agent was to be dismissed, or moved, a proceeding which involved a clash of personalities from the Reservation up to the Indian Office. It was announced in the face of rising disagreements that a Competency Commission would be appointed to select those Indians who might be advanced enough to operate without the Agent's constant direction.

Protests arose from both races. One Nebraskan, who spoke the Omaha language and had been familiar with their history for over forty years believed the tribe had been better off several years earlier for he said, "plans (which had been) executed for their benefit would have utterly ruined the same number of white people."[27]

The editor of the *Walthill Times* called it:

> ... an unwise system of government supervision ... every business action of the individual is supervised and hedged about with red tape and paternal restrictions ... that the Indian has been permitted to learn nothing ... no comprehension of business principles ... little incentive to prepare for citizenship.

The tribe spoke with one voice as they had not for a generation. The various contending groups forgot grievances against each other as they united in the determination to "scrap it out with the department and make no concession." A committee was appointed to proceed to Washington and make their demands known. The committee was made up of Hiram Chase (an attorney), Dr. Picotte, Daniel Webster (one of the wiser, older men), Simeon Hallowell (called Nebraska) and a member to be selected from the Indian Presbyterian Church.

This was the year that Mary had died and shortly afterward Susan had been desperately ill. Taken sick in March she was only able to be up and around the house in June. In September she worked strenuously to combat a diptheria epidemic and by November had plunged into this struggle for the tribe. She used her eloquent pen to good advantage before any start was made to Washington and wrote several articles to the *Omaha Bee* describing the burden placed on the individual Indian by the demands of red tape.

> We have rules and regulations to the right of us ... to the left of us ... behind us; do you wonder we object to the continuation of them in front of us? ... A new order is being enforced ... Indians can trade at certain stores up to a certain amount. The Superintendent inspects the bill and then if the department (in Washington) approved the number and size of prunes and the color of bananas, the government pays the bill out of the Indian's (own) money in the office. Shades of our ancestors! ... a distinct step backwards from what you knew ... you could trade your furs yourself ... Omahas have a trust fund ... application for (these) funds have been returned from Washington. ... One woman who had TB asked for her share; it was badly needed. The Superintendent asked for it to be a "special" ... an order came for her to sign certain blanks; the Superintendent wrote it was for *immediate* necessities ... they sent a new form to be signed. In the meantime she had died and was buried.

Despite their protests the combination of the Agencies was carried out. A mass meeting was held, attended by political friends of the Assistant Commissioner and remarkable unanimity of feeling was expressed, but the government maintained its position. The white business men of the area combined to bring pressure on the Indian Office and an Omaha delegation again left for Washington. On February 7, 1910, Susan addressed the Secretary of the Interior and spoke of the red tape of obtaining the Indian's own money and the difficulties imposed in travel to the combined Agency.

> Applications for these trust funds were made in January, 1908 . . . 84 or more Indians have died, deprived of the use of this money which was theirs. . . . I have several cases waiting for surgical operation who want to use these moneys for expenses. Every day I receive letters imploring my help.

In an earlier newspaper article she had expressed the feeling of most of the better educated Omahas:

> As for myself, I shall willingly and gladly co-operate with the Indian Department in any thing that is for the welfare of the tribe. But I shall fight good and hard against . . . anything that is to the tribe's detriment, even if I have to fight alone, for . . . I owe my people a responsibility.

The Competency Commission, thus prodded, acted quickly and three classes of Omahas were announced; Class I would have their land patents in fee and full control of their property, Class II would not receive patents but could rent and lease their own lands and manage that of their minor children, Class III were the "incompetents," the aged and mentally deficient, or ill, whose leases would be made by the Agency.

On March 11, 1910, the *Fremont Tribune*[28] wrote in congratulation:

> Omahas won a triumph . . . 250 full-fledged citizens of Nebraska, equal number elevated to that dignity with but a few restrictions. . . . Delegation was the wisest of the tribe, headed by a woman, a collage graduate and skilled in medicine. . . . Dr. Picotte drew . . . up a second declaration of independence. To say those who could frame such a scholarly instrument . . . should be denied (independent) citizenship would be to reject the possibilities of evolution.

Marguerite and Mrs. Harry Keefe were both charter members of the Walthill Woman's Club, which quickly became federated with the State and National organizations. Susan's name is lacking from the first list but there is no question but that she belonged from the first. She may have been visiting some sick Indian in a far corner of the Reservation on the day of organization. Her name appears in many accounts of the Club's early activities. Not only did she busy herself with the local projects but she was Chairman of Public Health for the Nebraska State Federation.

In this capacity she organized a state effort to obtain laws against the common drinking cup, started a fly eradication campaign and urged better education concerning contagion in tuberculosis. Her annual report for this committee is vigorously and concisely stated and indicates she was able to enlist others in her projects. She was also concerned over careless medical inspections at the large Indian Boarding Schools. She particularly objected to these schools sending home sick children who infected whole families, when the illness could have been detected. She wrote to the Office of Indian Affairs urging that all Indian Schools institute more frequent medical inspection. She herself made regular examination of the children in the Walthill school at no charge to the school district.

With all these things to be thinking over and planning it was no wonder that at times, lost in thought, she passed her friends on the street without seeing them. Carrie Dudley, a close friend who had charge of the music in the schools, chuckled over this years later and said when she saw Susan coming toward her in such a mood, she made no effort to get her attention. She knew Sue was "thinking about her Indians," puzzling over what was the best thing to do next.

Dr. Sue was a charter member of the Medical Association of Thurston County and a member of the Nebraska State Medical Society. She was on the Health Board of Walthill for several terms. During a smallpox epidemic most of the Health Board, including Susan, resigned under severe criticism. Because of an obvious panic in the community and the passing of years it is impossible to make any judgment on this incident.

She had her critics as have most physicians. Two or three stories persist of cases which went awry. There is no indication of neglect but possibly a wrong decision or the lack of some special, detailed knowledge. Susan's work must be judged in the light of medical knowledge and education in the 1880's and 1890's. Her preparation of two and one-half years of study with a few months as an aide in a hospital was typical, however meager it may sound today. For Susan this followed preparatory schooling less adequate than the best offered at the time—and she had no chance for refresher courses. Her work appears as an amazing accomplishment in spite of a few weak places in the record. She worked long and earnestly with no thought of the drain on her own strength.

From the early days on the Reservation she dreamed of having a hospital right at hand. Before her day, there had been a hospital built but the Indians would not let their sick leave the family circle and the building had become a school. But the tribe had learned a great deal since then and she knew they would have better care if a hospital were available. She had often discussed the possibility with Dr. Hildreth of Lyons and other practitioners in the area; roads were poor and it was a long drive to Omaha or to Sioux City.

Hope for a hospital was increased when Walthill was founded to be near the center of the Indian population, now well interspersed with white farmers. Then Dr. William Ream established himself in the infant community and gave his active support. Several efforts were made to interest some philanthropic organization but without success although for a time it seemed one Catholic nursing order might be interested. At last the suggestion was made to the Home Mission board of the Presbyterian Church which directed Susan's work at the Blackbird Hills Church. No doubt the presence of Mrs. Pingrey once of the Elizabeth Institute on this Board may have helped the decision.

After due deliberation this Board assumed certain obligations and made a grant of $8,000. The Society of Friends gave $500.00, through the Presbyterian Church; Walter and Marguerite Diddock gave an acre of ground on the northwest border of the village. Other individuals and organizations furnished rooms or gave equipment. Charles S. Cadman, coming into prominence as a composer organized a benefit concert in Pittsburg to raise funds, with the last group of selections being based on Omaha tribal music. It had been thought originally that the hospital would be for Indians only but the response was so generous that its services were open to all. As long as it operated it was a noteworthy example of a biracial effort. It opened January 8, 1913. The annual report two years later listed 448 patients cared for, 168 of these had been bed patients and of these 126 were Indians; the balance had been dispensary cases to the number of 280.

At last it was possible for Susan to work under standard hospital conditions. Carey's Elizabeth as a grown woman worked in hospitals as an aide, caring for patients and observing techniques and remembered how Aunt Sue had operated on every member of the family. She had been impressed as a child to see the sterile gown and gloves put on; as a more experienced woman she admired the deftness and skill and the care for details. The hospital also made it possible for Susan to limit her work to a pace more in accordance with her own strength. All doctors in the area brought patients there; she worked there for the most part, not attempting the old hard drives in bad weather.

Throughout its existence the hospital rendered a fine service. After Susan's death it was named the Dr. Susan Picotte Memorial Hospital by the Home Mission Board. It suffered greatly at the time of World War I when Dr. Ream was killed on active duty and another practitioner did not return to Walthill after the war. For some reason the Presbyterian Board turned the direction over to a committee in Omaha and interest was not continued. It was closed for several years; then largely through Marguerite's efforts it re-opened under two experienced hospital managers and still retained the name, the Picotte Memorial Hospital. Difficult times came again after the Second World War, when few doctors cared to reside in small towns and the government opened a hospital at Winnebago six miles north. Marguerite's grandson, Kent Baughn, practiced medicine in Walthill in 1947-48.[29]   The building, no longer a hospital, served the community as a nursing home for several years, under the direction of Clara Watland Score who as a young nurse, just graduated, had worked under Susan.

Dr. Sue was a working part of the hospital barely two years. The infection centering on her ears grew steadily worse involving a larger area and causing great pain. Only by 1914 was it called "decay of the bones"; later it was spoken of as "possibly cancer." Early in 1914, friends in the east began to learn of her trouble and sympathetic messages came to the Diddock home. Dr. Harold Gifford of Omaha, considered a leader in his field operated on Susan at the Methodist Hospital in Omaha in February 1915. The operation only seemed to indicate more surgery might be required as the assembled physicians tried to eradicate the diseased area. A second operation was performed in March. In June Caryl Farley wrote to his Uncle Frank saying Dr. Gifford felt Aunt Sue could not live over a month.

But the wiry little body kept up the fight and she came home to Walthill to her own tall house for her last few months. It was summer and her son Caryl was home from Bellevue College. He and his brother Pierre had gone to the Nebraska Military Academy in Lincoln, a private institution of fine reputation. They both made good records and Caryl was talking about going into medicine.

Marguerite's daughter Margie, across the street, was also home from Bellevue on vacation. She and Caryl, the two first born of their mothers devoted the summer to Sue. As she grew worse and it was impossible to shut out all the pain, she clung to them both, although for weeks a trained nurse was on duty. Marguerite spent hours preparing the few things Susan could eat, Sue felt they were better if Margy cooked them. She wanted only Caryl to give hypodermics and to see to her medicines.

Death claimed her on September 18, 1916, and grief shook the community. The messages poured in; the many, many people came to express their sorrow. The funeral service was held in her living room with the casket under the rhyme about "Hame's Best." Three Presbyterian clergymen conducted the service and the closing prayer was given in the Omaha language by Richard Robinson, one of the older members of the tribe. Burial was in the Bancroft cemetery beside Henry. The Walthill paper added an extra sheet to make a special edition to honor her. It was impossible, the editor said, for any one person to adequately describe her life. There were two long articles, one by Harry Keefe, her old friend and one by Rev. Jenkins of the Mission Board. Then an editorial saying that although she had helped mold the new community to which she had come, the welfare of her people had been the passion of her life. Of the more than 2,000 Omahas, she was said to have treated everyone and saved the lives of many.

The Southern Workman at Hampton spoke of her concern for her people, "Between them and those who sought to rob them she stood as a strong wall . . . to them her name came to be anonymous with right and justice."

Marguerite included Susan's boys with her own family although they were away at school. World War I came all too quickly and Caryl and Pierre immediately enlisted. In the fall of 1918 Walter and Marguerite Diddock drove from Walthill to Deming, N. M. where the boys were at Camp Cody, an attention which was surely beyond the call of an Aunt's duty considering the highways of that time. The boys were soon transferred to the artillery and within a month Caryl was at Camp Taylor in Kentucky at Officers' Training School, where he was commissioned as 2nd Lieutenant.

Marguerite continued to entertain the Missionary Society, to serve on the Library committee, to interpret for the Indians, to gather in the Farleys' and Walter's relatives on holidays, keep an eye on the hospital and enjoy the arrival of her grandchildren. It was certainly a milestone that she served on the election board the first time women voted under the Nineteenth Amendment.

Then suddenly Walter was taken by a heart attack in 1928 and life was different for Marguerite. She became more and more reserved, more withdrawn within herself and the young people of Walthill felt they had never known her. She lived with her daughter Marguerite who took good care of her, just as Walter had done. Marguerite the "delicate" one, ten years older than Carey lived almost as long as he did. She passed away in 1945 in the Dr. Susan Picotte Memorial hospital; figuratively speaking at least, these two sisters who had shared so many experiences and had been so close to each other, were together at the end.

CHAPTER VIII

TA-IN-NE'S CHILDREN

On November 20, 1916, Francis La Flesche wrote a letter on behalf of his sister Lucy, his brother Carey and himself, requesting adjustment of an allotment made to their mother Elizabeth La Flesche, known to the Omaha as Ta-in-ne. He said an allotment had been made to her in 1871, according to the treaty of 1865, but that her land had been in the two mile strip sold for the use of the Winnebago in 1874. Another allotment was to have been made to replace this cancelled one, but nothing had ever been done. Therefore, he now wished to present a claim for this land in the name of Ta-in-ne's children, her rightful heirs. He believed the Omaha, as a tribe, still held enough land in common to care for such requests.

It is not clear why Francis made this move at such a late date, more than forty years after the grant was cancelled and some thirty years after Ta-in-ne's death. The statement that an allotment had been made adds to the questions and confusion for neither the name of Ta-in-ne, nor her Anglicized name, Elizabeth La Flesche, are on the list of 1871.[1] Nor would one expect to find it there, for at that time Ta-in-ne was the recognized second wife of Joseph La Flesche and wives did not receive separate grants. There are many women on the list but they are widows, young unmarried women or orphans.

This procedure was in the manner of the white man's handling of land as property; a wife's rights were combined with or absorbed in her husband's right to the land. This was contrary to the Indian habit of thought. They believed everyone had personal property. Even a small child had his own eating bowl or plaything, which belonged to him and to no one else. Land as property was a new idea to the Indians for they had always felt land belonged to everyone, it was "no more to be owned than was a shower of rain."[2]

However, if Joseph had been able to get land for Ta-in-ne before 1874 when the allotment was cancelled (assuming it might have been made after the first list), it might help point to the time when Joseph "put her away" or as was usually said "provided for her." But Ta-in-ne had borne him a son in July of 1872, the boy Carey. This was four years after Joseph had sent home the third wife,

163

as reported by Rev. R. J. Burt. Joseph must have settled the matter of multiple wives before 1880, for he was an active member of the church when Homer W. Partch came to the Mission. The family story about Joseph ordering the Indians to attend church must belong in the 1870's. It was after discussion with Father Hamilton that he came to the conclusion that men could do some things, but God could do more. A leader could order a man to live in a house instead of a tipi and he obeyed; but he could not order a man to have a change of heart and expect to be obeyed—only God could accomplish that. Hamilton's closest association with the Mission church and his closest intimacy with Joseph ceased by 1880.

If Ta-in-ne's connection with the intimate family group came to an end in 1873 or early in 1874, Frank was seventeen years old, just coming into manhood, taking part in what remained of the old tribal pattern. This would have been near the time he had acted as runner for the hunt and when he had killed his first buffalo. Lucy must have been ten or twelve and Carey less than two years. Since, when any separation was made within the larger Indian family the Omaha custom was for the small children to live with their mother, Carey may have lived with Ta-in-ne in his childhood. At her death he might have returned to Joseph and Mary's home.

It is possible that Frank's thought turned toward clearing up this matter of inheritance by the experience the family had gone through in settling Joseph's estate. They faced the problem which through the years had burdened the whole tribe: property entirely in land which must be divided equally among many people. Tribal custom and Nebraska law held that all the children had an equal share in Joseph's land. By 1914 when they tried to settle the matter, Mary's life interest was cancelled by her death in 1909, but two widowers, T. H. Tibbles and Edward Farley, each had a life interest in the one-seventh portions which would have been Susette's and Rosalie's.

Such a division could only be made after land was changed into money. The demand for land had lessened, several possible sales faded away. Debts of family members to each other which must be considered and balanced against the proposed portions led to emotional differences of opinion, general suspicion and actual bitterness. Lucy was angry, Marguerite was hurt, Carey thought everyone wanted to cheat him, several felt Walter Diddock took advantage of his ability to act on credit and Frank was out of patience with them all. Caryl Farley admitted he had "had a row with Uncle Walter and

Aunt Sue." It had not been a pleasant experience and the ruffled feelings of them all may have moved Frank to wish to settle other family matters. There seemed to be no record, however, on what he may have accomplished.

By the time of Ta-in-ne's death in 1883, Frank was established in Washington although he had made one trip home to assist a Special Inspector and was soon to come for an extended period while Alice Fletcher made the allotment. Lucy had been married for some time and with her husband, Noah, had been at Hampton for eight months. Noah was a full-blooded Omaha, the son of Mah-zhah-ke-da, called Silas Leaming. This family was considered of lower position than Joseph's so he had taken Lucy's name and become Noah La Flesche. Silas Leaming had not had the advantages that had been Joseph's and apparently had been less eager to embrace new ways. He was still using his Indian name, even in transactions with white people when the annuity list was made in 1886, although the "citizen" name was recorded on the allotment list of 1871.

Noah had had four years at the Mission school, less then Lucy, and he spoke very little English. With Minnie and Philip Stabler they were among the first married couples at Hampton. Noah plodded along in the Indian school for over three years, which meant it took him that long to become fluent in English. Lucy spoke English and was mentioned in the first year as the star pupil of the school. She had three years in the Normal Division, at the last taking practice teaching. She had covered the same ground as Susan had when they graduated together in 1886.

Noah profited immensely from the whole school experience. He conquered the language until he spoke and wrote very well, although he always felt uncertain. He did well in the various crafts which were taught and was superior in all forms of carpentry. He made headway in his grasp of white living and gave serious thought to its effect on the Indians. He was concerned over his own place and how he might make a contribution to the whole group. He was so eager to get to work on his farm that he did not stay through the spring term of 1886 but went home in late winter to be ready for the spring work on his own land.

During the holidays between terms, he and Lucy, with Susan, made a visit to New England. Their host and hostess may have been of the Boston Committee, friends of Susette's, or may have been scientific connections of Alice Fletcher. Rosalie wrote to Miss Fletcher in the middle of January, saying:

... they are having such a good time; think of Lucy and Noah
visiting at one of the most beautiful homes in Boston and think
of where they were when you first took an interest in them.

Where they had been, no one can say; but if Noah had not had
the opportunities that Lucy had had, if his family had not adopted
white ways to any large degree, they might have been in one of the
poor shanties the uneducated Indians produced when they could no
longer maintain themselves in the old-fashioned more comfortable
dwellings used by their forefathers. The visit in the beautiful home,
no doubt, affected Lucy as such visits had impressed Susan. They
both quickly grasped and adopted for themselves the white manner
and habits conducive to cleanliness and order.

Noah asked that on his way to Nebraska he might be routed
through Washington, for he wished to talk to Frank and a few others
about the plans for self-government. It developed he was in the city
at the time a delegation from the tribe presented their idea to the
Commissioner of Indian Affairs. He attended at least one meeting
held in the office of General Whittlesey, Secretary for the Board of
Indian Commissioners, when General Whittlesey met the tribal representatives. Also present were Frank, no doubt as interpreter; J. Owen
Dorsey of the Bureau of American Ethnology, who understood the
language and personally knew many of the tribe; Edward Painter of
the Indian Rights Association; Edward Farley of Bancroft; J. W.
Davis of the "Boston Committee," and Thomas H. Tibbles.

The plan for self-government was completely discussed and the
books on the pasture business were carefully examined. Noah remained in the city during the whole discussion and was not pleased
with the attitudes of other men who had gone to Washington without
being sent by the tribe. He investigated after he was home and wrote
to Alice Fletcher that the younger men were disturbed over this. He
wanted her to understand and to tell others that the few who had
helped those men with their expenses did not "amount to anything."

Noah's first problem on his farm was a common problem—the
need for equipment. In the halls of Congress it sounded conclusive
and final to say that the Indians had land; surely they could farm
and support themselves on a quarter section of land. Annuities
sounded large when spoken of in the full sum total, but when divided
among the whole tribe they often came to only a few dollars for
each person. Few Omahas had had any way to earn more than mere
dribbles of cash for nearly a generation. Most of the land in the
allotments needed to be broken—plowed for the first time. The deep,

tough sod resisted even a good plow and good plows cost money. Moreover, the plow must be pulled through the matted, tangled grass roots by strong horses. The Indians always had ponies, but although good for the hunt they were too light for work horses. The horses also had to be properly attached to the plow. Plow, horses, harness were the first essentials, even before seed was needed or a house could be built.

Ed Farley went to the bank with Noah, helped him to establish credit, signing a note with him. Noah, as other homesteaders, started out with a large debt. Besides that, he was lonesome for Lucy and it was hard to weather through the long weeks of spring and early summer when he was working alone. He sometimes stayed with Philip and Minnie Stabler who were settled in the first "Connecticut Cottage" on the quarter diagonally across the section from Noah. Seeing them cozy in their house with each other and their babies made Noah all the more homesick for Lucy's fun and companionship. He would stop in often to see Rosalie and it taxed her usual cheerfulness and sympathy to hold him to his resolution to have many things ready when Lucy came. Lucy at Hampton was equally lonesome, thinking she could hardly wait to be with Noah again. But they stuck to their plans and proved, as one teacher said, the Stablers and the La Flesches had less "weak-kneeism" than most of the Indians.

They had been in one of the first separate cottages for married couples at Hampton when the fine gift of a cooking stove to the school had been put in Lucy's kitchen. On the reservation they had the second house built by the Connecticut Women's Indian Association. It was on Noah's allotment, a mile and a half north of Rosalie. By winter they were settled and Lucy took great pleasure in her new housekeeping arrangements:

> In our bedroom we have a very nice bedstead, berau (sic) and two chairs; but they are the only chairs we have and we carry them to the kitchen when we go . . . in the sitting room a nice bookshelf Noah made and a few pictures we brought from Hampton. In our kitchen . . . a good cooking stove, a nice table, a small table to keep the dishes on as we haven't any cupboard and a barrel to keep our flour in, that is all . . .

> After breakfast when my rooms are in order I sit down to sew. I have several sheets and pillow slips to make and several tables cloths and napkins to hem. I do my own washing and ironing and help Rosalie wash every other week. I love to help her. I helped Susette wash too before she went away, when their washing day came, they came over after me. I have good strong arms so I am willing to help them. . . . In the evening we both sit down to read or study.[3]

Reading meant a great deal to Lucy, and the friends who sent magazines or books were thanked over and over again. When it was suggested that some ladies might give her an organ, Lucy went about in a dream. She had never dared tell anyone but Noah how she longed to have an organ.

One winter she held a night school at her house for some of the younger men who knew they needed more training. Lucy enjoyed this until one by one the men moved too far away to make the school possible. Some of the moving on the Reservation came because allotments were being worked farther to the West; others came from a reaction that took several back toward the Agency. A few moved because houses on quarter sections seemed remote from each other. It was too great a change from the more companionable village grouping. The scarcity of wood in the Logan valley was another obstacle. For their first winter Lucy and Noah spent a great deal of time going back and forth to get wood. It was a three-day trip to the Agency, get a load of wood and return. The cost of heating the little house mounted higher and higher and they hardly had enough left over for food. But Lucy cheerfully went on, for "the winter is almost over and we will . . . get to work and raise plenty."

Lucy felt very responsible for Carey; she kept an eye on him and at times expressed her concern. Carey had gone to Hampton at the same time Susan and Marguerite had but did not see much of them. He lived in the "Wigwam"—the boys' dormitory. Both of the girls wrote home about his progress, but it is doubtful if they gave him much attention since they both became absorbed in love affairs as well as in their studies. Carey was at Hampton for six years although he came home for most of the summers. There seems no record of his having spent any summer with some family in the East as was the custom for Hampton students.

Susan once wrote in a big sisterly fashion of Carey doing well in his studies and looking so earnest but so little one day in the chapel seated between two larger boys. In the spring of 1886 Lucy wrote to Alice Fletcher:

> I'll tell you what I think about Carey. He ought to go home, he needs Father's stern talks more than anything at this time. There are so many boys, no one looks after (him) as he needs.

She may have meant that Carey should go home only for the summer. Even if plans had changed and he had gone home to enter the Government school, he would have had Joseph's directing advice and "stern talks" for only two years.

When he did come home to stay in 1891 he went first to Rosalie's which was the family home nearest the railway station. The children were delighted to see the handsome young uncle, but there were six of them by that time and they filled Rosalie's house all too snugly. Charlie Picotte was very ill and Marguerite was worried about him but tried to go on with her teaching. Susan was at the Agency most of the time when she was not out among the sick people all around the Reservation. Mary and Madeline Wolfe, the "oldest grandma" (sometimes the "littlest grandma"), who was now nearly 100 years old, were still in Joseph's house. Carey must have stayed with Lucy and Noah most of the time.

He was quite unattached, however, and after years of dormitory rules was ready to do a little roaming. Not that one roamed far on a Reservation, but with few opportunities for any employment and more and more land on lease, there were others like him and he had ample opportunity for companionship. Baseball was one delight and he became renown throughout the area for his performance as catcher. Teams sprang up here and there, representing different neighborhoods and villages and the young Indians could usually find a place on some team. Family stories say that for a time Carey played on one of the better professional baseball teams. Some of his comings and goings disturbed Lucy; she did not approve of all his companions and, knowing he would not listen to her, she wrote to Frank. She asked if he could not find some work for Carey near him where he might be able to watch out for and direct the younger brother.

Frank replied he did not feel he could spend his money on his brother and Carey could look after himself. Carey was just turning twenty and the older brother probably forgot that he, himself, had had little employment until he was several years older. Moreover, the circumstances within the Tribe and in the whole surrounding society had changed since his youth. He had been almost the only one of the young men and boys who could interpret, thanks to his Father's insistence that he became proficient in English. Interpretation had been the thing most needed at that time and he had stood out from the many and attracted the attention of Senator Kirkwood. Naturally Frank did not have the influence to open doors for Carey as Kirkwood had done for him, neither were there as many doors to be opened. Clerical work of all kinds was in great demand, however, and many papers still attest to Carey's excellent handwriting which was always needed. It may have been that Carey had not wanted to stay

East or had not been amenable to earlier suggestions of Frank's. Frank frequently got out of patience if other people did not perform as he had expected. He would be extremely critical and, with little investigation, denounce the action of others.

Under the tribal organization the male relatives most responsible for boys were the mother's brothers. Edward Esau is in the allotment list of 1871 and on the annuity list of 1886. Evidently it was this man who figures frequently in Rosalie's letters as coming for advice, interpretation and letter writing. Letters of J. Owen Dorey identify Edward as Elizabeth Esau's brother but nothing indicates that he entered the picture at this time. If Mary was considered as Carey's mother after his own mother's death, there were no brothers to call on there. Wajapa seemed to fill the place of the close male relative, although it is not clear just what his relationship to Joseph may have been. But Carey lived with Wajapa for months in 1893 and probably part of 1894.

Frank's answer to Lucy's suggestion threw Carey into a temper and he said that since Frank did not care what became of him, he would just stop telling Frank what he was doing or intended to do. In a typically youthful reaction he began to talk of finding a wife—without consulting Frank. The girl he found had tuberculosis; many of her family were ill and they were backward in their general attitudes. Lucy was extremely disturbed and Rosalie wrote to Frank insisting that employment for Carey even at low wages but off the Reservation would be better than his present situation. Apparently Frank made no move.

The whole episode was a turning point and Carey remained, living on the Reservation for the rest of his days. His children and grandchildren grew up in the familiar surroundings, the only members of the La Flesche family living there when the Reservation marked its one hundredth year. After a time Carey was made Assistant Clerk at the Agency and he also qualified as a notary public. His name appears as witness on many items of Agency business. In 1894 he was engaged as assistant teacher at the government school, receiving $15.00 a month with his board and clothes. He was still teaching at the school four years later. In 1904 he served on the Police Force.

Since he worked so long at the school, he made little effort to develop his own allotment but usually leased it. He did, however, become a farmer and had a comfortable home on land that was in his wife's family. He did not marry the girl he first talked about, but in or near 1897 was married to La-da-we, Phoebe Cline. There were three Clines on the list of 1871 and Wah-zhinga, Albert Cline, had built a house in the Make-Believe-White-Man's Village in the 1860's.

Carey and Phoebe became part of the family circle with the Farleys, the Tibbles, Noah and Lucy, the Picottes, and the Diddocks. As long as Rosalie lived, there was much going back and forth for meals, exchanging gifts of food and a great deal of visiting. Frank's Christmas boxes had gifts for everyone, and Rosalie was most liberal and thoughtful of Carey's family.

Lucy and Noah stayed on Noah's land for five years and then rented it to Rosalie. Noah had Lucy's land to care for and was "to farm the old place," which no doubt meant Joseph's. They decided to move nearer the Agency where there was wood for fuel and where, in the brush and timber, they could easily raise hogs. Lucy was happy about the move (Minnie and Philip had also left the Logan Valley). She was sure Noah would make her a nice house and it would be pleasant to see more people.

Noah did build a house, the first of two rather unique houses he built for Lucy. This was a small log house, carefully constructed of well selected logs fitted closely together at the corners and marked by expert workmanship in every detail. One unique feature was the good oak flooring which Lucy kept beautifully polished. There were good windows too where Lucy hung pretty lace curtains—no reason why pretty things could not furnish a house even if the basic material was rough logs.

Years later Noah built a Victorian cottage some distance behind the log house. Its steep gable faces were shingled and there were grill work brackets at the gable points and the corners of the porch posts. The front windows had narrow upper panes of stained glass and every bit of the structure was finely done. The younger members of the family always remembered the whole interior and spoke of Aunt Lucy's good housekeeping. Noah was famous as a carpenter (served as carpenter on the staff at the Agency for a year or two) and a good general mechanic, able to repair and fix over anything one might need around a house and farm.

The hogs did well the first year and they hauled them to Sioux City for sale. The income was evidently less ample a year later when Mrs. Kinney wrote that Noah had not paid the last of his debt to the Women's Indian Association and Ed Farley spoke to the Agent about finding work for Noah. It may be this was the time when Noah was appointed the Agency carpenter.

Lucy, at times, would disagree with others, but her usual kindness weighed heavily against her hasty criticisms. She and Noah depended very much on each other and between them differences became small. When Noah came before the Competency Commission, which was set up to recognize the fact that many Indians could handle their own affairs, he was passed with a high rating and with the remark that he did not use intoxicating liquor.

The move closer to the Agency brought Lucy and Noah closer to the events stemming from the old tribal pattern. They made visits to other reservations for Indian celebrations and special dances and did their share of the traditional gift giving. In 1898 Rosalie wrote that they had "gone by with some Indians" and that Noah had had eleven horses given to him. (Rosalie, always a member of the tribe, concerned with its welfare, nearly always spoke of "the Indians.")

More and more Noah was concerned with public affairs, all the things which affected the people as a whole. After his first experience in going to Hampton he began to carry responsibility. The next summer he escorted a group of new Students to Hampton. His opinions on matters concerning the tribe were carefully thought through and were respected by others. He served with the police and the council; at one time he was a precinct representative at a county political convention. He served on the council within the last ten years of his life, at the same time when Caryl Farley, Joseph's grandson, was a member of that body.

At different times Noah managed from 300 to 400 acres of land.[4] He had a fourth interest in his father's land. For a time he farmed Nicomi's land and Joseph's quarters, besides looking after his own and Lucy's. For many years, as legal guardian for an orphan, Lucy Mitchell, he cared for her land. At last he sold his own allotment and invested the proceeds. In 1907 he had $7,000 loaned at 8 percent interest. After clearing his early debts he took care to avoid others and always paid cash for his supplies. The Agency officials said:

> . . . this man supports his family better than most of his neighbors. He speaks good English, is industrious and a model for other Indians to follow.

He took a step followed by too few of the tribe when in 1916 he asked to withdraw his trust funds held by the government. Although he had been declared competent to manage his own affairs nearly ten years earlier, this required another investigation. The Superintendent (later term for the position formerly called Agent) recommended that the money be turned over to him and Noah drew out his entire balance of $3,348.75. Two years after his death some branch of the Indian Service inquired as to his estate in federal funds and the identity of any heirs. The Superintendent replied that Noah La Flesche had no trust property at the time of his death. In this particular at least, Noah lived in the white man's way.

He had suffered some rebuffs at the hands of bureaucracy. During one of the many recurring waves of alcoholism among the Omaha, Noah wrote to the Commissioner of Indian Affairs through the Superintendent, calling attention to the increase in drunkenness and the absence of any enforcement of the liquor laws in all the neighboring towns:

> . . . the welfare of the Omaha is close to my heart. . . . I am living among them and I know what I am writing about. You are so far away you have to depend on others for knowledge of affairs here. If we had a man who would take the drunken Indian, fine him, put him in jail till he sobered up, drinking would not be so bad. This is going to ruin the Omaha, I ask you to help us . . . we are in great need of help. Help us before another crime is committed.[5]

The local Superintendent sent this letter on to Washington without any letter of his own on the situation. The Assistant Commissioner replied, writing two letters, saying changes were being made in an area-wide plan for law enforcement. The bulk of the first letter,[6] however, was given to reproving the Superintendent for allowing it to appear that this appeal for help had originated with Mr. La Flesche. The Superintendent should have written a letter himself thus indicating that he was aware of the situation and reporting his own opinion on the matter. It would show that the Government was always watchful and the Indians did not need to take any initiative. The closing sentence in the second letter was striking, sounding a note too often in a system of overlapping administration and responsibility—the hope that action from another source would solve one's own problem. "We hope the fact that Iowa went dry the first of the year will benefit."

Lucy's pleasure in pretty things and her joy in an ordered household could not fill her life; she wanted children to love and care for. The old organization of the tribe, particularly within the gens, provided for many people to be responsible for children. In this way children were frequently cared for by others of the large family—by relatives—and relatives included connections by blood, by marriage, by adoption in an interwoven relationship white people seldom understand. In a letter to Alice Fletcher written soon after they were settled in the "Connecticut Cottage" Lucy said:

> Wajapa has given me one of his little girls, she is at the Mission now but will come to live with me just as soon as school closes. ... Wajapa wants me to keep her along and teach her . . . she is such a nice little girl and I like her very much. Badger wants me to keep his little boy, too, but I don't think we can afford to keep him. Badger is expecting his two boys home in the spring.[7]

That year Wajapa had five little girls under twelve and it would seem if parents can ever spare a child, he could have done so at this time.[8] There is no record of which little girl went to Lucy or how long she may have stayed. Ida Mitchell, whose mother had died in 1893, lived with Lucy for several years. Ida and her mother had been at Hampton when the La Flesches were there and Ida was four years old. Minnie Stabler and Lucy both would look after Ida when her mother went to classes.

Carey and Phoebe's family were made up of four girls and two boys, all with La Flesche family names—Elizabeth, Susette, Susan, Abby, Lucy, Frank and Joseph. Elizabeth spent weeks and months at a time in Lucy's home and was certainly "Lucy's little girl." Sixty years later she recalled with pleasure the incidents showing Noah's craftsmanship and Lucy's good housekeeping. She remembered how Noah would return from town or from a longer trip bringing things for Lucy and for her. He especially liked to bring pretty clothes for them and would carefully inquire of the salespeople if these were the latest fashion, for clothes must not only be pretty but must keep Lucy as modishly dressed as any women she might meet in town.

Carey's children all went to the Indian School founded in 1884 at Genoa, Nebraska. It was on the pattern of Hampton but in a different environment and entirely for Indians. Elizabeth always felt Genoa was a good school giving the right kind of training. She remembered her time there with affection and was grateful for the insistence that each student master each department of work. One of the periodic changes in the school system came during Abby's school days and for a time she attended the public school in Walthill.

Phoebe did not speak English when she was married and the language of the household was Omaha. Not until the children began to go to school did Carey talk to them in English. As this continued and the children spoke English to each other, Phoebe learned from them and English was common in the family.

Carey supplemented the education that the children gained in school by what means he had at hand. Frank sent them the *National Geographic Magazine* and, even before the children could read, Carey would gather them about him in the evening showing and explaining the beautiful pictures. Family time was often a time for stories, when Carey could draw on his wider experience as well as repeat the old folk tales of the Omaha.

Elizabeth became a practical nurse of outstanding ability and was most skillful with needle, thread and materials. Well trained at Genoa, she taught sewing at the Ft. Peck Indian School. She was called home from this work in Montana in the winter of 1919 when Uncle Noah became ill. Noah died of "influenza pneumonia"[9] in one of the last waves of the dreadful Spanish flu epidemic that had swept across the country since early autumn. In fact, Elizabeth came to be the one person in the family everyone called on in illness. As she had cared for Noah, four years later she helped Phoebe nurse Lucy for many months. Lucy's suffering was long and drawn out as inflammatory rheumatism disabled her, as it had Rosalie. She died in March 1923 and was buried in the Macy Presbyterian Cemetery.

Frank came home each year for his vacation and after Rosalie's death made his headquarters with Carey, although he spent time with the Farleys as, one by one, Rosalie's children established their own homes. Frank was always close to Caryl and in his later years wrote affectionate letters to Marguerite Farley Conn full of hopes for her children.

Frank's departure for Washington in 1881 marked a sharp division in his life. Only the journey with Standing Bear had served as a transition between the two worlds. For a short time then he had seen large cities and observed men living in ways undreamed of by his associates at home. It was a short interval, however, for in less than ten years after he had been a part of the buffalo hunt, he was a government clerk settled in the atmosphere he had glimpsed so briefly. It must have required great adjustment and could only have been accomplished by a man of superior intelligence.

The immediate family was proud of him; Rosalie's Mary showed her schoolmates a gift from Frank, explaining that it came from her uncle who lived in Washington and was "a relation of the government." Relatives and relationship figured so largely in Omaha society that, no doubt, Mary felt they must be extended to Washington. Joseph had known his children must find new ways to live but he could never imagine how it might come about. Now one of his, his eldest son, had found his way. Since, in the phraseology of the frontier, "cash money" was hard to come by, Frank's $900.00 a year seemed affluence. They hoped he could help the advancement of the tribe and interpret for them the mysterious and inexplicable plans of the Indian Office. It was a pleasant thing to have one of their own in work which concerned their race and its adaptation to a new existence.

But members of the tribe who had opposed Joseph, those whom Frank may have offended and those who were easily drawn under the influence of conniving white men resented this appointment and were positive that he only served as an intriguing spy on their personal affairs. Since he was a copyist for over four years before he received any promotion whatsoever and then served seventeen more years before he reached even the highest rank of "clerk," he can hardly have had much influence in the whole large staff of the Indian Office.

No person in the family has been the subject of as many hearsay stories, as many unfounded and inaccurate statements as has Frank. The jealousy and suspicion of the few thrived on the fact that he had talked very little about the other side of his two-sided existence. One part was pushed aside when he crossed the line into the other. These two lives merged but briefly when, for short periods, he was assigned a government task among the Omaha. In the first years this happened several times for he must have been the best Omaha interpreter in the Bureau and, moreover, he knew the terrain and the people. It would have been strange if the Department had not sent him on duty to the Omaha Reservation.

Frank's letters seldom speak of events in Washington, except as they concerned legislation affecting the Indians. Most of his letters available are those written to Rosalie, to Ed and their children. These are full of the affairs of the tribe and the Farley family, never about things he did or people he met in Washington. A few personal papers found recently and now preserved in the Bureau of American Ethnology give meager clues to his personal life and point to his wide acquaintance and participation in educational, scientific and artistic circles.

Since he was reticent about his own affairs, nieces and nephews never completely knew his personal life and the next generation knew even less. In that most personal of relationships—marriage, Frank was unfortunate, but whether from fault of his own or of others, no one can say. There were a number of women in his life, but in each case the story is blurred and full of contradictions.

In 1877 a Decatur newspaper gave a detailed account of Frank's marriage to a member of the Omaha tribe. A year later Joseph dictated a letter in the Omaha-Ponca dialect which is included in J. Owen Dorsey's study *The Çegeha Language*.[10] He said, "Our Frank was married last year, but she is dead." Did this mean actual physical death or that the wife had been unfaithful and was "dead" to the family? Under tribal custom infidelity was frowned upon, the marriage was considered ended and the husband could punish the wife.

In a letter written by Alice Fletcher in 1890, she said the couple had separated before Frank entered the Indian Service and that he had obtained a divorce as soon as he had been in Nebraska when the District Court was in session. She was not sure of the exact date, but did remember that it was about the time the allotment was completed. The record in the Court House at Dakota City, Nebraska, shows that Frank's petition was presented to the court on November 6, 1883.

Late in 1881, Frank was in Nebraska on government business concerning the Agency and probably stayed at the Mission, as Susette had done when she first returned from the East. Certainly Frank was at the Mission frequently for he paid marked attention to a young lady teacher who openly encouraged him. This annoyed Partch, especially after the young lady fell ill, too ill, she said, to enter the school room, but not to give private lessons to Frank in her room. When Partch remonstrated, she disclaimed any act of impropriety and assumed the attitude of a martyr being dealt with unjustly. She roused the sympathies of other teachers and of Frank until excited charges and countercharges spread to the tribe. Partch was beside himself and went to talk to Joseph. To his amazement he discovered Joseph felt the trouble had largely come from letters Susette had written to members of the Mission Board in the East. These women had hastened to support one side or the other without being fully aware of the situation.

It was equally shocking to Partch that during the time Frank had been on the Reservation he had ignored his wife and child who were nearby. The Indians felt this was an affront and, in Indian fashion, the father-in-law expected gifts from Frank. When no gifts were offered he came to the Mission and took a horse of Frank's and several of his sister's.[11] The Agent judged this to be improper (white men did not act so) and demanded that the horses be returned; naturally the tribe at the same time felt the Agent interfered with the proper adjustment of their affairs. The incident closed to the immense relief of Partch when the teacher resigned and departed and Frank's business was completed and he returned to Washington.

All this took place before Frank filed his petition for divorce which charged infidelity and named two prominent Omaha men as involved. It further charged the wife with having disregarded her marriage vows within a few weeks after they were spoken. The petition adds another point of confusion by giving August 1879 as the date of the marriage instead of July 1877 as reported in the newspaper. If this is the correct date, Joseph's letter of September 1878 might indicate an earlier marriage when a wife had died. Newspapers, however, do not report a wedding, mention the officiating clergyman and give the details of the wedding dinner, two years before it takes place. The difference in the dates can only be credited to the Indian attitude on time and its measurement and the lack of any knowledge of clocks or calendars. Most early dates concerning personal Indian affairs must be accepted as relative. Frank's own birth date is given from 1855 to 1862 in sources generally accepted as reliable.

The infrequency of legal procedures and the shift of records from one place to another, or at times, the change of county seats from one town to another has left several discrepancies in frontier and territorial Nebraska records. In Dakota County the decrees and decisions of the earliest court sessions have been lost. The only explanation seems to be that final divorce papers had all been filed together instead of with the petition in each case—then the file of decrees had been lost.

There is a notation in the file of this divorce case, however, indicating that Frank was granted a divorce on the grounds of infidelity. So considering the nonprophetic nature of the public press and the condition of frontier records, it may be said that Frank was married to Alice Mitchell in 1877 and divorced from her in 1884. Her name is given in the newspaper and in the court proceedings, but the wife in the story at the Mission is not named. Since this incident occurred between these dates, it would be assumed it was the same woman. Being persuaded of her infidelity, Frank probably did not consider the child was surely his and purposely ignored them. The only identity in the missionary story is through her father. The name used is neither the true Omaha name of the earliest records nor the citizen name of later lists, and it does not appear in the few places when both names are used together.

A community of interest and the tie of a shared experience drew together the Omahas who had been East to school and even when they were away for a period of years, they met again on the Reservation. Josephine Barnaby had gone to Hampton in the group with Susan and Marguerite and Carey. She was the "Josie" of Susan's letters. After Hampton, Josie went into nurses training but because of an accident she was forced to give it up. She returned to the Plains and taught in Dakota Territory. One year she had charge of music at Grand River in the Standing Rock Agency. When an epidemic broke out and the hospital lacked both a doctor and a nurse, she walked a considerable distance from Grand River to the Agency where the hospital was located and took charge of the institution, directing what unskilled help she would find.[12] Later she went to the Omaha Agency and assisted Susan. Frank must have seen something of Josie then, for the next summer Rosalie wrote to him saying Josie was to be married to a "young man by the name of von Felden." Late in the spring she told Alice Fletcher that if Frank came home the coming summer, they might see more of him since "now there is a new Mrs. Von Feldon." She went on to say that Frank did not seem heartbroken and, on hearing the news had said, "She must have had a sudden shock of love."

Kirkwood had expected Frank would make bigger contributions than was possible as a clerk; but even that position gave him special assignments which led to his real career as a student and then an authority on the Plains Indians. Because of his intimate knowledge of rites and customs, he was welcomed into scientific groups and into the philanthropic circles where the foremost interest was the welfare of the Indians. He was also thrown into contact with the slowly enlarging group of educated Indians.

It must have been through these groups that he met the woman whom he married and who survived him as his widow, although she was unknown to most of his associates and his family. Rosa Bourassa, half-Chippewa and a graduate of Carlisle, had been in the Indian Service for over ten years. Her mother was a full-blooded Chippewa and her father was half-French and half-Indian, giving her the same blood mixture as Frank, although the stories usually told around Macy and Walthill imply that she was white. Almost anything might have been said, since no one ever met her, and thirty years after Frank's death one of Caryl's sons did not know Frank had ever married. People who did meet her spoke well of her. The *Dispatch* of Columbus, Ohio, on September 17, 1911, said she was "brainy, cultured and quite French in appearance."

Frank and Rosa may have met at Carlisle, or possibly at Haskell Institute in Kansas, for Rosa had been a staff member at both schools. How they met or when they met is unknown. So far no exact date for the marriage has come to light, but it probably was in the latter part of 1906.

There must have been a preliminary time of courtship, at least they had done companionable things together and he had visited in her home. The marriage was of short duration; stories indicate they separated in a day or in a few weeks. In a letter written from Pinconning, Michigan, on November 28, 1906, which begins "Dear Francis" and closes "Your wife, Rose," she said:

> After you left me at the hotel at Bay City I went right to sleep and did not hear your [train]. I am busy . . . [my mother] will visit her father and I will do the work . . . the farm teams were plowing that field we crossed when we hunted ducks. Hope you enjoy your Thanksgiving dinner . . . remember me to your sisters and brother.13

Late the next June (1907), the Bancroft paper printed a dispatch from Washington, D. C.:

> Francis La Flesche a member of the Omaha tribe of Indians is being sued for divorce by his wife, Rosa B., a Chipewa (sic) Indian . . . the trouble started when he [went] to visit a kinsman at the Omaha Agency. The wife was left in Omaha, the husband went to the Indian Agency and later back to Washington, leaving the wife in Omaha.

The exact nature of Rosa's suit is in doubt, but no suit for divorce was filed against Francis La Flesche in that year.14 On April 24, 1908, in the Supreme Court of the District of Columbia, it was "ordered, adjudged and decreed" that the defendant in the case (Frank) shoud pay to the complainant forty dollars each month" and also pay the cost of the proceedings.15 The family at home were under the impression that Rosa had been unfaithful, for at the time Joseph's estate was settled, Susan asked Frank why he did not get a regular divorce since he had legitimate reasons. Others feared the complicated family settlement might be made more intricate if Frank could not sign certain papers which would require his wife's signature. As it turned out, the business was concluded in a way that no such signatures were necessary.

The little that is known about this chapter in Frank's life comes from the public records, the Carlisle personal folders in the National Archives, a few newspaper items and two letters Rosa had written. Frank had saved these letters with all his appointments to office, the patent to his land and the feather which may have been his particular symbol.

On January 1, 1907, Rosa applied for readmission to the Indian Service and listed the positions she had held since graduating from Carlisle, stating that on the date of writing she was married to Francis La Flesche. In 1914 she filled out a form for Carlisle as the school gathered data on their graduates and said that in 1907 she was a "housewife" residing at 214 1st Street S. E., Washington, D. C. The Washington address is that of the duplex apartment jointly occupied by Frank La Flesche and Alice Fletcher and owned by her.

Some implications might be glimpsed through the letters found among his personal belongings long after his death. What route these intimate possessions may have taken after leaving 214 1st Street is not known, but years later they were purchased from a second-hand bookstore in Washington by the Bureau of American Ethnology. The situation raises many conjectures, not the least of which is why Frank saved them for over twenty years. Both letters begin, "My dear Francis" and close, "Your wife, Rosa." The earlier one, from Michigan, has been quoted; the second was written in Washington on May 16, 1907, over a month before the newspaper dispatch concerning a suit for divorce.

This letter said:

> It is necessary for me to ask you for $25.00 to cover the expense of my trip from Chicago. Also . . . that you give me more than $30.00 per month allowance; that does not cover expenses here . . . regarding my re-instatement in the Indian Service . . . required I take Civil Service examination again, since I have been out over a year . . . this, too, is an added expense. Since you would give me no intimation of your wishes where I should stop . . . told me to do as I liked. . . . I went to my friend [here], who take[s] me in until you make other arrangements for me. In view of your desire that I not come to Miss Fletcher's . . . I assume you . . . prefer I do not send there. . . . I ask you to send [to] the above address, my summer hat and the contents of the box in which it was left and my tan voile dress. An early response to the above requests will greatly oblidge (sic).

Rosa returned to the Service; her first assignment was at Chilocco, Oklahoma, as assistant clerk. Later she went to the Crow Agency in Montana after an interval with a mining concern with offices in Long Beach, California. She left the Crow Agency in the fall of 1911 for Columbus, Ohio, to make the preliminary arrangements for the first Congress of American Indians in which active membership was limited to those of Indian blood. Several Omahas attended this meeting and an invitation was passed on to Frank after being sent to Charles Cadman, who had been working with Frank on Omaha music. Cadman asked Frank if he were going to the Congress, adding that he felt it was an excellent start toward a valuable organization. Rosa's name is included in the temporary executive committee. There is nothing to show that Frank responded to Cadman or made any comment, but he saved the invitation.

Rosa became one of the permanent staff of this organization which had headquarters in Washington, where she lived on 1st Street S.E.[16] a few hundred feet from the duplex where Frank resided. Later she returned to the Indian Service. Her brief appearance, through legal counsel, at the time of Frank's death is the last trace that has been found and there is little detail given. Every mention made by other people, however, speaks of her intelligence, her ability and devotion to the Indian cause.

The close association of Frank and Alice Fletcher and their frequent traveling together gave rise to much gossip. It began within the first half dozen years of their acquaintance. Marguerite was still at Hampton and General Armstrong, the Superintendent, had discussed it with her. He said the talk was undermining Miss Fletcher's influence with the Indians and he hoped the La Flesche family might be able to warn Frank and repair what damage had been done. The sensitive Marguerite was crushed and hurt. She wrote home, sorrowing. Maybe Ed could talk to Frank and why should any one say such horrid things about their dear friend who did so much for everyone? Besides, how ridiculous—didn't people realize that Miss Fletcher was an old lady! Alice Fletcher was just turning fifty at the time, but Marguerite, of course, was very little more than twenty and Frank about thirty.

Alice Fletcher became a cripple soon after Frank began to work with her. Many associates spoke of the indomitable spirit which drove her to negotiate even the steep sides of ravines on crutches, but she must still have needed assistance. Frank could supply the young strength to help her, but much more, he was the perfect collaborator for her studies of the Plains Indians. He possessed the needed set of mind, an appreciation of the spiritual message of the Indian rituals and had already determined to preserve what he could of the social customs of his people. Added to this background knowledge, he had the language-key by which they could reach the old men who knew the words of the neglected rites. Besides the difference of nearly twenty years of age, to her he appeared as a younger brother of the woman who had first introduced her to the several tribes of the Plains—Susette—and of the strong, understanding woman who became her close friend—Rosalie. In letters to the sisters Alice Fletcher always spoke of him as "Francis" or as "your brother."

Gossipers paid no attention, as gossipers seldom do, to the stretches of time when Alice Fletcher and Frank worked independently. For some time she continued to live in New York City with weeks and months in Cambridge, Mass., at the Peabody Museum. She spent many months with the Winnegabo while Frank was in Washington, and later she made allotments to the Nez Perces in Idaho. At the request of President Cleveland, she made a survey of education among the Indians which took her all over the country, even to Alaska. For several years before her death, Frank worked in Oklahoma while she was usually in Washington, except for trips to the far Southwest.

In 1890 Mrs. William Thaw of Pittsburg, formerly Mary Copley, made a grant of $30,000 to the Peabody Museum, establishing the Thaw Fellowship to support the ethnological studies of Alice Fletcher. This was the largest gift received by the Peabody up to that time and it carried the stipulation that it was for Alice Fletcher alone. She should continue to receive the income even if she should become incapacitated so that she required assistance or even if she could not work.

The Fellowship called the attention of the scientific world to Alice Fletcher. She was considered the foremost woman scientist of the day, and other women scientists gave a great reception for her at a Washington club, honoring her as a new Fellow of Harvard. It was logical to center her work in the Bureau of American Ethnology which had grown out of the earlier collections of John Wesley Powell and his associates. This was possible although the Fellowship was administered through Harvard. The great work, produced jointly by her and Frank—*The Omaha Tribe*—was published by the Bureau of Ethnology with Alice Fletcher properly identified on the title page as "Holder of the Thaw Fellowship, Peabody Museum, Harvard University." These same women persuaded her to make her permanent home in Washington and in order to overcome any objections she might make, with the assistance of Mrs. Thaw, they bought and gave her a house, the duplex on 1st Street.

Alice Fletcher was quite alone in the world, her nearest relatives were a stepbrother and his children and a few distant cousins. She was fifty-three years old and had not had a settled home of her own for many years. Her dear friend, E. Jane Gay, had attached herself to the summer working parties to be assured that Alice received proper food. But Jane Gay was a government clerk and lived in Washington and Francis La Flesche, her important coworker, lived in Washington, dependent upon a job there and working with her largely on his own time.

The thought of a home must have brought the thought of a family, for when the decision was made on the house, Alice Fletcher went ahead with an action which she may have considered earlier. In the spring of 1891, she drew up a legally worded and witnessed paper saying, "I have adopted Francis La Flesche to be my son" and requested this paper be placed with her will. The story that she adopted Frank thus had good foundation, except for the fact that she lived over thirty years longer, and a paragraph in the will which was probated at her death said, "I have for many years regarded and treated . . . Francis La Flesche as an adopted son and have for him the affection of a mother. I have not, however, formally and legally adopted him as a son for reasons well known to him and to me and which are explained in a paper also enclosed with my will."[17] Frank's statement was that when the final step in adoption was approached, he found he would be required to change his name; as the son of a Chief he preferred to keep the name of La Flesche.

It was only then, after ten years of work on the Omaha study, that in 1891, this three-sided household came into existence with E. Jane Gay supplying most of the furniture. It was a busy household and typically Washingtonian; each member went off each morning to a government office. At night Frank went to the law school at the National University where he was granted the degree of LL.B. in 1892 and the advanced degree of LL.M. the following year.[18] This living arrangement continued for over ten years, the years of the most concentrated study on Omaha customs. Important contributions were made by Frank during his summer vacations which were always spent in Nebraska, for this study was in no way a part of his regular work at the Indian Bureau. Several times Alice Fletcher and Jane Gay accompanied him to Nebraska to Rosalie's intense delight.

It was a delicate task to get the words of the rituals from the old men who had not performed the ceremonies for years. Frank made many visits, frequently sat quietly for hours until it might be proper to speak or the old Omaha would feel moved to recite the sacred songs. Frank had to have a place where the men felt at ease and where they might not be interrupted. At times he and Alice Fletcher went together to Mahawatha's house, knowing they would be alone. Lucy's home was frequently used. It was a part of the Reservation, a part of the tribal life and the men had a feeling of kinship for Lucy because of her father.

From her earliest acquaintance with the Omaha, Alice Fletcher had listened to their music and had been able to record it with sufficient accuracy so that professional musicians could set it down in acceptable musical form. She published, all told, three small books on Omaha music, one of which particularly emphasized the form. John C. Fillmore not only made the final arrangements, but contributed an article on the structure of Omaha music. Material from this book made a whole day's program at the Trans-Mississippi Exposition where Frank spoke and a group of the Omaha participated.[19]

Not only were the words and the music of ceremonies saved for the future, but the many articles used in the rituals were collected and studied. It was typical of the ever-thoughtful Omaha that when they were finally convinced the buffalo hunt and its attendant rites would never return, the older men talked together and decided on how these precious articles of the rituals should be cared for. They decided that each hereditary guardian of a Sacred Tent should maintain his watch and care for his lifetime. But he would not teach the sacred words to any young men; these things could never be a part of the young men's lives. As each Keeper would die, the objects under his care would be buried with him. In this way the old would pass out of existence and the young men would be compelled to build the new.

Joseph and Frank were not entirely in agreement with this idea. Frank wanted to preserve the past for the sake of the message it could pass on to the future. He felt that his people were not understood and was convinced that they had had a social philosophy worthy of preservation. White men could only understand the Omaha if they could understand the finest thoughts from their past. The first step toward saving the early culture came when the chiefs had danced the Calumet Dance for Alice Fletcher and had given her permission to study their rites and ceremonies.[20] Frank was of invaluable assistance in pointing out the old men who knew the ceremonies and he could properly approach these men who had decided literally to bury their past.

Alice Fletcher explained that the Sacred objects could be preserved and studied by white men for years to come, so that they
might understand what the Omaha legends had meant. Joseph was
probably a deciding factor since he was himself of the past. (As an
adopted member of the tribe he held no position of religious duty
toward a Sacred Tent.) Through his influence and Frank's persistent
efforts, and because of the confidence Alice Fletcher inspired, two of
the Sacred Tents of the Omaha and their contents were placed in the
Peabody Museum: the Sacred Tent of War in 1884 and the Tent of
the Sacred Pole in 1888.[21]

Alice Fletcher told the story of the Sacred Tent of War in a
letter to Fredric W. Putnam, Director of the Peabody Museum,
written June 6, 1884:

> It is with particular pleasure I commit for preservation . . . the
> entire belongings of the Sacred Tent of War of the Omaha Tribe.
> The articles are yielded to you by the descendents of the heredi-
> tary head chief of the tribe in whose custody they belonged. The
> relics and the presentation is made in behalf of the family by Mr.
> Francis La Flesche and myself. . . . The Sacred Tent of War was
> vital to the autonomy of the tribe. Without it citizenship was
> impossible; it gave rank to the tribe among other tribes and
> caused the Omahas to be feared by their enemies and consulted
> by their friends. The act by the keepers of the ancient symbols is
> without parallel and was done with a sober appreciation that a
> new era is upon the people wherein these objects have no
> place . . . this marks the Omaha tribe as possessed of men having
> an extra-ordinary degree of mind and character . . . the articles
> have a significance of courage. . .
>   Today Ma-hin-thin-ga . . . put his sacred charge into the
> keeping of the Museum. . . . "These . . . have been in my family
> for many generations, no one knows how long. My sons have
> chosen a different path from that trodden by their fathers." . .
>   It was late in the afternoon when we had reached his Lodge,
> the sun had set . . . he was alone . . . in the fading light, taking a
> last look at the ancient belongings . . . he lifted them into the
> wagon and said "They are all there" and turned away. We, too,
> turned and left as the round moon rose over the valley.[22]

Several years later Frank pointed out to Miss Fletcher a tent
carefully erected near a small frame house. Everything about was
clean and orderly, for within was the Sacred Pole of the Tribe. The
Keeper, Yellow Smoke, was not at home but his wife took them to
the door of the tent. The revered Pole, called the Venerable Man,
stood aslant in its proper position just as Frank remembered he had
seen it on a hunt when he had been a small boy.[23]

They stood respectfully in the doorway as Yellow Smoke's wife
said the Pole was now completely neglected. Only when it rained she

would come and close the door. Frank made several widely spaced, diplomatic visits on Yellow Smoke before the aged man allowed him to take the Pole and the objects related to it. More visits were necessary before Yellow Smoke went to Joseph's and gave Alice Fletcher and Frank the song and the words of the ritual.[24]

It was a brave act, for Yellow Smoke was one of the older men. But he had been able to adopt new ideas more quickly and hold to them more tenaciously than many who were younger. He had signed the treaty in 1854, then later he became an earnest Christian and a leader in the Blackbird Hills Church. He was famous as a speaker and had often on the spur of the moment swung the decision of a Council by his oratory. His acceptance of the new was intermingled with the long-seated habits of the old life. On a trip to Washington, he had been given a tall silk hat which he always kept to wear to church. With all dignity he would enter the building with his blanket correctly held around him and the shining hat on his head.[25]

There still remained the Sacred Buffalo Hide and its Tent to complete the ritualistic history of the Omaha. But the Keeper of the Hide was extremely old and the only one who knew the ceremonies. At first he would say nothing because there were still others who were involved in the rites and it would not be true to them. Frank waited, fairly certain of whom the old man spoke. Time and death took their toll, and when Frank went again the old Keeper admitted he would no longer violate any rule or bring harm to anyone if he gave the songs. So he sang and Frank said, ". . . watching him . . . was like watching the last embers of the religious rites of a vanishing people."[26] The old man begged to keep the White Buffalo Hide near him for a few more months, it was all he had of the old life. He would give it to Frank the next spring; then the Hide could go and be with the Pole.

In midwinter, while the old Keeper was at the Agency one day, the Sacred White Buffalo Hide was stolen from its Tent. The old man was grief-stricken. During the final preparation for the exhibits at the Omaha Fair, Frank was searching for the Hide. Alice Fletcher notified all other Museums to be alert if it might be offered for sale. Within a few days a number of the tribe were in Omaha for a trial. Rumors were circulated that "someone" had told "some of them" to appear at a certain building the next day and they could receive the Hide. But the trial continued, all the men were held in the court room and no one kept the appointment. The wife of one of these men told Rosalie that her husband did not know the person who talked to them or where the building was to which they should go. Another rumor said that "Jul. Meyer" had offered to pay the expenses of one man to come to Omaha and help him track the Hide. Meyer was a white man who had associated with the Indians over an extended period, had at times served as an interpreter and ran a curio and photographic shop in Omaha.

Mary was drawn into the affair by making a few visits here and there in the hope she might pick up any clues to the theft. At last Frank found the Hide had been sold to a man in Chicago, and he even learned the name of the thief. Every effort made to buy it back was rebuffed and later it was deposited in the Academy of Sciences in Lincoln Park in Chicago.[27] The old Keeper mourned over his own delay in handing the sacred symbol to Frank who understood its religious meaning and thus allowing it to fall into the hands of someone who only wanted to get money for it. The contrast between the spirit of lofty resignation in which Ma-hin-thin-ga (No Knife) and Shu-da-naci (Yellow Smoke) had surrendered their sacred objects and the mercenary desire of some tribal member is one mark of the changes which occurred between 1883 and 1898.

From his first efforts to preserve the Omaha lore, Frank tried to write it in stories or short sketches. In this way he did preserve some things which might have escaped him, but he realized his accomplishments would not attract and hold the attention of the persons he wanted to inform. There was widespread interest in the Indians, and editors were eager for such material but most of them assumed any story about Indians should follow the ideas they held, while Frank tried hard to keep to his own experience. His earliest efforts were talks at scientific meetings, and Alice Fletcher rigorously coached him and edited his writing. As the program on Omaha music was planned for the Exposition, she wrote to Rosalie:

> Prof. Fillmore will come from California, [give] a paper and I shall have one and your brother will give one on "Songs of War and Peace." He thinks I am very hard [in] this hard work of writing but I desire him to be honored in the matter and be ranked high.

The demand for excellence from her pupil was an integral part of her own nature. Thoroughness was a basic element in any task she undertook. At the memorial service after her death, Charles F. Lummis who had known her through the School of American Research in Santa Fe, said:

... some have greater genius, but genius is not always Power ... and Knowledge always is ... she knew to the roots whatsoever she attempted to write about. This Power-by-Knowing was mated with serene ... vision untinged by self-concern; her knowledge adjusted her judgement, her judgement adjudicated her knowledge."28

Frank had several stories published in newspapers and magazines, most of which were of small circulation or short publishing life and are difficult to trace. He thought of getting together a book of stories and sketches, collecting those that were published and adding others. A few publishers evidenced mild interest but made exact demands before seeing the stories. They had preconceived ideas about Indians and would not accept a different approach. One requested that the stories be told with humor on the order of Uncle Remus. Another one thought such a book would fit into a series for boys, one title of which was "Cattle Ranch to College."29

By late 1899, he had ready a manuscript of book length about his own school days at the old Omaha Mission. At first this met with a cool reception. It did not correspond to the publishers' ideas about Indians. Frank wanted to show that small Indian boys were like all small boys, but one publisher rejected it saying, "... this shows too little difference from *any* boy." Another said, "... wish you would undertake something showing the actual life of the Indian in his wilder state." The manuscript was, of course, a most exact account of the actual life near the old Mission in the time when the Omaha were still going out on the hunt. It was as "wild" a state as had existed at the time. No wonder the educated Indians had trouble associating with white people when those who influenced the reading of the country did not admit there could be anything but "wild Indians."

Finally Alice Fletcher sent the manuscript to Bliss Carman who was on the board of the publishing house of Small and Maynard in Boston. Carman had a better comprehension of the Indians' position and he knew good writing when he saw it. He sent the manuscript to Small and Maynard with his recommendation and wrote to Alice Fletcher:

I should like to congratulate Mr. La Flesche ... for having gained so strong a hold on our difficult English speech. His sense of proportion and dramatic values is excellent, he knows when to stop and what to omit.... I would have liked more on the Indian people, his parents etc.... The current vulgar notion of [the Indian] ... is enough to make angels weep.

The publishers promptly accepted it with a few suggestions. The most important item was that Alice Fletcher should write an introduction explaining the Omaha tribe. It was desirable to use a recognized name in presenting a new writer and apparently the company hesitated to let the book—and Frank—stand on their own. It was part of her system of training that Alice Fletcher refused to do this. Frank wrote a preface that still stands as one of the best statements of the Omaha situation in the late 1860's and includes interesting points on the changes in names and customs.

Herbert Small caught Frank's purpose and heartily approved of the dedication, "To the Universal Boy," for he said, ". . . the chief charm is not that the Indian boy is different but is so like the white boy. The average reader will come to the book unconsciously influenced by ideas of Indians." Small wished to have one good picture to illustrate the book and fortunately he gave the assignment to Angel DeCora, a Winnebago Indian who was teaching at Drexel Institute. She had been to a similar school herself and then on to Hampton, and congratulated Frank on the realism of his story. Her picture, used as a frontispiece in the first edition, showed a school boy in the school uniform trying to comfort a weeping little new boy. The younger lad had been brought to school in his best clothes, long trousers and a long jacket-like shirt of deer skin.

The book was published in August of 1900 and Frank received his first royalty check in February of 1901, with an accompanying letter saying it was hoped he was not too disappointed, the publishers believed the book would "gradually win its way." An order for 250 copies from the Wisconsin State Library was encouraging and there were many complimentary comments in different magazines. Frank made a scrap book of the notices and they ranged across the country coming from most of the good periodicals. He also saved a little sketch about himself from *The Land of Sunshine,* a magazine published in Los Angeles by Charles Lummis, who had come to know Frank and Alice Fletcher well, and it may be assumed that the facts in this sketch are correct.

Personal letters expressing pleasure and approval gave Frank a sense of achievement. Pratt wrote from Carlisle expressing his great interest and the idea that Carlisle might help in the sale. He suggested it would be a help to the Carlisle boys if Frank would write a book about the Indian, away from the school and quite by himself in white society. George Bird Grinnell spoke of it as an admirable book in its simplicity and its fidelity to nature.:

... the portrayal of Indian thought and action make the volume most useful . . . which will convince the reader that Indians are just like other people and share the same feelings that other human beings have. . . . One such book . . . will do more to convey a just idea of Indian Character . . . than a thousand ethnological books, telling about habits and customs.30

Frederic Putnam of the Peabody Museum was "delighted"; John Webster of Omaha sent his congratulations as did Richard Sylvester from "Headquarters Police" in Washington, D. C.

It was a heady draft to Frank and he tried to help the sale as he could. He wrote to Caryl to inquire at the book stores in Lincoln to see if they had the book, perhaps persuade them to stock it. He wrote to Ed asking if anything was being done about preserving the old Mission building. He felt that if his book continued to increase in sale it would arouse an interest in the area and people would want to come and see where the school had been. Poor Ed, with his own household still in a chaotic condition, hardly had time for a crusade to save the Mission.

The book might have had a greater sale and brought better returns to Frank if Small and Maynard had not failed in business in 1902. After bankruptcy proceedings Frank received a pro rata share of the assets in place of the full amount due him. There was a later reorganization and the book was still sold through February 1913, according to the Royalty Statement among Frank's papers. The total payments to Frank came to less than three hundred dollars in thirteen years. Those persons back home who felt he was wealthy could have been assured he did not become so on the proceeds of his book.

The reorganized Small and Maynard Company suggested a combined effort with a firm which only handled school books. This meant a cheaper edition but with prospects of a much larger sale. Frank felt it was placing the book in a category of lower value, and he would not agree. It meant that he would receive 6 percent instead of 10 percent royalty with the book at a much lower price. The fact of less income was not the deciding factor (in two years he had received only $42.33); "school edition" did not sound fitting to him. The publishers assured him they would not drop the trade edition and that they had had school editions which sold as many as 2,500 copies-in one state. They did add that if he could not agree to this, "we might not take much interest in gaining a wider audience."

Frank missed an opportunity to speak his message on the Universal Boy and to exert the influence that Pratt and Grinell had wished from the book. Did he only visualize the poorly printed, worn and tattered books used in the Mission School and feel that his book must never be like that? For all his attainment and the broad education which he eventually acquired, he had had only one limited and brief experience of school as a child. Small and Maynard did not drop the trade edition but must not have pushed the book because in a few years it was out of print. Fortunately it returned in a paperback edition more than sixty years after its first appearance, *The Middle Five: Indian Schoolboys of the Omaha Tribe*, still addressed to the Universal Boy.[31]

In the space of a few years many changes came. At home the family was changed with Susette and Rosalie gone and the children growing up. Frank always was intensely interested in Caryl's education and when Caryl returned to the University the fall after his mother's death Frank began to write to him about getting a degree there and then planning on graduate work. He talked to Caryl more about the things he did and saw, the beauty of Lake Mohonk, where the annual conference on Indians was held, the color and excitement of Inauguration Day in Washington, the advantages of living in a city and learning city ways.

Caryl did not get a degree[32] but with his Father and Jack continued in stock business and built up the real estate firm known as Farley Brothers. At one time they had an office in Walthill under Fletcher, one in Sioux City under Caryl, one in Rapid City, South Dakota, under Louis—with Jack and Ed managing things from Bancroft. Caryl was married in 1905 to Jennie Butcher, a trained nurse who had come to care for the younger Ed Farley, the nephew, after an accident. Frank and Jennie were most congenial and Caryl's home became one more welcoming spot for Frank on vacations.

Vacations were a round of family visits in the year after the Omaha study was finished, a high point in his routine. The prairies and his own people were always calling to him through his enjoyment of the city, its formality and glamour. One year he wrote to Ed:

> I'm getting bleached out again, but I get homesick. . . . I enjoy the hunting very much. Get a good pup and train him well. . . . I may come next year. I shall send a gun home but I will not give it to Father, but let him keep it so you could use it too when you want it. I am afraid he might let Tibb have it.

On vacation Frank entered fully into the life of the family and of the Reservation, leaving the other half of his life far away. He visited Caryl's city home and enjoyed playing cards with Jennie. The children would say, "Now, get out the cards, Uncle Frank's coming!" He would visit in Walthill with Marguerite and Susan whose homes had acquired a sophisticated tone, taking part in an evening musical or attending a number of the lecture series and visited on the Reservation with Lucy and Carey. He liked to be home at the time of the Fair or the Pow wow.

In 1918 the Pow wow was an amalgamation of Omaha ways and the current demands of white society—of all society—across the nation. The Indian custom of gift giving, of honoring individuals or groups, with special attention given to guests, was made modern by becoming fund raising for the American Red Cross. Articles of all sorts were donated; livestock, fancy work and garments. These were handled by a committee headed by Noah. They selected Silas Wood as the auctioneer and the sale brought almost $1,700.

> Caryl Farley bought a silk quilt for $15.00 Jack Farley bought two geese for $6.00. Many presents were given to the Osage visitors by the Omaha. Henry Red Eagle, an Osage, presented Francis La Flesche $10.00 to do what he wished. Frank turned it to Thos. McCauley for the Red Cross. Frank La Flesche also gave $20.00. In lieu of the old Indian custom of taking a tobacco offering to a friendly tribe, the Osage of Oklahoma sent cash of $60.00, which was put into the hands of Harry Lyon, who proposed the tribe give this to the Red Cross. All Omahas consented.[33]

There could have been no more appropriate meeting of persons and events to dramatize Omaha history and the changes since the Treaty. Here Francis La Flesche, the son of Chief Instamaza, Iron Eye, and his nephews, Caryl and Jack, grandsons of Iron Eye who definitely lived twentieth century lives, took part in this custom of Iron Eye's forefathers. Silas Wood was the son of Gahige,[34] one of the signers of the treaty. He had been in the Mission School when Frank's older brother Louis had been enrolled; he served in the Union cavalry in 1865 and 1866; had been interpreter at the conspiracy suit brought by Rosalie in 1892. Here he played the leading part in a white men's device, the auction, for a white men's organization, the Red Cross, taking place at an Indian event, the Pow-wow, made up of the ancient dances.

Participation in Reservation events was not always so pleasant for Frank. In August of 1890 he attended a Sunday School picnic and was unexpectedly called upon to make a speech. Not having thought of such a possibility, Frank spoke extemporaneously on the matter of temperance since he felt the persons present would appreciate the urgency of the matter and possibly be the ones to exert the right influence on the tribe. He returned to Washington unaware that anything had been built up from his speech.

A disgruntled lay-worker in one of the outlying centers of the Presbyterian Church distorted the meaning of the speech to be slander against all white men and wrote heatedly to the Commissioner of Indian Affairs. He said that Frank had not only slandered the white race but that for years he had robbed the Omaha of money due them, and he had worked in collusion with government officers and members of the tribe to bring about his own advancement and the downfall of others.

The Commissioner forwarded this letter to the Agent at the Winnebago and Omaha Agency asking that he make a complete investigation. The investigation added many, many pages to the files of the Indian Office. The Agent, Robert Ashley, did a thorough job, completely clearing Frank and turning up statements as to the unreliability and easy-trigger temper of the accuser. Several persons who heard the talk had found nothing wrong in it; the accuser himself had not even been present to hear the speech. As for the other charges, persons near at hand refuted them. Basically the accuser was poorly informed, since he included situations and used phrases typical of the white man's frontier which did not apply to the Indians.

It would all seem like a high hurricane in a small teapot except that the man must have talked as well as written and his accusations may have been the basis for sneering stories still told around the neighboring towns.

Turning from the long study of the Omaha, Frank gave his attention to the Osage, a cognate tribe of the Omaha, by 1900 located in Oklahoma. In 1910 he was temporarily transferred from the Office of Indian Affairs to the Bureau of American Ethnology and was sent to Pawhuska, Oklahoma, with an added allowance for field work. This temporary arrangement was repeated a number of times and at last made permanent in 1920. The new rank was "Ethnologist," a vastly different category from the "copyist" of 1881; a long wait before the "more important work" foreseen by Kirkwood was recognized as having the first claim on Frank's time. In the Osage study he was on his own, not associated with Alice Fletcher.

She was making studies of other tribes and was one of the incorporators of the School of American Research associated with the Museum of New Mexico in Santa Fe. She served on the board of managers and exerted every effort to advance scholarly study at this institution. In the courtyard of the old Governor's Palace where the Museum is located there is a bronze tablet expressing in her words the essence of her life's endeavors:

> Living with my Indian friends, I found I was a stranger in my native land. As time went on, the outward aspect of nature remained the same, but a change was wrought in me. I learned to hear the echoes of a time when every living thing, even the sky, had a voice. That voice devoutly heard by the ancient people of America, I desired to make audible to others.

She, herself, made no exhaustive study of any tribe in the southwestern part of the United States, but she felt Santa Fe was an excellent location for a study center since it was surrounded by tribes whose culture had been less disturbed by white settlement than in other parts of the country. She determined to make as large a contribution as she could. She was greatly indebted to an institution's support made possible by a private philanthropist; such a boon she would pass on to others.

Therefore, her will drawn in 1919 provided for a trust made up of the largest part of her estate. The income from the trust was to go to Francis La Flesche during his lifetime and then the body of the trust would be delivered to the School of American Research "to establish a Fellowship in my memory and to bear my name."[35]

Before Alice Fletcher had made the long detailed study of the Omaha she had published in the Twenty-second Annual Report of the Bureau of American Ethnology a fine study of the Hako Ceremony of the Pawnee Tribe. This ceremony, considered a fundamental expression of Indian philosophy, was found in slightly varying forms among the tribes whose hunting grounds had been in the Plains. Traditions said it had come into being during a great council to promote peace among the Arikara, Cheyenne, Omaha, Ponca, Iowa and Otoe tribes. This had been in the far distant days recounted in the Omaha Sacred Legend. It is accepted historically since similar ceremonies, with the same theme, have been found in these tribes, only modified slightly by the subsequent experience of the different peoples. Alice Fletcher's work on the Hako attracted a great deal of attention from ethnologists, philosophers and students of religion.

Frank began his study of the Osage with a volume of that tribe's rituals and ceremonies which again showed fundamental likenesses in thought and symbolism to the Hako. The rite was called the

Wa-wan by the Omaha. With this volume Frank took his place as an authority on Indian mythology. Besides recognition, it brought a wider audience, many honors, many invitations to write and to speak, interesting scholarly friendships and opportunities to share in the expression of the several arts.

He was elected to membership in the Washington Academy of Science open only to those who had made noteworthy scientific contributions. Later he was made a vice-president of the Academy, representing the American Anthropological Society to which he had belonged since 1886. He was officially appointed to represent the Bureau of Ethnology at the Nebraska State Historical Society in January 1912. This was most acceptable as an honor but also meant an extra trip home beside the usual summer vacation. He made the trip from Oklahoma and was able to spend a short time on the Reservation and listen to the tribe's problems. At the Historical meeting he made the principal address one evening but was requested to speak briefly at each meeting since different people would be present. On another day he addressed a convocation for the University students and attended a banquet in the evening. In the same year he was elected as vice-president of the American Anthropological Association.

In 1926 the University of Nebraska conferred on him the honorary degree of Doctor of Letters.[36] He was rather overcome by this and wrote to Carey's family, in the Indian fashion, saying the University would "make a feast for him." Naturally Omaha society had not conferred college degrees but had shown honor and homage to their great men by making feasts. Frank was escorted in the Commencement procession by Prof. Paul H. Grumann, Director of the School of Fine Arts, and was formally presented to the Chancellor for the degree by the ranking dean, Dr. Lucius A. Sherman. Chancellor Edgar A. Burnett had said that the University honored a man who was born to the chieftainship but who had acquired scholarship and distinction and in so doing the University itself was honored. At a luncheon following Commencement Frank was asked to make a talk, possibly in reminiscence of his boyhood. He showed his sense of fitness by being brief, saying that as a lad he had planned to be a great buffalo hunter but the white people came and ate up the buffalo, so he turned to writing and was with the Bureau of Ethnology; then he added gracefully that on the whole he was glad the whites had driven out the buffalo or the present agreeable occasion would not have come to be.

He was beseiged by collectors of Indian artifacts asking him to buy, asking if he had anything to sell, or urging him to visit their collections and pass on their value or authenticity. Frequently he was approached to establish the truth of fantastic or misinterpreted frontier tales or to criticize a paper or a speech. This took a great deal of time, and from the letters still among his papers in the Smithsonian he must have given careful attention to each request. Any scientist or student whose labors took him near the Omaha Reservation wrote to him first; many also wrote cordial letters after their visit, often mentioning they had met Carey. In 1910 one noted that the Fair put on by the tribe had been an excellent one and that Carey had been one of the officers.

One outcome of the Historical Society meeting in 1912 may have been Frank's introduction to Hartley Burr Alexander, head of the Philosophy Department at the University. Alexander was intensely interested in the history of his native state but even more interested in the culture of the Indians. He studied and wrote widely on Indian ceremonials and the poetry and philosophy of Indian thought. A poet himself, he embodied the high emotion of Indian songs and ceremonies into literary form in poems, stories and drama as well as writing and lecturing on Indian myths.

He had taken the theme of the Hako ceremony and written a pageant, "The Mystery of Life," which for years had impressive performances by amateur groups. In 1913 he wrote to Alice Fletcher saying he hoped she did not feel he had borrowed too heavily from her work on the Hako, for he felt her study was "a veritable inspiration, especially as reflecting the spirit of my own native prairies." He was delighted with Frank's article, "The Symbolic Man of the Osage," in *Art and Archeology*. It presented ideas he wished to use in work he was doing on "Primitive Worship" for Hasting's *Encyclopedia of Religion and Ethics.*

On his part Frank said he had kept Alexander's *Mythology of North America* close at hand for years. The man who as a child had known the seminomadic life of the tribe and who had had but a hit-and-miss education and the man who was the product of and a part of the scholarly life, found much in common. They had a steady exchange of ideas and Frank met Alexander quite on his level, discussing the philosopher's term "psycho-eideism" at some length and urging him to "give critical thought to the use of the word 'primitive.'"[37]

From 1915 to 1917 the University of Nebraska and the Lincoln

Commercial Club presented annual pageants in celebration of the State's semicentennial in 1917. Hartley B. Alexander wrote the words for all of these productions; the music for the first and third pageants was by Howard I. Kirkpatrick, for the second by Henry P. Eames, both of the School of Music. Each of these three productions used Indian themes, and a portion of the music was based on Omaha songs. The second pageant, in 1916, symbolically indicated the location of the future city of Omaha. As an introduction, Alexander devoted the first half to an Omaha ritual on the search for peace and unity among the people. He drew heavily on the He'dewachi ceremony of the Sacred Tree which according to the Sacred Legend had existed before the rites and the social structure surrounding the Sacred Pole. Acknowledgement was made to *The Omaha Tribe* and no doubt Frank served at times as a consultant. He was a special guest at the first pageant in 1915. The music of this second pageant was used off and on for years and was called "The Sacred Tree of the Omaha" although some themes from other tribes had been included.

Shortly after this the State of Nebraska began planning for a new capital building, with Bertram G. Goodhue of New York as architect. The building was to be symbolic in its very form. A low structure as a broad base would represent the great sweep of the prairies; within the square were wings forming a cross pointing to the four points of the compass, quite in keeping with Indian feeling for the directions. The decorations throughout were to illustrate the History of Western Man, Law as the Basis of Democratic Government and the Heritage from the Indians. Hartley Alexander was asked to help plan this symbolism and to select the several inscriptions to be carved on the walls. He wrote to Frank:

> Goodhue plans a high portal and two wings bearing buffaloes, conventionalized . . . inscriptions can be cut upon their bodies. I'd think it fine to have Indian sayings on these. Can you find bits of political or social wisdom if possible from the Omaha or other Nebraska tribes . . . that would be appropriate?

Frank could not suggest anything suitable from the Omaha. His memories were of axiom-like sayings by which the elders taught thrift, obedience and thoughtfulness to the children, nothing which applied to the larger group. Alexander then chose passages from the rituals of the Pawnee, Sioux and the Navaho. On the inner panels of the wings flanking the great front stairway he placed the name of the tribes that had lived or hunted in Nebraska: Omaha, Otoe, Pawnee, Arapahoe, Kiowa, Sioux, Cheyenne, Winnebago, Ponca and Arikara.

Frank had an impressive idea for placing the history of the Indians within the setting in order to include them in the whole story. He suggested a statue of several Indian hunters placed on a broad pedestal, on which should be carved the dates when the Omaha, the Ponca, and the Otoe had had their last buffalo hunts. This would mark the end of the Indian Society, the forerunner of the society which would produce and use the monumental building. But this meant a separate and detached work of art and was entirely outside Alexander's assignment. Frank felt the Indians themselves would contribute largely to such an object, but he added, "Their money is so tied up that they are not free to give what they might feel able to do." Since, as Susan had found, they could not get their own money for medical care, it might be quite difficult to use it for a work of art.

After the appearance of Alice Fletcher's book of Omaha Songs, the programs at the Exposition and the work of one or two other ethnologists, there was increased interest in Indian themes for music, poetry and drama. Both Marguerite and Frank were often asked to criticise and edit scripts written by white people.

Frequently the authors drew heavily on their own imagination instead of keeping to the basic ideas of the Indians. Melvin Gilmore advised Marguerite not to collaborate with or in any way encourage a "Mrs. B" in writing a pagent since he found the woman persisted in using the term "princess" which the Indians felt was entirely incorrect, since Indian social structure contained nothing similar to the European aristocracy by birth.

The Reverend William N. Guthrie, Rector of St. Marks in-the-Bouwerie in New York City, dedicated one Sunday each spring as Indian Day. He regularly communicated with Frank for he said, "I wish to avoid exhibitionism but bring out the best." In 1922 Indian Day at St. Marks fell on May 25th and consisted of a long devotional service compiled from "American Aboriginal Rites and Ceremonies."

This service followed the traditional form of Christian ritualistic worship, from Voluntary and Exhortation to the Benediction; the only exclusively Christian element was the Doxology sung before the Benediction. The hymns and an anthem were entirely from Indian themes, for the most part written by Alice Fletcher and Hartley B. Alexander. A period of Silent Prayer was closed by Indian prayers. A ritualistic responsive reading was from the "Immediate Revelation" in the Hako. The congregation joined the minister in a responsive reading taken from the Omaha Ritual of "The Child Introduced to the Great World at Birth." After the closing hymn (from the Hako rendered into English by Alexander) both Alice Fletcher and Frank gave talks concerning Indian ceremonies.

Frank worked steadily at writing, striving to get the thoughts of his forefathers into beautiful English words, to devise some form through which the aspirations and the tragedies of their lives could be made clear to others. Until then the greatest outlet for Indian themes had been in music, usually in short songs. Occasionally songs were used in pageants but neither Frank nor Alice Fletcher were pleased with most of the production, and the Indian portion was often only one scene or a short prelude to dramatic presentation of the white man's deeds.

The earliest years of the twentieth century brought what one magazine spoke of as "an epidemic" of Indian music. Different schools of thought arose over whether a new scale must be developed or whether the Indian music must be adapted (some said it was forced) to the orthodox musical scale. While Arthur Farwell and Edward MacDowell were becoming recognized for their Indian music, a still younger composer was coming into the musical picture. In 1907, Charles Wakefield Cadman of Pittsburg asked Alice Fletcher for permission to use certain themes from her book of Omaha songs. He had four songs ready to be published and he had tried to keep to the Indian themes and deviate as little as possible.

He had difficulty finding a publisher but at last these "Four Indian Songs" were published by White, Smith and Company of Boston, and were dedicated to Alice Fletcher. A few scholars felt they were acceptable songs but not truly Indian. Nevertheless, they represented Indian music to a large section of the public for several decades. These four were: "Land of the Sky Blue Waters," "Far Off I Hear a Lover's Flute," "The Moon Drops Low," and "While Dawn is Stealing." All but the last were based on Omaha songs.

Cadman came into great popular demand and gave lecture-recitals across the country, talking about Indian music, playing his own compositions and accompanying a vocalist who sang the songs. He was always beseiged by journalists begging for interviews. Alice Fletcher and Frank protested a number of times on statements ascribed to him on Indian customs and research. Once Frank became very indignant when it appeared Cadman took entire credit for dis-covering and recording certain music. Frank wrote a scathing letter, dropping from his usual "Dear Charles" and "As ever, Frank" to a formal "My Dear Mr. Cadman" and "Yours very truly, Francis La

Flesche." Cadman replied with "'My dear Mr. Cadman,' indeed!" and went on to explain the questioning of the reporter and to insist that he had given the right information but it had been written up in a different way, giving a different meaning.

Whatever breach there may have been, it was quickly healed and together these two men conceived the idea of an Indian grand opera. Cadman would have the opportunity to use a wider variety of music and Frank would have a form through which he could express the poetry, the drama and the high tragedy of his people.

The project developed by leaps and bounds, and a third collaborator was required,[38] since Frank's written words must conform in meter and accent to the music. Mrs. Nelle Richmond Eberhart, a poet and experienced writer, was given this difficult task. She rearranged Frank's work in some of its larger pattern for, she insisted, it must be true to the traditional form of grand opera. The villain must perish (he always did), and the only question was the method by which this was brought about; things might not be true to life "But operas never are." At times Frank was confused, wondering if he could meet all demands and maintain the Indian aspect of the work.

The libretto and the score of "Da-o-ma: an Opera in Three Acts" was offered to White, Smith and Company in 1912. The company was doing very well with Cadman's songs, but an opera was a different matter. Victor Herbert had produced an Indian opera, "Natoma," the year before; it and one or two other similar attempts had been "semi- to rank failures" and White and Smith preferred not to take the risk.

Cadman spent ten years going from one publisher to another, offering the work to the Metropolitan Opera and to Boston's and Chicago's opera companies with no success, but always urging Frank to be hopeful. By 1920 he and Mrs. Eberhart talked of rewriting, but Frank, deep in his work on the Osage, did not wish to undertake revision.

In 1922, unexpectedly, Edouard Albion, representing the National Opera Association, asked to see the score of "Da-o-ma" and talked of producing it in Baltimore. Frank, with renewed hope, asked Mrs. Eberhart to at least send the libretto and the piano score, since at the moment Cadman was away and could not send the complete score. To Frank's amazement, instead of the title page reading "Libretto by Nelle Richmond Eberhart and Francis La Flesche," it was "Da-o-ma: the Land of Misty Waters; Libretto by Nelle Richmond Eberhart after a story by Franics La Flesche."

Frank was angry and expressed his anger with considerable heat. Apparently Mrs. Eberhart appeased him for on August 4, 1922, Frank wrote again to her saying, ". . . now we understand concerning the libretto we can pull together . . . and discuss terms." He added that both Mr. and Mrs. Albion had liked the title "Da-o-ma."

However, Cadman's listing in *Who's Who in America: 1914-1915* included among his compositions "The Land of Misty Waters (Indian grand opera)." Apparently he, as well as Mrs. Eberhart, wished to drop the Indian name. It might seem this inclusion of the opera in this biographical sketch means it had been published, although nothing in the correspondence available would indicate this. It had not been produced before 1922 and as far as can be ascertained it was never produced. A typescript copy of the libretto is in the Fletcher-La Flesche-Cadman Papers at the Nebraska State Historical Society.

After 1900 both Frank and Alice Fletcher traveled a great deal but with headquarters still in the duplex in the block next to the Congressional Library. E. Jane Gay had left to spend her last days with members of her family in England. She left the furniture, though, and it continued to add charming background to the delightful dinner parties given at 214 1st Street. After Miss Gay left there were short periods when some other woman friend took her place, but on the whole the gentle crippled scholar and the son of the tipi and the earth lodge were alone until she died in 1923.

Letters indicate the understanding companionship and affection which existed between them; one might say like that of a settled married couple and yet also like a mother and son entirely alone, or the relationship between a teacher and beloved pupil. As fond as she was of him, her position as teacher was always evident. She taught him and groomed him and changed him from an awkward, untutored Indian boy, dressed in ill-fitting clothes, uneasy in many situations (but showing it very little) into a polished, educated man of the twentieth century, well groomed, poised, an able writer, a gracious host and effective speaker who moved at ease in the best circles of cultured and educated people.

For his part Frank always spoke with a note of deference, almost of reverence: "It was fortunate for me that I became associated with her," "It is a comfort to me when people speak of her achievements." His private name for her was "dear Lady." He would speak of "dear Lady" being off on a lecture tour, and after her death he said, "I miss the dear Lady at every turn." Back in Washington after receiving the honorary degree at Nebraska he replied to a friend's note of congratulations showing he still had the teacher-pupil relation in mind:

> ... the dear Lady would have been joyed at the honor conferred on her pupil. The homecoming was a bit sad as I thought of her and how happy she would have been over my recognition by a great University.

During Alice Fletcher's last illness Jane Gay's niece, E. Jane Gay Dodge, came to help care for her. Mrs. Thaw supplied a nurse, and Frank cared for her correspondence and her business. Several letters from Mrs. Thaw[39] to Jane Dodge show how much Mary Thaw had contributed to Alice Fletcher's life and that she was a little uncertain about Frank having carried any share of the household finances.

> Wired you Miss Fletcher has no relative living. What about the disposition of the house? Some of the contents were your aunt's, now yours. I felt she meant Francis La Flesche to have all ... beside paying the major part of the cost of the house ... I have contributed a considerable amount for improvement and repairs, so it is only proper if some of the expenditures of her illness ... be a loan to Francis La Flesche if he is to be the sole heir. I feel it due you and me to have an understanding of the financial situation. If more help is needed do not hesitate to call on me. (Francis La Flesche is a most worthy young man but "circumstances alter cases" as the old copy book ran.)

Why Mrs. Thaw met the expense of nursing care when Alice Fletcher owned securities in the neighborhood of $30,000 is not quite clear. the house was apparently unencumbered and was left to Frank if he cared to live in it, provided he would pay the taxes and keep up the repairs. There were gifts to a few distant cousins and stock and bonds up to around $15,000 which were to set up a trust from which Frank would receive the income. A long list of personal possessions was left in Frank's charge with instructions on the distribution. These items were largely jewelry, Indian craft work and a few of purely sentimental value.

Frank carefully followed the directions, checking off each item as he delivered an article to the proper person. A Ponca ceremonial basket with woven feathers, "a valuable specimen" was left to Mrs. Thaw. A desk set was to go to Dr. Hewitt of the School of American Research, and a lace handkerchief to his wife. A scarf pin and a fifty dollar Liberty Bond were to go to Rosalie's grandson, Fletcher Louis Conn. (Rosalie's son, Fletcher, had been a casualty of World War I.)

To Rosalie's daughter, mother of the younger Fletcher, a Florentine necklace of green stones set in silver.

Frank had hardly started distributing the personal possessions to the proper persons when the children of Alice Fletcher's step-brother contested the will. The usual claim that the testator was unduly influenced and not competent when the will was drawn was made but was easily refuted. Frank wrote to close friends asking they return letters sent to them to show that Alice Fletcher had been mentally alert. The scholars of the nation joined in the praise; again and again her great cultural studies were cited. Frank wrote the tribute for *Science,* the organ of the American Association for the Advancement of Science. Some sympathetic journalist on the *Omaha Bee* spoke for the people of the Omaha Tribe:

> . . . there is no state in the Union which has a better right with gratitude to claim her than has the State of Nebraska. Her service to mankind was long and active and rich, but its most significant chapters are more intimately connected with . . . our own Nebraska soil than any other. . . . (Her) whole career stamps her like the Apostle Eliot as a "friend of the Indian." She was in Nebraska only last fall . . . and many will remember the dear old lady with the cane whose bright eyes and eager voice . . . bespoke the youthful enthusiasm of her spirit . . . she leaves a heritage of love and admiration such as falls to few. . .

Frank finished his books on the Osage and started on the work which he intended to be the crown of his life's work, an Omaha dictionary. In 1925, for some reason which is not clear after this span of time, Frank again took a Civil Service examination. In the test for retention of material read, the average of those taking the test was 82.5 per cent, between the minimum of 65 per cent and the maximum of 100 per cent. Frank at sixty-eight years of age rated 90.40 per cent. With understandable pride, this man who had learned English after he was six or seven years old and attended school for four years and then once more studied after he was an adult, put away the record of this test with other papers he considered valuable.

He suffered an illness early in 1927 and then, past seventy years, he realized the trust fund established by his foster mother might soon go to the School for American Research for which she had worked so faithfully. He determined that he would add to her fund and establish a Memorial Foundation bearing both names, Fletcher and La Flesche. Anxious that there be no misunderstanding as to his intentions, he assigned 125 shares of stock of the Homestake Mining Company to the School with the understanding he should receive the dividends during his lifetime.

In February of 1927, Dr. Edgar I. Hewitt, President of the School of American Research, wrote to Frank, expressing sympathy over the illness and added:

> Mr. Kappler has informed me of the disposition you have made of your Homestake Mining stock and the trouble you have taken to make its transfer to our School absolutely certain. I want to assure you of our gratitude and say you may absolutely count on it that your wishes will be carried out. Added to what will eventually be realized from Miss Fletcher's estate, I can see that this will produce in time a Foundation that will yield great returns. Our greatest hope, however, is that you will regain your own health as to long postpone the operation of that Memorial Foundation.

In July of that year Frank was still much below his usual strength and he was placed on "detached duty" until October. He was to work on the dictionary just as he was able to, keeping account of the hours and receiving pay on the basis of an eight-hour day. The illness had involved paralytic strokes from which he made a partial recovery. His eyesight had been a matter of concern for over twenty years. Cadman wrote in warning on eye strain soon after their acquaintance started and now his sight was much worse. A Mrs. Grace Woodburn had acted as nurse and secretary when he was most incapacitated.

The work on the dictionary was extremely important; he could not give it up but drove himself day after day to work. Taking Mrs. Woodburn with him, he went to Nebraska and settled at Carey's. He reported every two weeks; the first two weeks in July he put in the equivalent of seven and one-half days and was "much improved," "have been dictating." From July 27 to August 12 he was able to work approximately thirteen days; then for the last part of August he did a little better and optimistically reported that he continued to improve. The next fortnightly report was poorer but he wrote, "I would like to continue for two more years in order to complete this work."

Back in Washington he went on a different schedule, not counting the hours but being allowed a certain number of days, on sick leave, but he had only one such day from January until May. His eyesight was failing and he moved with great difficulty. In November of 1928 he asked Charles Kappler, his attorney, to come to his house and he again went over the matter of transferring the Homestake stocks to the School of American Research. Feeling this matter was settled and secure, he had Kappler draw up a will.[40]

This document made small bequests to his sister Marguerite, to the six living children of Rosalie (Louis and Fletcher had died), said nothing about Susan's boys; bequeathed the 125 shares of stock to the School in New Mexico, with a long explanation of the action taken to endorse the stock certificates. One paragraph read:

> I have in mind my former wife, Rosa La Flesche, but as I have provided for her during my lifetime, it is my wish she take no part of my estate.

He made a bequest of $3,000 to Mrs. Grace D. Woodburn:

> ... in appreciation of service, kindness and attention during my illness and of valuable assistance rendered in my literary work ...[41]

He left the balance and residue of his property to Carey and asked that Charles J. Kappler and Charles H. Merrilat be appointed executors. This Will Number One was put away in a safe deposite box and eighteen months or so later Frank left for Nebraska. At first he talked of buying a house in Walthill but instead he helped Carey make some repairs and moved in with Carey's family on the Reservation. He kept doggedly at the Omaha dictionary trying to keep the one side of his life still going in the environment of the other. He grew worse, probably suffered more stroke, and Carey's Elizabeth came home again to be nurse. Although he got around with some difficulty, he could have a walk in the yard, enjoy visits with old friends or get into Walthill. He talked of getting back to Washington and straightening out the things left at 214 1st Street, but never went.

In May of 1932 he had Carey call an attorney from Walthill, A. D. "Al" Raun. Raun went to Carey's house and drew up a will for Frank. This Will Number Two left everything to Carey and named him as executor. Frank became weaker and by the end of a long hot summer was confined to his room for a week or two and died on September 5th, mourned by both the Indians and their neighbors. It may have appeared as a greater loss to many in the other side of his life than to those who had seen him return yearly to the Reservation and then leave to what they felt was a world of self indulgence. The academic world did him honor, many tributes appeared speaking of his unique position, his three college degrees and his scholarly contributions. The article in American Archaeology was written by his friend Hartley B. Alexander.

The funeral was indicative of the separate strains and diverse influences which made his life. There were three services for the Chief's son who had been an Elder in the Presbyterian Church. The first was led by Amos Lamson of the Latter Day Saints; then, at the cemetery, the Masonic Order conducted a graveside service. Frank had been a member in Washington and had associated with Masonic groups while he worked in Oklahoma. After the white people left, the Indians performed their rites. Henry Turner was in charge of this service and White Bear, one of the oldest members of the tribe, spoke of Frank as a boy and as a man. Then, in closing, Henry Morris, after removing his shoes, offered a long prayer in Omaha.[42]

If the funeral had been significant, the two separate wills spoke even more clearly of the two separate sides of Frank's life. No one in Nebraska knew about Will Number One and no one in Washington knew about Will Number Two. In making Will Number Two, Al Raun had assumed Frank was a single person, nothing was said about there being a wife, so no mention was made of Rosa in Will Number Two. There was no mention of Mrs. Woodburn or Marguerite and the nieces and nephews. Nor was anything said about the Mining Stock or the School of American Research.

Will Number Two was immediately filed for probate in Thurston County and at the same time Kappler and Merrilat, as executors under Will Number One, requested the proper official to open Frank's safe deposit box, and the mining stock certificates and Will Number One were disclosed. Through their attorneys Mrs. Woodburn, Dr. HeWitt representing the School of American Research, and Rosa speaking from her residence in the State of Washington, filed separate suits in Washington, D. C., to stay the probate of Will Number Two in Nebraska until their positions were determined by the courts.

There followed nearly a year of legal maneuvering until a Court in the District of Columbia declared Rosa had a right to share in the estate and that the gift to the School had been valid. Then all three of the suits to delay probate were withdrawn by a settlement out of court. Frank had not collected dividends on the stock for several years. A stock dividend had been declared making the total value larger than when he had made Will Number One. The Court ordered that a portion of the shares be sold and from their shares of the receipts, Carey and Rosa should make payments to Mrs. Woodburn. This still left Carey and Rosa heirs to an estate totaling over $90,000 before the costs and deductions were made.

In this way, by 1933, in the middle of the depression, Carey, the youngest, whose childhood had not followed an even course, who had never been able to be important beside his famous brother, found himself in possession of a great deal of money. It meant more value at that time than at many others. Money was in short supply, so were work and food; but money went a long way for prices were ridiculously low. At the same time the society around him maintained all the old Omaha tradition of hospitality and the importance of gifts. Carey liked doing things for other people, having guests in his house and he was ready to help others. Winnie Farley remembered how, when Susette died, Carey and Phoebe had come to her early the next morning wishing to know what they could do for her.

These years of the 1930's were extremely difficult on the Reservation and Carey's help, here and there, was gratefully received. The Indians did not mind if he indulged in luxury foods for his own table. Leasing had become a general practice; an Omaha could lease his land, retain the house to live in, maintain himself on the rents and travel far afield. Carey delighted in automobiles, good automobiles, and he and Phoebe made many visits to tribal connections South, North and West. The money did not last long.

Phoebe, who was known for her beautiful shawls, for her beautiful garden, who struggled to learn English from her children, became ill and died in November of 1942. This left Marguerite and Carey the last of the family. Even then Carey was not well. He was often in the hospital or would be with his second daughter, Susette, gradually losing interest in things around him. He died in the Indian Hospital at Winnebago on June 28, 1952, almost ten years after Phoebe's death and only a few days before his eightieth birthday.[43]

The student pastor of the Dutch Reform Church of Macy (the successor to the Blackbird Hills Presbyterian Church) conducted the service at Susette's home. Carey was buried in the Macy cemetery not far from Ta-in-ne's other children, Lucy and Frank, just ninety-eight years after his father had signed the Treaty. The cemetery is high on the hill above Macy, crossed by winding roads and with a view that sweeps off toward the River and the spot where Iron Eye and the Young Men's Party built the Make-Believe-White-Man's Village nearly one hundred years before.

CHAPTER IX

A NEW ROAD

Families go on and on, one generation after another, each building on the experiences of those who have gone before. Then periodically throughout history, there have come times of sudden change which may be likened to geographical faults, when the ground has suddenly dropped, fallen down hundreds and hundreds of feet until there is no connection between pieces of land which had been one continuous area.

When a "social fault" comes there is a break between the past and the present. The people are caught with no guide posts for living; the old markers have no meaning. The habits and the routine of living used by past generations cannot be used: the supply of food and clothing has vanished, the material for arts and craft cannot be found, the method of exchange for goods and services no longer works, tools used for years are not needed. Their language is unknown to the small group around them until they are misunderstood and isolated. The skills taught to the children are no longer useful. The old and tested laws are inoperable. Even their expressions of beauty, of meaning in the world and in themselves are suddenly inadequate and all sense of morality is gone. Everything that generations have relied upon, have known and worked with suddenly has no value.

This has never been better expressed than by a man of another race, from an ancient civilization, which had undergone a long process of erosion before the drastic fault and loss of values. As an adult he was forced to adapt himself to a new road in an alien environment. In his book *The Wilting of the Hundred Flowers: The Chinese Intelligensia under Mao,*[1] Mu Fu-sheng said:

> ... When values are shifted, it is like the ground sinking under one's feet. ... There is need to break free, there [is] nostalgia; there [is] courage but panic as well. To cut oneself loose from one's cultural moorings is a frighting and demoralizing experience at any time. Until one's culture is threatened one does not readily realize how much one lives by the culture to which he belongs and how the basis of culture is an arbitrary standard of values.

Such a cataclysmic experience came to the North American Indians within the scope of United States history. It came to the Plains Indians within the one hundred to one hundred and fifty years just passed. The brunt of this blow falls most heavily on two generations; the one that is adult and in charge of the affairs of their society when most of the people realize that acceptance of the change is inevitable. Second, the next generation must in some way find new rules and new values and carry life forward. Those of the first generation make surface changes; few of them personally make all the adjustments in language, economy, crafts, commerce, art and religion. A few change in one way, a few in another. The second generation, however, must make the greater part of these changes within their own lives or they are lost. They must help the society as a whole find new guide posts to direct them along a new road.

Joseph La Flesche, called Iron Eye, had a glimpse of the changes when as a youth he had traveled with his father. He had helped make the surface change by signing the treaty and building the Make-Believe-White-Man's Village. His generation watched the disappearance of the game, the end of the buffalo hunt with its effects on religion and the whole social structure. He personally suffered from denial of the ancient authority and then the abolishment of the chiefship. He saw the loss of law, the loss of morality, the loss of all standards which gave meaning to men and to their living with each other.

Only strong men survive such losses; only men who believe deeply enough in fundamentals that they can recognize those truths of life in other guise, in other forms and customs. Joseph's belief in a Power which pervaded all nature, filled the world about him and gave him work to do and a responsibility to others was as truly expressed for him in the God of the Missionary's Book as in Wakonda to whom the Omaha prayed.

On the other hand, Joseph never mastered the new language and had a distressing time over many aspects of the white man's economy, although by hard work he had earned rather large sums of money for his time and situation. He held in respect the old arts and their expression in the tribal ceremonies but he felt they would not help on the new road. He believed the important thing was what was in a man's heart. God's Book in the white man's church talked of His "straight path" where a man would not stumble and he knew the long line on the pipe of the Wa-Wan ceremony was straight and meant the "straight path of life"; it was red because if a man followed it "the sun of life and happiness would always shine on him."

Joseph sensed the force of the new set of techniques and values which destroyed the old ways of the Omaha. Nevertheless he believed men of different customs still shared certain things and he taught his children that the "white man has come to teach us how to live." He may have been fortunate in knowing white men of integrity and good will at an early date, although he had his share of unfortunate encounters. Still he believed in the white man's road; since hunting no longer provided for the tribe, the Indians must learn the things the white men knew and the ways in which they provided for their families.

Neither Joseph nor any of his children ever cut themselves away from the geographical setting of their old culture. The hills, the prairies, the creek valleys where Joseph's great-grandparents had probably hunted and cultivated their little corn patches were still part of home to his children and are today to his great-grandchildren. Frank and Susette lived far away for months, even for years, but they were always coming back. Frank's work centered his time and thought on the Reservation and its past. Susette, who had worked desperately for her people had her attention pulled into other arguments and controversies. Yet, they both returned to the homeland and both died on the Reservation.

None of the children ever removed their names from the Tribal Roll. Even if they stepped along a new way they held their place in the old. Certainly they all believed they could help the Tribe more if they were one with the people. Marguerite and Susan developed households based on the acceptance of the new culture and yet Mary could comfortably be a part of these homes. These homes were open to tribal problems and were a meeting place for the Omaha and their white neighbors.

As members of the generation which first stepped out from the tribal pattern Joseph's children all spoke and read English; all wrote it in a beautiful legible copy-book hand. They handled money competently enough to be released from government supervision. However, all of them did not completely change their attitudes about money and property from the ancient Indian way of counting a man great by his deeds and his gifts to the white man's measure in terms of property owned and money saved. To a large degree they learned and used the new method of business and commerce as in the office work done by Carey and Frank and in Rosalie's large business ventures. They acquired skills and techniques, the use of farm machinery and of sewing machines and most of the women played the organ. New skills were evident in Lucy's fine housekeeping and Noah's carpentry and, in another field, in Susan's work in medicine and surgery.

To Joseph's relief, kind friends here and there made it possible for his family to share in the white man's system of education. His loss of the trading post and the slow uncertain return from "first breaking" farming had made him fear they could not receive the education he coveted for them. While most of them had scholarship help as they went East to school, certain expenses were met from home. Lucy, with Noah, Marguerite, Susan and Carey all attended Hampton. Carey had more years of formal schooling away from home than any, unless it was Susan. Even Frank's night study could hardly equal Carey's six years at Hampton, for all it was on a different level. Rosalie had the least formal education and yet she was the advocate, the champion of education. Plainly she was an educated woman and she instilled a desire for education in her children.

Nominally, at least, they all followed their father in making the change in religion. A few writers speak in either a jocular or scornful tone of what they contend are the mere surface effects wrought by the Missionaries. But much of it went below the surface and no one can doubt the sincere faith of Susette, Rosalie, Marguerite and Susan. All of Joseph's children were buried by the Christian Church; Frank, Carey and Lucy with Noah lie in the graveyard at Macy, Marguerite at Walthill while the graves of Rosalie and Susan and Susette are at Bancroft. Those graves are by the big stone for Joseph and Mary with Madeline Wolfe and her half sister Nicomi close by.

Each in their own way met life with the new values and moved along a new road—or along two branches of the same road, branches that ran parallel to each other and frequently nearly merged. Rosalie, Susette, Susan and Marguerite, on the whole, kept to the road among white ways and manners, leading to increased participation in the affairs of the wider, multiracial, multicultural society. Their children and grandchildren have continued along that road. Lucy and Carey took the path that turned toward the Reservation and the Indian fashion of living. They exercised their new skills and their new thinking in an atmosphere including more of the old culture.

Frank seemed to walk between, or he changed from one path to the other in the constantly two-sided way of his life. He probably knew and was known by more white people of culture and learning than any of the others. When he was alone and in need of help he returned to the familiar surroundings and could quickly throw himself into the life of the Tribe.

He had been an Elder in the Church in 1880; in the 1890's he became irritated at a bungling, overofficious representative of the Church and withdrew becoming quite detached from matters of religion. He was by the nature of his work, given to an impersonal view of philosophical and religious matters. He seemed to observe from a distance without any intellectual or emotional involvement. The three groups in charge of his funeral were symbolic of his attitude.

Few other families of the generation that was forced to find a way to new values have as many outstanding figures. Other families have illustrious names, but frequently they are from more than one generation or are connected by secondary relationships. The seven La Flesches were children of one father and they all took on new values within fifty years after the old culture had crumbled.

The next two generations, Joseph's grandchildren and great-grandchildren have given to society a few bankers, an architect, farmers, musicians, business men, lawyers, soldiers and two physicians. One grandson is a Lieutenant Colonel, a veteran of Bataan. Two great-grandsons graduated from Medical College in the city of Omaha less than one hundred years after Joseph had signed the treaty, under which white men came and built the city. Many of the family have been in Civil Service, several have been and some are now in the Indian Service. There have been artists and teachers in all types of education from college teachers with doctorates, through the secondary and primary schools and the specifically Indian schools.

As Mu Fu-Sheng has said, the process of finding one's place in a new culture is mixed with struggle, nostalgia, even panic and it requires courage. It was hard work and it took a frightful personal toll; no wonder that the older ones who met the change first died young. These seven typify an era in American history; the lives of Joseph and his family cover more than one hundred years.

These hundred years were in a period of remarkable technological change for all the world. The situation of the Tribe was utterly changed, the relationship between the government and the Indians was changed many times, but never back to what it had been when Joseph was a young man. The mechanical and industrial world was quite different when Carey worked at the Agency than it had been when Susette first went East. Carey faced a purely monetary economy and the automobile era at the same age that Frank had been when white as well as red men walked or rode horseback over the miles they must travel. Although Carey was Joseph's son, in actual living there was more than one hundred years between the young Joseph La Flesche who walked from St. Louis to Bellevue and the overweight Carey La Flesche who rode in his chauffeur driven car from Macy to Ponca, Nebraska.

The seven represented many facets of the old and the new in those years of change. Carey, who faced the changes later than the others, worked within a Tribe quite different than the one Frank knew in 1879. Carey was the Educated Indian on the Reservation, the keeper of records, who could serve as the public relations man, the host to the visiting scholars, preserving traditions on the spot and adding the excitement of baseball on a league team to the pleasure of leading the old dances at the Powwow.

Lucy was the Teacher, foster mother and homemaker. She tried always to pass on the things the new education had brought to her; teaching formally when she could, but always unconsciously teaching.

Francis the Scholar, lawyer, lecturer, author, internationally known scientist, the accepted member of academic and artistic circles.

Susan the Doctor of Medicine, the beloved healer, crusader for public health on and off the Reservation, missionary, temperance leader and public speaker.

Marguerite the Teacher, community leader, gracious hostess, interpreter for her people in many ways, whose children continued to work for the Indians.

Rosalie the Merger of two Cultures, leader of the Tribe, center of the family, business woman, stock raiser, advocate of education.

Susette, "Bright Eyes" the Symobl of the Indian Maiden, the famous one, public speaker, artist, writer, defender of the Indians.

These were the children of the man who prayed that God would help him along the "good road" and who said:

> God has given us the hands with which we can work . . . look back on the lives of your fathers and grandfathers; then look at yourselves and see how far you have gone ahead, and seeing this, do not stop and turn back to them, but go forward. [2]

NOTES

When possible I have named sources used in the text in order to avoid constant interruption by footnotes. A complete list of sources is given in the Bibliography.

The hyphens used to space syllables in Indian names decrease as the book progresses. They are used when a name appears for the first time or when the sources relied upon uses them. The custom of omitting the hyphen increased as the Indians used more Anglicized names.

Chapter I
INDISTINCT BEGINNINGS

1. Alice C. Fletcher and Francis La Flesche, 27th Annual Report of the Bureau of American Ethnology, *The Omaha Tribe*, Washington, 1911.

2. Papers of Alice C. Fletcher and Francis La Flesche, Bureau of American Ethnology, Smithsonian Institution. No. 4558.

3. *Ibid.*

4. A granddaughter of Iron Eye (Joseph La Flesche) on mention of Wajapa spoke quickly and with evident pleasure, "We always called him 'Grandpa'." When Wajapa died a grandson of Joseph's wired to Francis La Flesche in Washington, D.C.

5. La Flesche Family Papers. A paper found in a journal of Dr. Susan La Flesche Picotte. Nebraska State Historical Society.

6. Joseph Hamilton, Indian Agent to Joshua Pilcher, Superintendent, May 19, 1840. *Letters Received* by Office of Indian Affairs from Council Bluffs Sub-Agency, 1836-1843. National Archives.

7. *Oo-Ma-Ha Ta-Wa-Tha* by Fannie Reed Giffen, illus. by Susette La Flesche Tibbles, Lincoln, Nebraska, 1898. p. 72.

8. Joshua Pilcher, Superintendent to T. Hartley Crawford, Commissioner of Indian Affairs, April 10, 1841. *Letters Received, op. cit.*

9. *The Omaha Tribe, op. cit.* p. 632.

10. *Ibid.*

11. *Oo-Ma-Ha Ta-Wa-Tha, op. cit.* p. 29.

12. Fletcher and La Flesche Papers, *op. cit.* Bureau of American Ethnology. 4558, VIII B. 17.

13. Thomas H. Harvey, Superintendent to T. Hartley Crawford, Commissioner of Indian Affairs, February 9, 1844. *Letters Received* by Office of Indian Affairs from the Council Bluffs Sub-Agency, 1844-1847. National Archives.

14. Major John Miller, Indian Agent to Brigham Young, April 1845, *ibid.*

15. Thomas H. Harvey, Superintendent to T. Hartley Crawford, Commissioner. July 23, 1845, *ibid.*

16. Daniel Miller, Indian Agent to D. D. Mitchell, Superintendent, Jan. 25, 1844. *ibid.*

17. The word "chief" is even more loosely used today, even by Indians seeking the spotlight or in flattering white men.

18. Treaty of 1854. United States Statutes at Large. vol. X, p. 1043.

19. Fletcher and La Flesche Papers, *op. cit.* Also in *The Omaha Tribe, op. cit.* p. 623.

20. *Oo-Ma-Ha Ta-Wa-Tha, op. cit.* p. 39.

21. Alfred Cumming, Superintendent to George Manypenny, Commissioner, Jan. 27, 1854. *Letters Received* by the Office of Indian Affairs from Council Bluffs Agency, 1852-1857, National Archives.

22. George Manypenny, Commissioner to Robert McCleland, Secretary of the Interior, March 1, 1854. *Letters Received, ibid.*

23. George Hepner, Agent to Alfred Cumming, Superintendent, December 27, 1854. *Letters Received, ibid.*

24. *North American Ethnology* vol. VI, p. 458, Washington, D.C., 1890.

25. *American Indian Correspondence,* Presbyterian Historical Society, Philadelphia, Pennsylvania. Hereafter referred to as *Missionary Letters.*

Chapter II
THE EARLY RESERVATION: IRON EYE AS A TRIBAL LEADER

1. Article 1, Treaty of 1854. *United States Statutes at Large,* vol. X, p. 1043.

2. *Savannah* (Missouri) *Sentinel,* clipping enclosed in letter, Alfred Cumming, Superintendent to George Manypenny, Commissioner, February 20, 1854. *Letters Received, op. cit.*

3. *Nebraska Palladium,* July 15, 1854. Nebraska State Historical Society.

4. *Ibid.*

5. George Hepner, Agent to Alfred Cumming, Superintendent, November 1, 1855. *Letters Received, op. cit.*

6. *Ibid.*

7. *The Middle Five* by Francis La Flesche, Madison, Wis., 1963 p. xviii-xix. This presents the difficulties of translation and the failure of interpreters.

8. Report of Indian Commissioner, 1856.

9. *Ibid.*

10. History of Nebraska by J. Sterling Morton and Albert Watkins, Lincoln, Nebr. 1907, vol. II, p. 251-252.

11. J. D. Rolfe to Walter Lowrie, October 12, 1858, *ibid.*

12. Charles Sturgis to J. C. Lowrie. January 25, 1858, *ibid.*

13. *Diary of Dr. Joseph A. Paxton,* edited by Dr. James L. Sellers. *Nebraska History,* vol. 27, Nebraska State Historical Society. 1946.

14. Charles Sturgis to J. C. Lowrie, October 21, 1859. *Missionary Letters, op. cit.*

15. *Oo-Ma-Ha Ta-Wa-Tha, op. cit.* p. 32.

16. *Ibid.* p. 36-37.

17. *Robert W. Furnas as Omaha Agent,* 1864-66 by Robert C. Farb. *Nebraska History,* vol. 32, No. 3 and No. 4.

18. *Ibid.* p. 36-37.

19. R. J. Burtt to Walter Lowrie, March 5, 1866, *Missionary Letters, op. cit.*

20. R. J. Burtt to Walter Lowrie, April 14, 1866, *ibid.*

21. Robert W. Furnas to Dr. J. C. Lowrie, July 29, 1866, *ibid.*

22. Samuel G. Daily to Robert W. Furnas, March 31, 1864. Farb, *op. cit.*

23. *The Omaha Tribe, op. cit.*, p. 34.

24. *Oo-Ma-Ha Ta-Wa-Tha, op. cit.*

Chapter III
JOSEPH AS A FAMILY MAN

1. *The Omaha Tribe, op. cit.*, p. 638.

2. *Ibid.*

3. Rev. William Hamilton to Walter Lowrie, August 16, 1862. *Missionary Letters.*

4. *Ibid.*

5. *Journal of Rudolph Frederich Kurz.* Edited by J. N. B. Hewitt. Bureau of American Ethnology, Washington, D. C. 1937, p. 334.

6. Ages are estimated from the dates on gravestones whenever possible, then adjustment made with variations appearing in Annuity Rolls.

7. Capt. W. E. Moore to Hon. A. B. Greenwood, Commissioner of Indian Affairs, May 10, 1860. *Letters Received, op. cit.*

8. *Oo-Ma-Ha Ta-Wa-Tha, op. cit.*

9. Rev. William Hamilton to J. C. Lowrie, February 1, 1868. *Missionary Letters, op. cit.*

10. *Ibid.*

11. The author's paraphrase from the literal translation given in *The Omaha Tribe*, p. 130.

12. *Fletcher and La Flesche Papers, op. cit.*

13. Çegeha Language by J. Owen Dorsey. U. S. Geographical and Geological Survey, vol. VI. p. 466.

14. Theodore F. Gillingham, Agent, to Edward Smith, Commissioner, July 10, 1875. Letters Received by Office of Indian Affairs from Omaha Agency, 1871-1876.

Chapter IV
SUSETTE AND ROSALIE: THE INDIAN PROBLEM AND THE LAND

1. *Reports on Poncas,* 46th Congress, 2nd Session, Report 670, United States Senate, Washington, D. C., 1880.

2. *Ibid.*

3. December 27, 1879. *The Woman's Journal,* Boston.

4. Records of Office of County Judge of Burt County, Tekamah, Nebraska.

5. *Ibid.*

6. Account of Alice C. Fletcher by Jane Gay Dodge. *The Jane Gay Dodge Papers,* Women's Archives, Radcliffe College.

7. Alice C. Fletcher speaking to the Lake Mohonk Conference, 1907, the 25th such conference, recounted her first contact with the Omaha over twenty years earlier.

8. Act of August 7, 1882. U. S. Statutes at Large, vol. XXII, p. 341 as cited in *The Omaha Tribe*, p. 624.

9. *The Middle Five: Indian Schoolboys of the Omaha Tribe*, Small & Maynard, Boston, 1900. University of Wisconsin, Madison, 1963.

10. See Bibliography.

11. See Bibliography.

12. Edward A. Ross to T. H. Tibbles, 1909, *Tibbles Papers*, MS 1644, Nebraska State Historical Society.

13. See Bibliography.

14. Dr. Addison E. Sheldon to T. H. Tibbles, 1920. *Tibbles Papers, op. cit.*

15. Alice C. Fletcher, Tribute by Francis La Flesche, *Science*, August 17, 1923.

16. *An Indian Allotment*, a speech by Francis La Flesche at the 18th Lake Mohonk Conference of the Friends of the American Indian, October 12, 1900. This later appeared as an article in *The Independent*, November 8, 1900.

17. Copies of the Proposed Plan of Self-Government are in a bound volume of Alice Fletcher's Papers in the Library of the Peabody Museum at Harvard, although it was not her work alone. A copy is also among Alice Fletcher's Papers in the Bureau of American Anthology, Smithsonian Institution. No. 4558.

Chapter V.
ROSALIE: THE FAMILY AND THE PASTURE

1. *Beyond the Hundreth Meridian: John Wesley Powell* by Wallace S. Stegner. Boston, 1943.

2. Homer W. Partch to J. C. Lowrie, December 1, 1881. *Missionary Letters, op. cit.*

3. Charles W. Conn of Bancroft, Nebr., who married Marguerite Farley, Rosalie's younger daughter.

4. Map in *The Omaha Tribe, op. cit.* Map based on a study of the Omaha Indian titles made by H. F. Keefe.

5. *Twenty-two Years Work at the Hampton Normal and Agricultural Institute* by Helen W. Ludlow and Cora M. Folsom. Hampton, Va., 1893.

6. Alice Fletcher to Rosalie, January 7, 1884. *La Flesche Family Papers, op. cit.*

7. The La Flesche and Farley families freely bestowed nicknames on each other. Rosalie was "Ro," Marguerite was "Mag," "Maggie" and "M," La Flesche became "Kig" and "Fletcher" was "Fletch."

8. Francis La Flesche to Frederic W. Putnam. *Report* of Peabody Museum, 1884, vol. III, p. 179.

9. No. 15561. *Letters Received,*OIA, 1884, *op. cit.*

10. *Report of the Commissioner of Indian Affairs*, 1885.

11. Susan was in Philadelphia at the Women's Medical College of Pennsylvania.

12. *Report of the Commissioner of Indian Affairs*, 1893.

13. Records of the United States Circuit Court, District of Nebraska, Number 18, Docket Q 2.

14. Records of the United States Circuit Court, District of Nebraska, Number 18, Docket Q 25.

15. Records of the Supreme Court of the State of Nebraska, Case File 6996; Opinions, 723. Office of the Supreme Court of Nebraska, in the State Capitol Building.

16. *Report of the Commissioner of Indian Affairs, 1895.*

17. *Ibid.*

Chapter VI.
ROSALIE AND SUSETTE: THE TRIBE AND THE FAMILY: WHICH WAY?

1. "A Tribute to Wajapa" by Melvin R. Gilmore. *Walthill Times,* August 30, 1907.

2. *The Omaha Tribe, op. cit.* p. 224.

3. A. M. Gardner of St. Louis to Mrs. Edward Farley, January 12, 1888. *La Flesche Family Papers, op. cit.* Nebraska State Historical Society.

4. *Nebraska, Old and New* by Addison E. Sheldon. Lincoln, Nebr., 1937.

5. *Warpath and Council Fire* by Stanley Vestal, New York, 1948.

6. All the following excerpts, describing Rosalie's life are taken from the *La Flesche Family Papers, op. cit.*

7. *Jane Gay Dodge Papers,* Women's Archives, Radcliffe College, Cambridge, Mass. *op. cit.*

8. *The Weekly Independent,* Lincoln, Nebraska. October 11, 1895.

9. Alice C. Fletcher letter February 10, 1898. Correspondence of the Peabody Museum, Harvard University.

10. *Omaha Daily Bee,* Omaha, Nebraska. July 1, 2 and 3, 1898.

11. *Ibid.* August 4 and 5, 1898.

Chapter VII
MARGUERITE AND SUSAN

1. Many treaties with the Indians included the statement that the treaties would be in effect "as long as the grass shall grow and the waters shall run."

2. Report of George W. Wilkinson, Agent at the Winnebago and Omaha Agency. In *Report of the Commissioner of Indian Affairs,* 1882.

3. *Missionary Letters, op. cit.*

4. General Armstrong's Report from Hampton in *Report of Commissioner of Indian Affairs,* 1880.

5. General Armstrong's report, October 1, 1883 in *Report of Commissioner of Indian Affairs,* 1883.

6. *The Southern Workman,* Hampton, June 1886.

7. *The Woman's Journal,* Boston, June 12, 1886.

8. *The Southern Workman, op. cit.,* December 1884.

9. *The Omaha Tribe, op. cit.* p. 319.

10. General Armstrong's Report, *Report of the Indian Commissioner,* 1883.

11. *Twenty-two Years Work at the Hampton Normal, op. cit.*

12. *The Southern Workman, op. cit.,* September, 1884.

13. *Twenty-two Years at Hampton Normal, op. cit.*

14. *Ibid.*

15. *Ibid.*

16. Item 23847, *Records of Office of Indian Affairs*, National Archives.

17. *The Omaha Tribe, op. cit.* p. 104. In the list of animals known to the Omaha, the skunk is given as "Monga." This was later confirmed by Elizabeth La Flesche Fontenelle in conversation with the author.

18. Letter of Mitchell Barada, an Omaha in *The Red Man*, the paper of Calisle; reprinted in the *Thurston County Republic*, Pender, Nebraska, March 5, 1897.

19. Rev. W. A. Galt, typescripts of sketches on Omahas. Nebraska State Historical Society.

20. *The Southern Workman, op. cit.*, June 1892.

21. *Bancroft News*, Bancroft, Nebraska, editor Evelyn Vogt. "Now and Then" Column by J. R. (Rob) Kelley, 1956.

22. *Bancroft Blade*, June 29, 1905.

23. In 1965 the town of Bancroft and the Nebraska State Historical Society placed a "Landmark" on the edge of Bancroft. This states Bancroft was the place where John G. Neihardt wrote his *Cycle of the West* and mentions Susette and Susan as one source of his knowledge of Indian life. This actually applies more to Susan, since Dr. Neihardt has told the author that his acquaintance was really with Tibbles rather than with Susette. He did, however, know Susan well and she felt he expressed the spirit of Indian life better than other writers.

24. Stories persist that the Diddock house was finished in walnut from the old Mission. Before 1906 a minister of the Presbyterian Church took wood out of the old dilapidated building to repair other church property. Other materials were used and at last Noah La Flesche owned the building and tore it down for its salvage value. The Diddock home was finished in oak.

25. Both of Marguerite's daughters had good voices. The older one, Marguerite (Langenberg) did concert work for years and is remembered as "a magnificent soprano." She always opened a concert with "The Omaha Prayer" as arranged by John C. Fillmore in Alice Fletcher's book on Omaha Music.

26. *The Omaha Tribe, op. cit.*, p. 642. Letter from Superintendent John M. Commons, September 10, 1909.

27. State Senator George Wiltse quoted in *The Walthill Times*, November 12, 1909.

28. Editor of *Fremont Tribune*, Ross Hammond, influential citizen and politician went to the Reservation in January 1910 to personally investigate.

29. Kent Baughn practiced medicine in Helena, Montana in 1965. A grandson of Rosalie, Marguerite Farley's son, Fletcher, is also a physician and practices (1965) in Klamath Falls, Oregon.

Chapter VIII
TA-IN-NE'S CHILDREN

1. The Allotment List of 1871, based on the Treaty of 1865 was discovered in the United States District Court Office in Omaha in the winter of 1965. It gives the Indian name, the "citizen name," the age of the allottee and a

description of the allotment. This list is now in the Nebraska State Historical Society by the courtesy of Judges Robert Van Pelt and Richard E. Robinson of the United States District Court, District of Nebraska.

2. Alice Fletcher in *The Woman's Journal,* Boston, February 11, 1882.

3. Lucy to Alice Fletcher, February 21, 1887. Bureau of American Ethnology, No. 4558.

4. All the information on Noah which follows is taken from his folder at the Agency Office, Winnebago and Omaha Indian Agency, Winnebago, Nebraska. Permission to quote is granted in a letter to the author from G. W. Branchaud, Acting Superintendent, September 7, 1965.

5. Letter from Noah to Superintendent Johnson of the Omaha Indian School, January, 1916, *ibid.*

6. Letter, E. B. Merritt, Assistant Commissioner of Indian Affairs to Superintendent Johnson, January 17, 1916, *ibid.*

7. Badger was a relative of Joseph's, but the exact degree is uncertain; his sons were at Carlisle.

8. Annuity List of the Omaha Tribe, 1886. *Records of the Office of Indian Affairs,* National Archives.

9. Death Certificate in the Agency file.

10. *The Çegeha Language* by J. Owen Dorsey, *op. cit.*

11. When a person had been insulted it was customary to expect gifts would be given as an apology. Since gifts were not given the father of the injured family felt privileged to take the horses.

12. *Twenty-five Years at Hampton Normal, ibid.*

13. Letter, Rosa to Frank, Bureau of American Ethnology, No. 4558 IIA, Folder 5.

14. Letter of the Clerk of Court of the District of Columbia to author, 1965.

15. Report from the Supreme Court of the District of Columbia, No. 27,167, Equity Docket 60.

16. Address, 310 First Street, S. E. on letter Rosa to "Nellie," November 1, 1911. *Carlisle Records,* National Archives.

17. *Fletcher-La Flesche* Papers, Nebraska State Historical Society. Frank's statement on his name explained in a letter to the author from Dr. Thurmond Wilkins, July 22, 1962. Wilkins had made a study of Alice Fletcher.

18. Letter to author from Charles Nutting, Administrator of National Law Center at George Washington University, Washington, D. C., September 13, 1965. The National University was merged with George Washington University in 1954.

19. See Chapter VI.

20. See Chapter IV.

21. *The Omaha Tribe, op. cit.,* p. 221.

22. Letter from Alice C. Fletcher to Frederic W. Putnam, June 6, 1884. *Report of Peabody Museum of Harvard University,* 1884.

23. *The Omaha Tribe, op. cit.,* p. 248.

24. See Chapter VI.

25. *Oo-Ma-Ha Ta-Wa-Tha, op. cit.,* p. 47.

26. *The Omaha Tribe, op. cit.,* p. 251.

27. *Ibid.* p. 283.

28. *El Palacio,* Vol. XI, No. 5, Museum of New Mexico and School of American Research.

29. Correspondence of Francis La Flesche and items concerning *The Middle Five,* Bureau of American Ethnology. No. 4558.

30. (George) Bird Grinnel, *ibid.*

31. *The Middle Five,* University of Wisconsin Press, Madison, 1963.

32. Caryl continued a connection with the University through his children. When they were of college age he moved to Lincoln to simplify their attending college. Of two sons and two daughters, the three younger ones all received their Bachelor degrees. The older daughter, Rosalie Winnifred, also received both a Master's degree and a Doctorate. In the 1960's she was an Associate Professor at the University of Nebraska and had held positions in National Educational Organizations.

33. *Walthill Times,* September 6, 1918.

34. *Çegeha Language, op. cit.*

35. *Fletcher-La Flesche-Cadman Papers, op. cit.*

36. *Lincoln Evening Journal,* Lincoln, Nebraska, June 5, 1926.

37. *Francis La Flesche to Hartley B. Alexander,* May 10, 1900. La Flesche Letters, Bureau American Ethnology, *op. cit.*

38. *Ibid.*

39. *Jane Gay Dodge Papers,* Women's Archives, Radcliffe College.

40. Charles J. Kappler, editor of *Indian Affairs, Laws and Treaties,* a three-volume study considered an authority, Government Printing Office, 1902, 1913.

41. Copy of the first will of Francis La Flesche given the author by the late A. D. Raun, attorney of Walthill, Nebraska.

42. *Walthill Times,* September 15, 1932.

43. Death Certificate of Noah La Flesche. Bureau of Vital Statistics, Department of Health, State of Nebraska. Copy issued May 27, 1965.

Chapter IX.
A NEW ROAD

1. Published in the United States of America in 1963 by Frederich A. Praeger, Inc., p. 99. Quoted by permission of the publisher and the author.

2. See Chapter II.

BIBLIOGRAPHY

Books

Chittenden, Hiram M., *Life, Letters and Travels of Father Pierre-Jean De Smet, Sr.,* New York, 1905.

Dorsey, James Owen, *Omaha and Ponca Letters* (in translation) Bureau of American Ethnology, Washington, D. C. 1891.

Eastman, Elaine Goodale, *The Red Man's Moses,* Norman, Okla., 1935.

Fletcher, Alice Cunningham and La Flesche, Francis, *The Omaha Tribe,* 27th Annual Report of the Bureau of American Ethnology. Smithsonian Institution, Washington, D. C.

Giffen, Fannie Reed, *Oo-Ma-Ha Ta-Wa-Tha,* Lincoln, Nebraska, 1898.

La Flesche, Francis, *The Middle Five: Indian Schoolboys of the Omaha Tribe,* Boston, 1900. Reissue: Madison, Wisconsin, 1963.

Ludlow, Helen W. and Folsom, Cora M., *Twenty-two Years Work of the Hampton Normal and Agricultural Institute,* Hampton, Virginia, 1893.

Morton, J. Sterling, *History of Nebraska,* Lincoln, Nebraska, 1907.

Olson, James C., *History of Nebraska,* Lincoln, Nebraska, 1955.

Sandoz, Mari, *Love Song to the Plains,* New York, 1961.

Schwarz, Rev. Julius F., D. D., *The Presbyterian Church in Nebraska* (Synod of Nebraska: 1911).

Sheldon, Addison E., *Nebraska, Old and New,* Lincoln, 1937.

Tibbles, Thomas H., *Hidden Power: A Secret History of the Indian Ring,* New York, 1881.

Tibbles, Thomas H., (Zyluft), *The Ponca Chief: An Attempt to Appeal from the Tomahawk to the Courts,* Boston, 1880.

Tibbles, Thomas H., *Ploughed Under,* New York, 1881.

Vestal, Stanley, *Warpath and Council Fire, 1851-1891,* New York, 1948.

Newspapers and Magazines

American Anthropologist, Vol. 35.

Bancroft Blade, Bancroft, Nebraska, 1892, 1894-1919; 1932, 1937, 1954, 1964.

Bancroft Enterprise, Bancroft, Nebraska, 1895-96.

Belleview Gazette, Belleview, Nebraska, 1857.

Boston Daily Advertiser, Boston, Mass., November and December, 1879.

The Council Fire, A Monthly Journal, A. B. Meacham, edit. Vol. I, No. 1 to 5; 10-12, 1878; Vol. II, No. 1 to 6; 9 and 12, 1879; Vol. IV Nos. 5, 8, 9, 12, 1881. Washington, D. C.

Dakota City Herald, Dakota City, Nebraska, 1858.

Decatur News, Decatur, Nebraska, 1895-96.

Evening State Journal, Lincoln, Nebraska, 1926.

Hartford Daily Courant, Hartford, Conn., 1880.

Lincoln Independent, Lincoln, Nebraska, 1895.

Nebraska Palladium, Belleview City, Nebraska, 1854.

Omaha Arrow, Nebraska Territory, 1854.

Omaha Herald, Omaha, Nebraska, February 1879-June 1879.

Omaha Daily Bee, Omaha, Nebraska, 1898.

Southern Workman, A Monthly, S. C. Armstrong and H. W. Ludlow, editors, Hampton, Virginia, 1879, 1881, 1884, 1885, 1886, 1887, 1892.

Thurston County Republic, Pender, Nebraska, 1895 to 1900.

The Vindicator, Decatur, Nebraska, 1877-78.

Walthill Citizen, Walthill, Nebraska, 1918-22, 1947.

Walthill Times, Walthill, Nebraska, 1906-1912; 1917-1918; 1919-1921.

West Point Republican, West Point, Nebraska, items 1878 and 1895.

Manuscript Collections, Reports of Historical Societies,
Organizations and Government Departments

American Indian Correspondence Collection, The Presbyterian Historical Society, Philadelphia, Pennsylvania.

Bangs, S. D., *History of Sarpy County, Transactions and Reports*, Nebraska State Historical Society, Vol. II, Lincoln, Nebraska, 1887.

Baptismal Records of Father Hoechen and Father DeSmet, Library of St. Mary's College, St. Mary's Kansas.

Commissioner of Indian Affairs, *Reports*, 1839, 1845, 1846, 1847, 1849-50, 1851, 1852, 1853, 1855, 1856, 1857, 1858, 1860, 1861, 1862, 1863, 1865, 1866, 1867, 1868, 1869, 1870, 1871, 1872, 1873, 1874, 1875, 1877, 1878, 1879, 1880-1886, 1891, 1892.

Cutter, Dr. Irving S., *Dr. John Gale, Pioneer Army Surgeon*, Journal of Illinois State Historical Society, Vol. XXIII, No. 4, Springfield, Ill., January 1931.

Dodge, Jane Gay, *Papers*, Women's Archives, Radcliffe College, Cambridge, Mass.

Dorsey, James Owen, *The Çegeha Language, Contributions to North American Ethnology*, Vi, Washington, D. C. 1890.

Dorsey, James Owen, *Omaha Sociology*, 3rd Annual Report Bureau of Ethnology, Washington, D. C., 1885.

Farb, Robert C., *Robert W. Furnas as Omaha Indian Agent, 1864-1866, Nebraska History*, Vol. 32, No. 3 and 4, Nebraska State Historical Society, Lincoln, 1951.

Fletcher-Cadman-La Flesche Papers, Nebraska State Historical Society, Lincoln, Nebraska

Fletcher and La Flesche Papers, Bureau of American Ethnology, Smithsonian Institution, Washington, D. C.

Galt, W. A., *Manuscript Collection*, Nebraska State Historical Society, Lincoln, Nebraska.

Hamilton, Wm. H., *Autobiographical Sketch, Transactions and Reports*, Nebraska State Historical Society, I, Lincoln, Nebr., 1885.

Indian Rights Association, *Reports*, 1885-1889, 1891, 1893.

Journal of the Atkinson-O'Fallon Expedition, North Dakota Historical Quarterly, 4; 1929.

Journal of Department of History, Vol. 20 and 21, The Presbyterian Historical Society, Lincoln, Nebraska.

Kurtz, Rudolph Friedrich, *Journal:* 1846-1852, Translated by Myrtis Jarrell. Bureau of American Ethnology, Bulletin 115. Smithsonian Institution, Washington D. C. 1937.

La Flesche Family Papers, Nebraska State Historical Society, Lincoln, Nebraska.

Lake Mohawk Conference, *Reports*, 1894-1900, 1903, 1906, 1907.

Minutes of Nebraska Synod, Presbyterian Church, 1892-1903.

Paxson, Dr. Joseph, *Journal.* Edited by Dr. James L. Sellers, *Nebraska History*, Vol. 27, Nos. 3 and 4. Nebraska State Historical Society, Lincoln, 1951.

Peabody Museum *Reports and Correspondence*, Harvard University, Cambridge, Mass.

Records of Office of Indian Affairs, National Archives
    Letters Received from Council Bluffs Sub-Agency, 1836-1857.
    Letters Received from Omaha Agency, 1856-1876.
    Census, 1848
    Annuity Roll, 1848, 1886.
    Microfilms in Nebraska State Historical Society

Reports on Poncas, 46th Congress, 2nd Session, Report 670, United States Senate, Washington, D. C., 1880.

Green, Norma Kidd
　　Iron Eye's family: the children of Joseph La
Flesche.　　Lincoln, Neb., Johnsen Pub. Co. [c1969
　　xv, 225p.　illus., ports.　22cm.

　　"Sponsored by the Nebraska State Historical
Society."
　　Bibliography: p.223-225.

1.La Flesche, Joseph, 1822-1889.　2.La Flesche family.
I.Nebraska State Historical Society.　II.Title.